WAR AND SOCIETY IN IMPERIAL ROME
31 BC–AD 284

Brian Campbell

London and New York

First published 2002
by Routledge
11 New Fetter Lane, London EC4P 4EE

Simultaneously published in the USA and Canada
by Routledge
29 West 35th Street, New York, NY 10001

Routledge is an imprint of the Taylor & Francis Group

© 2002 Brian Campbell

Typeset in Bembo by Florence Production Ltd, Stoodleigh, Devon
Printed and bound in Great Britain by Biddles Ltd, Guildford and King's Lynn

British Library Cataloguing in Publication Data
A catalogue record for this book is available from the British Library

Library of Congress Cataloging in Publication Data
A catalog record for this book has been requested

ISBN 0–415–27881–3 (hbk)
ISBN 0–415–27882–1 (pbk)

FOR KAREN

CONTENTS

CONTENTS

ILLUSTRATIONS

Plates

Figures

PREFACE AND
ACKNOWLEDGEMENTS

In this book, which is aimed primarily at students of the ancient world and at the general reader, I have tried to explain the nature of warfare and its impact on the life and society of the Roman empire from the reign of Augustus up to the military reorganization carried out by Diocletian. Conveniently for the historian, during this period both the system of government and the structure of the army remained relatively unchanged. The army was a professional force permanently stationed in those provinces the Romans considered crucial for their military, economic and political interests, and the soldiers in many ways came to be closely linked with the society in which they lived and operated. Therefore the nature of the military community in its day-to-day existence, and not just in time of war, forms an essential part of the book. Many provincial communities heard the tramp of the legionaries' feet, whether or not there was any actual fighting. Each chapter is constructed round a general theme: Why did wars start? Who served in the army and why did they fight for Rome? What was battle like in the Roman world? How did war and the presence of the army affect society, especially in the provinces? How was war manipulated to suit imperial politics? How was the emperor's military role presented and public opinion managed?

In preparing the book I derived many useful ideas from a broadly based colloquium on *Warfare and Society* organized by Kurt Raaflaub and Nathan Rosenstein in June 1996 at the Center for Hellenic Studies in Washington, DC. I owe an especial debt to several colleagues. Not for the first time, Professor David Buck offered advice, encouragement and detailed suggestions. Dr John Curran read the entire text, and as usual provided a stimulating and civilized environment for discussion. Frederick Williams, Professor of Greek at the Queen's University of Belfast, read the proofs with his customary skill and erudition. I should also like to express my appreciation of the professional and friendly support from the editorial staff at Routledge.

Finally I dedicate the book to my wife Karen, whose love and support have made modern university life tolerable.

ABBREVIATIONS

AE	*L'Année épigraphique* (Paris, 1893–).
AHB	*Ancient History Bulletin.*
ANRW	Temporini, H. *et al.* (eds) *Aufstieg und Niedergang der römischen Welt* (Berlin, 1972–).
BASO	*Bulletin of the American Schools of Oriental Research.*
BAR	*British Archaeological Reports.*
BASP	*Bulletin of the American Society of Papyrologists.*
BMC	Mattingly, E.H. *et al.* (eds) *Coins of the Roman Empire in the British Museum,* Vols 1–6 (1923–66).
CAH²	Bowman, A.K., Champlin, E. and Lintott, A. (eds) *The Cambridge Ancient History* (2nd edn), Vol. X: *The Augustan Empire, 43 BC–AD 69* (Cambridge, 1996).
CCG	*Cahiers du Centre G. Glotz.*
CIL	Mommsen, Th. *et al.* (eds) *Corpus Inscriptionum Latinarum* (Berlin, 1863–).
Digest	Mommsen, Th. (ed.) *Digesta; Corpus Iuris Civilis,* Vol. I (Berlin, 1872).
Diz. epig.	De Ruggiero, E. (ed.) *Dizionario epigrafico di antichità romane* (Rome, 1895–).
FIRA	Riccobono, S. *et al.* (eds) *Fontes iuris Romani anteiustiniani* (3 vols, 2nd edn of Vol 1, Florence, 1940–3).
HSCPL	*Harvard Studies in Classical Philology.*
IGBR	Mihailov, G. (ed.) *Inscriptiones Graecae in Bulgaria repertae* (Serdica, 1958–70).
IGR	Cagnat, R. *et al.* (eds) *Inscriptiones Graecae ad res Romanas Pertinentes* (Paris, 1906–27).
ILS	Dessau, H. (ed.) *Inscriptiones Latinae Selectae* (Berlin, 1892–1916).
JARCE	*Journal of the American Research Centre in Egypt.*
JDAI	*Jahrbuch des Deutschen Archäologischen Instituts.*
JRA	*Journal of Roman Archaeology.*
JRS	*Journal of Roman Studies.*
MAAR	*Memoirs of the American Academy in Rome.*

*OCD*³	Hornblower, S. and Spawforth, A. (eds) *The Oxford Classical Dictionary* (3rd edition, Oxford, 1996).
PBA	*Proceedings of the British Academy.*
PBSR	*Papers of the British School of Rome.*
PCPhS	*Proceedings of the Cambridge Philological Society.*
RAL	*Rendiconti della Classe di Scienze morali, storiche e philologiche dell' Accademia dei Lincei.*
REG	*Revue des Études Grecques.*
REL	*Revue des Études Latines.*
RIB	Collingwood, R.G. and Wright, R.P. (eds) *The Roman Inscriptions of Britain*, Vol. I *Inscriptions on Stone* (Oxford, 1965).
RIC	Mattingly, E.H., Sydenham, A. *et al.* (eds) *The Roman Imperial Coinage* (London, 1923–94).
RRC	Crawford, M.H. *Roman Republican Coinage* (Cambridge, 1974).
RSA	*Rivista storica dell' Antichità.*
SCI	*Scripta Classica Israelica.*
SEG	Hondius, J.J.E. *et al.* (eds) *Supplementum Epigraphicum Graecum* (1923–).
Sylloge	Dittenberger, W. *Sylloge Inscriptionum Graecarum* (3rd edn, Leipzig, 1915–24).
TAPhA	*Transactions and Proceedings of the American Philological Association.*
TAPhS	*Transactions of the American Philosophical Society.*
ZPE	*Zeitschrift für Papyrologie und Epigraphik.*

EMPERORS FROM AUGUSTUS TO DIOCLETIAN

The names by which emperors are commonly known are italicized.

27 BC–AD 14	Imperator Caesar *Augustus*
AD 14–37	*Tiberius* Caesar Augustus
37–41	*Gaius* Caesar Augustus Germanicus (*Caligula*)
41–54	Tiberius *Claudius* Caesar Augustus Germanicus
54–68	*Nero* Claudius Caesar Augustus Germanicus
68–69	Ser. Sulpicius *Galba* Imperator Caesar Augustus
69	Imperator M. *Otho* Caesar Augustus
69	A. *Vitellius* Augustus Germanicus Imperator
69–79	Imperator Caesar Vespasianus Augustus (*Vespasian*)
79–81	Imperator *Titus* Caesar Vespasianus Augustus
81–96	Imperator Caesar Domitianus Augustus (*Domitian*)
96–98	Imperator Caesar *Nerva* Augustus
98–117	Imperator Caesar Nerva Traianus Augustus (*Trajan*)
117–38	Imperator Caesar Traianus Hadrianus Augustus (*Hadrian*)
138–61	Imperator Caesar T. Aelius Hadrianus Antoninus Augustus Pius (*Antoninus Pius*)
161–80	Imperator Caesar *Marcus Aurelius* Antoninus Augustus
161–9	Imperator Caesar L. Aurelius Verus Augustus (*Lucius Verus*)
176–92	Imperator Caesar M. Aurelius *Commodus* Antoninus Augustus
193	Imperator Caesar P. Helvius *Pertinax* Augustus
193	Imperator Caesar M. *Didius* Severus *Julianus* Augustus
193–211	Imperator Caesar L. *Septimius Severus* Pertinax Augustus
198–217	Imperator Caesar M. Aurelius Antoninus Augustus (*Caracalla*)
209–11	Imperator Caesar P. Septimius *Geta* Augustus
217–18	Imperator Caesar M. Opellius *Macrinus* Augustus
218	Imperator Caesar M. Opellius Antoninus *Diadumenianus* Augustus
218–22	Imperator Caesar M. Aurelius Antoninus Augustus (*Elagabalus*)

222–35	Imperator Caesar M. Aurelius *Severus Alexander* Augustus
235–8	Imperator Caesar C. Julius Verus *Maximinus* Augustus
238	Imperator Caesar M. Antonius Gordianus Sempronianus Romanus Africanus Senior Augustus (*Gordian I*)
239	Imperator Caesar M. Antonius Gordianus Sempronianus Romanus Iunior Augustus (*Gordian II*)
238	Imperator Caesar D. Caelius Calvinus *Balbinus* Augustus and Imperator Caesar M. Clodius *Pupienus* Augustus
238–44	Imperator Caesar M. Antonius Gordianus Augustus (*Gordian III*)
244–8	Imperator Caesar M. Julius Philippus Augustus (*Philip*)
249–51	Imperator Caesar C. Messius Quintus Traianus Decius Augustus (*Trajan Decius*)
251–3	Imperator Caesar C. Vibius *Trebonianus Gallus* Augustus
251–3	Imperator Caesar C. Vibius Afinius Gallus Veldumnianus Volusianus Augustus (*Volusian*)
253	Imperator Caesar M. Aemilius Aemilianus Augustus (*Aemilian*)
253–60	Imperator Caesar P. Licinius Valerianus Augustus (*Valerian*)
253–68	Imperator Caesar P. Licinius Egnatius *Gallienus* Augustus
268–70	Imperator Caesar M. Aurelius *Claudius* Augustus (*Claudius II*)
270	Imperator Caesar M. Aurelius *Claudius Quintillus* Augustus
270–5	Imperator Caesar L. Domitius Aurelianus Augustus (*Aurelian*)
275–6	Imperator Caesar M. Claudius *Tacitus* Augustus
276	Imperator Caesar M. Annius Florianus Augustus (*Florian*)
276–82	Imperator Caesar M. Aurelius *Probus* Augustus
282–3	Imperator Caesar M. Aurelius *Carus* Augustus
283–5	Imperator Caesar M. Aurelius *Carinus* Augustus
283–4	Imperator Caesar M. Aurelius Numerius Numerianus Augustus (*Numerian*)
284–305	Imperator Caesar C. Aurelius Valerius Diocletianus Augustus (*Diocletian*)

1

THE ORIGINS OF WAR

Warfare in the ancient world was a personal business. Decisions were taken by an individual or by a few people and were carried out by soldiers fighting face to face. Wars differed in type and intensity; in the early period war was virtually a private affair, fought between individuals and their retinues, and could even be resolved by single combat. Later, war was waged by the state against external enemies, or involved civil conflict or rebellion against occupying forces, and was settled by full-scale battles, guerrilla campaigns and sieges. There were also naval engagements, though Rome fought no specifically naval wars. War was sometimes used as a political tool, to confirm a ruler in power, or as social cement, to bind a whole people together for purposes other than fighting in the war itself, or to establish the dominance of one group. Some fought to seek revenge or with that pretence, others as an expression of religious belief or ritual enactment. However, state-sponsored wars were usually fought for imperial and economic aggrandizement and territorial expansion, the acquisition of booty, and the achievement of honour and glory for the leaders (though this, too, could often have political significance). Wars fought against powerful neighbours to ensure survival might be described as defensive, however disingenuous that was, but wars begun ostensibly for defensive purposes might in time lead to further conquest. Of course many wars arose for complex reasons, or from accidents and misunderstandings, and indeed those instigating war may have had different, even inconsistent, motives. Therefore it is useful to start with a general definition, namely, that war occurs when 'those who decide public and military policy believe that war is in their material self-interest, considered from the perspective of their position within social and economic organization'.[1]

In the Roman imperial period it is of course notoriously difficult to discover why a particular war occurred, or what the people thought about the wars fought in their name. This is because we rely mainly on literary sources that are often incomplete and ill-informed, or prejudiced by preconceptions or dislike of individual emperors. In fact historians tend to be more interested in politics, government, and even civil wars than in foreign conflicts.[2] What we need is access to the diaries of emperors and their advisers, the records of meetings that normally took place behind closed doors, and the letters or memoirs of army commanders. In their absence it may be instructive to examine societies in other ages and common sociological features that can help explain the origin of war and illuminate the impact of warfare on society and political development. War seemingly has deep roots in human personality and the aggression of man living in society, whether that is instinctive or environmental.[3] However, we must be cautious, since the application of over-schematic theoretical analysis based on inadequate knowledge of the ancient world may produce only superficial and ultimately misleading similarities.

The Roman Republic

One Roman historian believed that it was the number and valour of Rome's soldiers and the skills of her generals that, with the help of fortune, had made Rome unconquerable.[4] Now, the willingness of any state to go to war surely depends in part on the expectation of success, and past experience of war and its consequences. So, in developed societies, determination to fight will be centred on the nature of the army and its organization and command, which in turn depend on the nature of society and the political structure. Consequently war decisions were taken which embodied the motives of governments and assemblies, or groups or individuals within those bodies, and such decisions were closely linked to the success of government itself. Therefore Cicero could refer to 'the institutions of our ancestors which experience and the long duration of our government vindicate'.[5]

In fact most wars in the Roman world depended on the decision of a relatively small number of important people, or, in the imperial period, of the emperor. In the early Republic the Roman army was effectively a peasant militia, in which Roman citizens took up their arms for the duration of a campaign. Warfare tended to follow a routine pattern, with mobilization in early spring for campaigns against neighbouring communities. At the end of the summer the soldiers were discharged. Citizens were habituated to warfare as an annual event and continued to be available for call-up while they were of military age. But there was also a property qualification; thus fighting for the state was a duty and responsibility, but also a kind of privilege associated with citizenship.[6]

The same citizens who took up arms for the state also constituted the people's assembly, which controlled decisions about war and peace.[7] Therefore, when proposals were put to the assembly, the leaders might need to take account of the feelings of the ordinary citizen-soldiers and their willingness to serve in person and go into battle. Many factors applied here: the soldiers' confidence in their commander, their hope of booty and the profitable acquisition of land and slaves, and perhaps the prospect of an exciting change in the usual humdrum routine of peasant life. Doubtless patriotism also played a part, in that what they fought for could be represented as the defence of Rome. It is likely that at least down to the 150s BC Roman citizens were not reluctant to engage in regular warfare.[8]

Although popular opinion remained important, in that the people were theoretically sovereign, in my view the preponderant influence in deciding all questions of foreign policy lay with the senate, which under the guise of offering advice issued instructions to senatorial magistrates or army commanders. These officials, because of the difficulties of communicating quickly with Rome, often exercised considerable discretion and could significantly influence policy. Of course, army commanders also had to justify their conduct with reports or displays of military success. Therefore decisions were subject to the prevailing emotions and opinions of the upper classes, and the traditional structure of Roman society and government.[9] Many of the aristocrats who sat in the senate were attuned to a militaristic outlook and experienced in military service, and had warfare firmly implanted in their mindset. Moreover, military success could be personally advantageous in bringing enrichment, prestige, and even political advancement. Collectively, senators might compete to vote for more wars to enhance their own glory and also to enrich the state by expanding the empire. Strategy and long-term planning may have taken second place to greed and imperialist aggrandizement. Of course they could readily convince themselves that what was in fact personal gain was to the advantage of the Roman state.[10]

There was also the effect of a gradual habituation to war and the possession of a successful army, and in particular the contribution from Rome's Italian allies. Every year they were obliged by their treaties with Rome to contribute a considerable body of infantry and cavalry, in lieu of taxes. There may have been a perceived need to find something for them to do, to convince the allies of Rome's worth and power.[11] It is also true that the Romans did not always win their battles and sometimes encountered a real threat to their success or even their existence, notably during the invasion of Hannibal. Fear that powerful neighbours might be able to do them serious damage could be a factor in decisions to go to war, even if this fear was often irrational. Finally, as an established state Rome doubtless found it relatively easy to wage war on less militarily developed communities.

However, even if the social and cultural context in the mid-Republic was conducive to the unrestrained waging of war, we may still exaggerate the single-mindedness of Rome's devotion to war and her greed and imperialist aggression. Especially in the second century BC the level of warfare fluctuated and the momentum of Roman conquest was inconsistent as her military commitments changed. There were also constraining factors. For example, rivalry among the upper classes for military glory may have been two-edged, in that it could restrict war, as successful senators tried to prevent others from benefiting by denying opportunities for military command.

3

Furthermore, for a time in the late second century there were increasing worries about the availability of sufficient manpower. Therefore it may be argued that the Roman senate was sometimes able to reach decisions on war and peace dispassionately, in the light of the general public good, although that of course was in line with entirely selfish Roman interests.[12]

The causes, character and intensity of Roman warfare changed throughout the first century BC, and by the late Republic the senate and upper classes were increasingly sidelined and decisions on war and peace were taken to satisfy the ambitions of a few great military commanders, who aimed for wealth and personal aggrandizement to secure their political dominance. Thus Marcus Crassus, who dragged Rome into a disastrous war against Parthia in the hope of winning military glory, said that no man could call himself rich unless he was able to support an army from his own pocket.[13] Julius Caesar's conquest of Gaul, in which he built up a deep personal rapport with his army, was partly motivated by a desire to win wealth, renown and political standing.[14] Nevertheless, the underlying intention was to win glory by conquering through war and adding territory to the empire.[15]

The army, too, had changed. Men now joined up in the expectation of enrichment in the successful campaigns of a distinguished commander, served for longer (sometimes stationed in a permanent base), and looked forward to a satisfactory pay-off, usually in the form of land that would set them up for the rest of their life. Therefore a bond of personal loyalty was created with their commander rather than with the state.[16] In the eighteen years after Caesar crossed the River Rubicon, invaded Italy and initiated civil war, Roman life and society were convulsed until the Republican establishment was finally overthrown with the emergence of Octavian as master of the Roman world in 31 BC. Taking the name Augustus in 27 BC, he established an autocracy that lasted until the fall of the city of Rome itself.

Augustus and warfare

Augustus reorganized the Roman army, and absorbed into himself the mechanisms for controlling the military and deciding questions of war and peace. Making use of earlier developments, he established a professional army, in which the soldiers were paid to spend their best working years (eventually twenty-five) as full-time soldiers; they could devote all their time to military duties, free from farming and commercial concerns or formal family responsibilities. Augustus intended that this standing army should be capable of meeting all the military requirements of the empire without the need to resort to disruptive special levies. This transformed war-making possibilities. The empire was virtually in a permanent state of war, in which year-round sustained campaigns could be fought where necessary. Augustus' shrewd recruitment of non-citizen auxiliary troops from the less Romanized provinces or the periphery of the empire, and their eventual incorporation into the formal structure of the army, offered significant reserves of manpower.[17]

Strabo described Augustus as 'Lord of war and peace', and Dio speaks of the right of emperors 'to declare war, make peace, and rule both foreigners and citizens in every place for all time'.[18] The senate and people now counted for little, and if Augustus consulted them it was out of politeness. By the end of his reign most governors in charge of troops were directly under his control and incapable of taking any real initiative. So Augustus was not bound by the jealousies and prejudices of the aristocracy that had previously controlled senatorial debate and the appointment of governors, or by any high command of generals.[19] All our literary sources, when describing Augustus' military campaigns, indicate that he was effectively in charge. For instance, according to Florus' history, the German wars resulted from a personal decision of Augustus.[20] Dio describes how Augustus intended to wage war on Britain, but then changed his mind during a visit to Gaul.[21] This is also the story in Augustus' autobiography, the *Res Gestae*, though he is normally at pains to conceal his political dominance. 'At my command and under my auspices two armies were led almost simultaneously into Ethiopia and Arabia Felix.'[22] Similarly, embassies from foreign peoples seeking to confirm or develop relations with Rome came to Augustus, wherever he was.[23] Eventually he appointed a committee of ex-consuls to hear embassies from peoples and kings, but only when he was too old to do so himself.[24]

The emperor's control of military affairs was limited only in so far as he chose voluntarily to consult more widely.[25] Here he could ask friends (*amici*) whose advice he trusted to attend his informal council, the *consilium principis*. He was not obliged to consult the council, or take its advice, and there was no formal membership or schedule of meetings. However, in the debate over the future of Judaea after the death of King Herod in 4 BC, we have a rare glimpse of the council's involvement in the important question of whether peripheral lands in which Rome had an interest should be annexed or managed in some other way.[26]

Augustus' decisions on war and peace should therefore indicate precisely how *he* wanted to use the Roman army, but they cannot tell us why he went to war or if he had some kind of general strategy. We still need to deduce this from the nature of the campaigns he conducted and the political and cultural context. We can have little confidence in the (rare) attempts by ancient sources to explain the motives for the wars waged by Augustus. Florus implies that Augustus generally had personal motives, alleging that he embarked on the German wars because he sought to emulate the campaigns of Julius Caesar in Gaul.[27] This may, however, be a stock literary topos. Dio, on the other hand, describes Augustus' military activity mainly as a response to the immediate situation and, indeed, suggests that the

5

emperor was reluctant to pursue an expansionist policy.[28] But Dio himself was opposed to territorial expansion in his own day, and may have allowed his prejudices to colour his narrative of Augustus' reign.[29] Suetonius says that Augustus had no desire 'for aggrandizement or military glory', and downplays his military conquests.[30] Furthermore, the carefully selected information provided by Augustus in the *Res Gestae* is hardly a reliable guide. He gives the impression of a steady, planned advance of Roman power, and territorial aggrandizement on all fronts under his leadership as the unrivalled world conqueror. Other rulers are subservient to him, all wars fought by Rome are just, and peace achieved by victory is inevitably part of the fulfilment of her imperial destiny.[31]

The difficulty is that in military affairs, as in so much else, Augustus' own views and personality remain enigmatic. His personal record as a military commander was poor, and he had no major military success to his name in his early career. Over the years, hostile and sarcastic stories were circulated by his political enemies,[32] and the campaigns he conducted in Illyricum between 35 and 33 BC were intended partly to reinforce or create a suitable military reputation. But, although he was wounded twice, he did not complete the conquest.[33] He was also greatly embarrassed by Sextus Pompey's naval campaign in Sicily, and had probably accepted before the battle of Actium in 31 BC that he should rely on others to look after the details of military command for him. Suetonius relates some anecdotes about his views on army command, which, if true, suggest a conservative, cautious leader. He used to say that a war or battle should not be undertaken unless the expectation of gain was greater than the fear of loss. Memorably, he compared this to fishing with a golden hook, the loss of which could not be outweighed by any likely catch.[34]

However, despite this unpromising background Augustus in fact became Rome's most successful conqueror, and added an enormous amount of territory to the empire, almost doubling its size. North-west Spain, Raetia, Noricum, Pannonia, Moesia and Germany all saw prolonged fighting and wars of expansion. Egypt was added to the empire, there was fighting in Arabia and Ethiopia between 25 and 22 BC, while Galatia and Judaea were absorbed peacefully into Roman control. Indeed, more conquests were threatened or predicted, in Britain, in Parthia, and even in China. Augustus took the title *imperator* ('general') as his forename, celebrated three triumphs, and was acclaimed on twenty-one occasions as *imperator*.[35] He also admired Alexander the Great, the most famous conqueror of all, used his image in his signet ring, and visited his tomb in Alexandria, declaring that Alexander was a real king while the remains of the Ptolemies were mere corpses.[36] He was of course the adopted heir of Julius Caesar, a most distinguished general who at the time of his death had been planning campaigns against the Dacians and the Parthians.[37] In any case, whatever military activities Augustus undertook, he controlled the means by which his image and activities were presented so as to make the best impression on public opinion. At a pinch he could dress up routine military action as a great victory.

What were Augustus' reasons for going to war so often?[38] In reality, it is likely that political and dynastic reasons predominated. The new ruler needed to show himself as a successful conqueror who brought glory to Rome, and to conceal the more obvious picture of the victor in a squalid civil war. The enhancement of Augustus' military glory, his status, prestige and place in the canon of great Roman leaders were important not just with the soldiers but also in the wider political world, as he tried to establish himself in a position from which he could not be challenged. What is more, Augustus by birth was one of the upper classes, for whom war-making had been an important part of their cultural and social identity. The influence of his background and environment should not be under-estimated. His sons and grandsons, marked out for great things in the dynasty, also needed an opportunity to show themselves to the soldiers, to display their military prowess, and to bring home the laurels of victory.

Warfare was therefore largely a personal decision, affecting the emperor and his family. But how far was he influenced by outside factors, such as public opinion or the perceived military needs of the empire? The traditionally bellicose outlook of the upper classes and the formidable record of the Roman people in waging war could create their own momentum and a public opinion eager for war. This might inspire a drive towards wars of imperial aggrandizement or revenge, or condition government think-ing to a kind of permanent war footing.[39] Furthermore, it is possible that the permanent presence of an army of 300,000 men could itself encourage an atmosphere where warfare was begun easily without fear of criticism or serious repercussions. Now, the size of the army was in my view determined by what Augustus thought would suit his interests and resources. He aimed to secure his personal protection and also enhance his dignity as the pre-eminent military leader.[40] He had after all succeeded by overcoming in battle his rivals for supreme power and wished to avoid the same fate.[41] Since the army was stationed in the provinces (it might be dangerous to his security to keep it in one spot), Augustus perhaps felt that he ought to give the army something to do, and by sending the troops on campaign keep them militarily active and also out of the way of the provincials.[42]

We must not necessarily assume a rational approach, and there is no disputing that Augustus was audacious if not reckless in his pursuit of polit-ical power at the age of 19. However, there is no evidence that the size or location of the army contributed significantly to his decisions to go to war. He was a shrewd and often ruthless man, and it is difficult to believe that he was dragged into fighting any wars against his will. Although Augustus had huge resources and many opportunities for significant military action, he also had diplomatic opportunities, especially in the context of

Rome's relations with Parthia, and excellent channels of communication with local communities and rulers, which he took over and exploited. It is indeed more likely that he manipulated or encouraged public opinion to suit his own ends. It will not have been difficult to obtain approval from the upper classes for campaigns of legitimate conquest after the civil wars. Ordinary people will have enjoyed the triumphal ceremonial, displays and handouts associated with the victories of Roman armies.

There were also genuine military needs in some parts of the empire. Augustus reacted to all this by exploiting circumstances and opportunities, with a shrewd idea of his own benefit both in military and political terms. He did not launch the empire on a new phase towards world conquest (even on the basis of the limited Roman concept of the world), or set out to keep the army constantly occupied with wars. But equally he did not have a minimalist defensive view of his responsibilities, based on the security of the empire or some notion of the best defensive line. Augustus went to war to confirm control of lands widely accepted as Roman but insufficiently pacified, such as Spain, or to secure territory arguably crucial for Rome's vital interests and neglected by previous Republican governments. Appian, commenting on Augustus' subjection of the Alpine tribes, expresses surprise that so many Roman armies crossing the Alps had neglected to deal with these peoples and that even Julius Caesar had not brought about their subjection during the ten years of his campaigns in Gaul.[43] The Alps were certainly important for communications and the security of northern Italy. Similarly, the whole region including Illyricum, Pannonia and Moesia, which absorbed much of Rome's military energy, was pivotal for east–west communications. In these areas Augustus could have been considered derelict in his duty as *princeps* if he had not taken action, though such action was of course unremittingly imperialistic. Elsewhere simple financial profit may have persuaded Augustus. The annexation of Egypt brought huge booty, and Strabo thought that the invasion of Arabia was motivated by hopes of large gains in revenue.[44]

Therefore, although Augustus' foreign policy was expansionist and imperialistic, it was also expedient and exploitative. He fought wars of imperialist aggression where he thought he was likely to be successful, and where he could increase his standing and that of his family in public opinion. In fact most of his imperialist wars, except perhaps that in Arabia, seem to have been fought for territory as well as for booty and prestige. On the other hand, he could not afford to be humiliated by serious military setbacks; it would not do to lose a war or to have Roman territory overrun. Augustus was furious at the defeat of Quinctilius Varus and the loss of three legions in Germany.[45] Therefore decisions to fight needed to be carefully balanced. When Augustus elected to launch large-scale campaigns across the Rhine, but not across the Euphrates into Parthia, even though he had the opportunity of supporting a pretender to the Parthian throne, he may have been thinking that Julius

Caesar had conquered Gaul relatively easily in ten years, whereas Crassus had fared disastrously in Parthia, and Antony had made heavy weather of his attempted invasion a few years previously. Consequently, when it suited the emperor, he used diplomacy judiciously, as in the settlement of relations with Parthia and the eventual conclusion of a treaty. Elsewhere he avoided expeditions that some at least expected: for example, to Britain.[46] Throughout his reign Augustus very effectively used a combination of warfare, threats, the power of his reputation, and occasionally his personal presence on campaign, to get what he wanted. The greater his reputation became, the better this worked. Thus a contemporary writer commented on his dealings with the Parthians: 'Augustus achieved more through the grandeur of his reputation than another commander [Antony] had achieved through force of arms.'[47]

In a way Augustus defined his position by conquering so much territory and proving himself a worthy heir of Julius Caesar.[48] Throughout his reign he also maintained the army as an effective fighting force, and made sure that funds were always available to support it. Therefore decisions to go to war were not influenced by anxiety about the readiness or skill of the army, and this remained true well into the third century. At the same time Augustus was not a warrior and he left a complex legacy for his successors, which is perhaps summed up in his enigmatic advice to Tiberius to keep the empire within limits.[49] He was surely not thinking of formal boundaries or a complete end to military advance, but meant that Tiberius, using his own experience as a commander, should exercise appropriate discretion in his use of the Roman army, according to circumstances and the nature of those peoples presently on the edge of Roman control. Tiberius was strong-minded enough to eschew further military conquests (though Rome continued to acquire more territory); he had his own military glory based on long commands and two triumphs. But no emperor could escape totally the trappings of military power with which Augustus had surrounded the imperial position, or the precedent he emphasized of achieving peace through military victory, symbolized by closing the doors of the temple of Janus on three occasions during his reign.[50]

Warfare after Augustus

We are no better informed about the causes of war in the period after Augustus, but we need to ask, first, how emperors made their personal decisions on questions of war and peace; second, why individual emperors committed the resources of the Roman world to war; and, finally, how far long-term strategic considerations may have affected the pattern of warfare.

All emperors after Augustus retained personal charge of the deployment of the army, and controlled decisions on war and peace. Our sources assume this without debate and are probably right. Tacitus explains how Tiberius personally decided not to pursue a war against the Frisii, a tribe living on the east bank of the Rhine, and instead suppressed information on Roman losses.[51] The great wars of conquest in the first and second centuries – in Britain, in Dacia and Parthia, and in Mesopotamia – are all ascribed by the ancient writers to the personal decision of emperors.[52] More strikingly, Trajan's control of the supply of information on the Parthian War is demonstrated in his adoption of the honorary title 'Conqueror of the Parthians' (*Parthicus*) in 116:

> On 20 (or 21) February a dispatch decked with laurel was sent to the senate by the emperor Trajan Augustus. For this reason he was named 'Conqueror of the Parthians', and for his safe deliverance a decree of the senate was passed, offerings were made at all the shrines, and games were carried on.[53]

Previously, in 102, Trajan had messengers from the Dacian king Decebalus sent on to the senate to confirm the terms of the peace treaty, which he had already negotiated. Later, when he adjudged Decebalus to have broken the treaty, the senate obediently declared the king a public enemy (*hostis*), and war began again.[54] The prayer of the priestly college the Arval Brethren for Caracalla's campaigns in the north in 213 also shows imperial responsibility for the detail of military policy: '11 August . . . because our lord, the most revered pious emperor M. Aurelius Antoninus Augustus, chief priest, is setting out to cross the border of Raetia and enter the [land] of the barbarians in order to annihilate the enemy, may this turn out fortunately and luckily for him.' [55]

Emperors, of course, continued to take informal advice from their *amici*, but it is hard to say how decisive this was. Our sources were poorly informed about council meetings, which will have normally taken place in secret. However, the satirist Juvenal gives us a comic version of what he imagined such a meeting was like in the reign of Domitian. The advisers were summoned in haste ('Hurry! The Emperor is seated'), and arrived nervously fearing a military disaster – 'panic-stricken dispatches might have been pouring in from all parts of the empire'. In fact they were asked to suggest ways of cooking a large fish, and duly gave their advice.[56] A more serious debate took place under Nero on the situation in Parthia. After a military setback he consulted his council of advisers with the question: Should they accept a humiliating peace or risk a hazardous war? They immediately decided that they must go to war.[57] On the other hand, after the death of Marcus Aurelius, his son Commodus ignored advice from his father's advisers and made peace with the Marcomanni, although the opinion was that the Romans could have destroyed them.[58]

To go to war was a serious decision for a Roman emperor, and we need to know what factors influenced his decision. There were many reasons for hesitation: inertia, precedent and the importance of the status quo, which might tell against extravagant military decisions. In most aspects of government, emperors usually responded to events and pressure from below, and those who took the initiative, or who were compelled to do so, stand out in our sources.[59] Then the expenses of a campaign might or might not be recouped by the profits of victory, and there were potential logistical difficulties in assembling large numbers of troops for military operations, given the static nature of the dispositions of the Roman army. On the other hand, it is not clear to us how an emperor could calculate or oversee these matters, or even if he thought that they were important.

On a sinister note, some emperors might want to avoid war to prevent others from acquiring the glory associated with military leadership. Senators still commanded the legions as part of their traditional duties as provincial governors, but emperors could ensure that they were denied the responsibility of an independent command in a major campaign. For example, Claudius prevented his governor of Lower Germany, Domitius Corbulo, from crossing the Rhine to engage the Germans. Corbulo wryly commented: 'once upon a time Rome's generals were lucky!' Indeed, Pliny believed that jealousy and fear of imperial displeasure in the reign of Domitian paralysed military commanders.[60]

An emperor could also restrict the role of senators by taking personal command of major campaigns, as generally happened from the late first century onwards. However, in the two centuries after the death of Tiberius, most emperors had little or no military experience, except for Galba (who ruled for only one year), Vespasian and his son Titus, Trajan and Hadrian. Marcus Aurelius and Lucius Verus, who by circumstance were forced to spend many years fighting in the east and the north, had no military experience whatever. Furthermore, up to the reign of Septimius Severus the reigning emperor rarely had a member of his family on whom he could rely to take charge of major wars. An exception was Vespasian, who did indeed employ Titus to stamp out the Jewish rebellion. Therefore an inexperienced emperor on campaign might be anxious about the possibility of defeat and its repercussions, notably the potential damage to his image, which could help to undermine his standing in Rome. For defeat would be his personal responsibility and could not easily be blamed on one of his generals.[61] Furthermore, it might be wise to avoid long wars, since it has been plausibly suggested that over time the will to war fades as the costs mount up; people do not like living in perpetual fear, and protracted war can lead to internal divisions. Of course, once a decision had been taken either to wage war or to seek a resolution by other means, the government could rationalize this and make a suitable presentation for public consumption.[62]

There was also possible political danger in leaving Rome for long periods in order to conduct military campaigns. Rome was the centre of the nexus of administrative, political and social contacts that helped to underpin the imperial position, and in the capital there was a well-established pattern of protecting the emperor through the praetorians and the urban cohorts. Tiberius, declining to leave Rome to deal with the mutinies of AD 14 on the Rhine and the Danube, vividly described it as the 'head of everything'.[63] Tacitus recognized this when he made events at Rome the centrepiece of his narrative in the *Annals*. In the emperor's absence from Rome, dissension or even revolt could perhaps be more easily fomented.

Emperors who were nervous of command, or preoccupied with administrative duties, or indifferent to conquest, could find an alternative to war by pursuing and developing the relatively sophisticated diplomatic contacts that had been established by the late first century AD. These involved envoys of high status, formal meetings and dinners, negotiation, written treaties and recognition of the importance of good faith. Of course, diplomacy generally meant that the Romans got what they wanted (or a convincing version of it) without fighting, and had proved particularly effective in dealing with the Parthians.[64]

We might therefore think that emperors would need strong reasons to commit Roman troops to lengthy campaigns, but three other factors are relevant. First, the military trappings of the emperor's position, his titles and attributes, and his depiction in art, which owed much to decisions taken by Augustus, all contributed to a warlike image that never faltered through the first three centuries. Some emperors may have felt the need to live up to this and acquire military honours to enhance their prestige and that of their house.[65]

Second, the psychology of war in Rome was important. Military attributes remained common in society and culture, and war was never likely to be thoroughly unpopular. It could be said of imperial Rome that 'war was a noble and necessary activity for any state desirous of demonstrating its power and virtue'.[66] The Romans continued to be impressed by military success and an ability to master the qualities and attributes of a general. They were interested in both the technical and moral aspects of commanding men in battle, as we can see from the many handbooks and guides written about the character and role of a general.[67] It is interesting that Appian's history of Rome is arranged in a series of war narratives according to the various peoples whom the Romans had fought and conquered. Presumably he expected that this demonstration of how the Romans 'acquired unparalleled foreign domination, and brought the greater part of the nations under their control' would appeal to his audience.[68] Florus, writing in the mid-second century AD, composed a work entitled *Abridgement of All the Wars of Seven Hundred Years* to encapsulate the history of the Roman people, who had carried their weapons throughout the world, so that their exploits seemed like the history not of a single people but of the human race.[69] More substantial historians, like Tacitus and Cassius Dio, dealt seriously with warfare, the status of Rome and relations with foreign peoples. The fact that senators like these despised the ordinary soldier does not mean that they despised military command itself. Indeed, Dio commanded two legions as governor of Upper Pannonia.[70]

This interest in warfare often brought with it an implicit assumption that the Romans' military superiority was absolute and that they could arrange peoples and kingdoms to suit their interests, and continue conquering when and where they wished.[71] To take one example, Livy in his history recounted with many stirring anecdotes Rome's glorious military heritage, and in the Preface wrote that the Roman people's military glory was so great that it was reasonable for them to think that they were descended from Mars, the god of war.[72] The story of the reappearance in a vision of the first king, Romulus, was certainly fictitious, but his message to the city reflected the reality of what Romans thought about their empire: 'my Rome shall be the capital of the world; so let them foster the art of war, and let them know and hand down to their children that no human strength can resist Roman arms.'[73] It is hardly surprising that emperors gave expression in word and deed to these long-established feelings. Thus Tiberius, no warmonger, was furious because of his generals' inability to end the war in Africa against Tacfarinas, who had sent envoys to the emperor with demands. 'No insult to him or the Roman people, it is said, ever annoyed the emperor more than that this deserter and brigand should behave like a hostile king.'[74] Such sentiments did not abate with the passage of time. In AD 375 the emperor Valentinian received ambassadors from the Quadi, who came to meet him at Brigetio (Szöny) to negotiate a treaty, but in private audience they defended their previous conduct so insolently that the emperor in a rage suffered an attack of apoplexy and died soon afterwards.[75]

Third, a Roman emperor had few constraints upon him. There were lands and peoples where it was feasible for the Romans to seek further conquest with a good expectation of victory. At least before the mid-third century there was no shortage of funds, supplies and recruits to support military expansion. Furthermore, since the army was becoming gradually less Italian in composition, there will have been correspondingly less pressure from public opinion about the possible loss of Italian lives on needless campaigns.[76] The emperor was commander-in-chief of a large army, but there is little sign that any emperor was greatly concerned about soldiers' opinions on military matters, or came under pressure from the soldiers for action and booty.[77] Mutinies about imperial military policy rarely occurred, or at least are rarely reported, and most of our information concerns random disturbances related to the conduct of individuals, or isolated military incidents.[78] Although in the serious mutinies of AD 14 an important factor was the soldiers' concern about what would happen to them after Augustus' death, in my view the underlying impetus was discontent with pay and conditions. In general, although emperors identified themselves closely with the army, they remained aloof from and even contemptuous of the ordinary soldiers, and seem to have felt able to devise military policy free from any significant concerns.

This is the background against which individual emperors decided to go to war. The empire was an autocracy, and the character and behaviour of emperors are important factors in imperial politics, but we are poorly informed about precisely why emperors took decisions. As Cassius Dio points out, it was often difficult to get information about what happened in the provinces and on the periphery of the empire.[79] When ancient writers do give a specific reason for a war, they usually emphasize an emperor's desire for glory, renown and personal prestige. This is Dio's explanation of Trajan's Parthian war, and he must have thought that this was at least plausible.[80] Trajan had had an unusually long period of service as a military tribune, and was governor of Upper Germany when he became emperor. He liked to be seen as a soldier's man, participating in military exercises, marching at the head of his men on campaign, and allegedly tearing up his own clothing for bandages during the Dacian Wars.[81] Now, although Trajan had a reasonable pretext for his invasion of Dacia, in the apparently unsatisfactory nature of Domitian's settlement with the Dacian king, Decebalus, he was perhaps attracted by the idea of waging war on a seemingly powerful and arrogant people on the periphery of the empire.[82] His success probably accustomed him to the military life, which he tried to re-create with the war against Parthia. All the emperor's military exploits brought him extraordinary honours and were celebrated in art and architecture, most notably in the column that adorned his forum.[83] Therefore Dio's explanation rings true, though we cannot be sure what other ideas were in Trajan's mind, and hopes of plunder and loot cannot be discounted. However, the emperor wanted more than merely to conquer people and amass booty, since he annexed Dacia as a province, and then Arabia (probably in 106), and later was apparently planning to create new provinces beyond the Euphrates.[84]

In the aftermath of the murder of Gaius, Claudius had to rely on the embarrassingly open support of the praetorians as he plotted to become emperor. He was physically unappealing, suffered from a stammer and was unpopular among the upper classes. There seems little doubt that an important motive for the invasion of Britain in AD 43 was the exploitation of the glory that came with military success to enhance Claudius' political standing. Suetonius was sure that Claudius ordered the invasion of Britain because he wanted a campaign where he could earn a proper triumph. He therefore had to go in person, and the invasion commander Aulus Plautius, as instructed, summoned him at a crucial moment of the campaign, although he stayed in Britain for just sixteen days. On his return to Rome, amid massive celebrations he ceremonially extended the formal boundary of the city (*pomerium*) symbolizing the addition of new territory, which even Augustus had not done, and honoured many of the upper classes who had served in the invasion.[85]

From AD 82/3 Domitian embarked on a series of wars on the Rhine and the Danube. Rome was encountering difficult relations with peoples in this area, but the emperor was probably not unhappy to see war and the opportunity for military glory. He had poor relations with the senate; and, in AD 89, L. Antonius Saturninus, governor of Upper Germany, revolted, so that the loyalty of the army was severely tested, and perhaps was only partly confirmed by a timely pay rise. Domitian himself was short of military prestige in comparison to his father and brother Vespasian and Titus, both of whom had distinguished military reputations.[86]

After his seizure of power in AD 193, Septimius Severus fought two bitter civil wars, which brought huge Roman casualties and much resentment among the upper classes. He needed a respectable war against foreign enemies, and this is probably the reason for the two campaigns he conducted in the east. Since the reign of Trajan, Rome's relations with Parthia had been unstable, and that land always offered a venue where limited wars could be fought and military glory gained in the footsteps of Alexander the Great. Once again there were enormous celebrations in Rome. Interestingly, Severus tried to explain his Parthian war on strategic grounds, arguing that the land acquired would be a defence for the province of Syria; but in the view of his contemporary, the historian Dio, Rome was now embroiled unnecessarily in expensive conflict with peoples on the periphery of the empire. Then, late in his reign, Severus led a campaign in Britain; and, although there was a pretext of some turbulent British tribes, ancient writers believed that the real motive was personal and political – namely, to give his sons something honourable to do and to procure dynastic stability.[87]

Warfare did not always involve great campaigns of conquest. Apart from low-level violence, where the army was involved in putting down rebels, disposing of bandits and keeping order, the preservation of the territorial integrity of the Roman empire was itself an important motive for war. It was in an emperor's self-interest to ensure that land long recognized as Roman was not overrun or abandoned, since this, too, could have political implications. Criticism of an emperor's foreign and military policy could easily become criticism of his capacity to rule.[88] Hostile commentators alleged against Nero and Hadrian that they toyed with the idea of giving up Britain and Dacia respectively.[89] In fact, emperors were prepared to fight to retain or consolidate such peripheral areas. In the second century Britain detained three legions and perhaps a total of 50,000 troops in its garrison.[90]

But perhaps we should not see this as entirely a matter of Roman imperial self-interest. Some emperors perhaps really did want to ensure the security, peace and well-being of the inhabitants of the empire.[91] Emperors did, after all, respond from time to time to deputations and appeals from their subjects, both individuals and communities. Velleius, a strong supporter of the imperial regime, was probably quite genuine when he celebrated the return of Tiberius to army command as being for 'the defence of the empire'.[92] Frontinus believed that by defeating the Germans Domitian had acted for the benefit of the adjacent Roman provinces.[93] Plautius Silvanus Aelianus, Nero's distinguished governor of Moesia, can speak for himself in the inscription in which he celebrates his career, and lists various military and diplomatic achievements 'by which he confirmed and extended the peace of the province'.[94] Much later the emperor Constantine was to be celebrated by the community of Tropaeum Traiani as a 'restorer of Roman *security* and liberty'.[95] Other writers speak of the army as a kind of protective ring around the empire. Appian describes how the Romans 'surround the empire with large armies and garrison all this land and sea like a single fortress'.[96] Similarly, Tacitus summarizes the situation in AD 14: 'The empire was fenced round by the ocean or distant rivers; legions, provinces, fleets were all linked to one another.'[97] Of course a fear (real or imagined) of powerful neighbours, who might or might not threaten Roman territory and subjects, could lead to a pre-emptive attack by the Romans, which could then become a campaign of conquest. Marcus Aurelius began his northern wars as a response to incursions by German tribes, but at the end of his life seemed to be contemplating the creation of a new trans-Danubian province of Sarmatia.[98]

Frontier policy?

No coherent analysis of the causes of war in the imperial period is possible because of our flawed or inadequate source material.[99] But it is worth asking if we can overcome this problem by taking a wider view based partly on comparative material derived from the discipline of defence analysis. On this basis war and military dispositions may perhaps be explained in terms of the evolution of an empire-wide strategy and an overall response to long-term strategic, tactical and diplomatic concerns, based on what have been described as 'scientific frontiers'.[100] These were modified occasionally by individual emperors, who were essentially therefore taking rational decisions, which to some extent depended on perceived wisdom and practice, and amounted to virtually a common policy, at least in certain areas of the empire.

Indeed, this theory suggests that Roman strategy was successively modified in the light of experience and changing circumstances. The Julio-Claudians maintained a 'hegemonic' empire, in which strategically situated forces could be concentrated where necessary, supported by the forces of friendly kings. From the late first century onward there emerged the idea of preclusive defence, with sharply delineated frontiers, defended by forces in fixed locations, which dealt with hostile activity outside the frontiers. This was a 'territorial' empire, which achieved the maximum influence for Roman power with an economy in the use of force. In the third century, as the empire came under greater threat from external forces, the Romans resorted to 'defence in depth', using self-contained strongholds with mobile forces deployed between or behind them.[101]

If true, this theory could have serious implications for how we view the causes of war in the Roman world. Although emperors doubtless had differing levels of interest in strategic and military concerns, it would certainly be wrong to assume that the Romans did not have a judicious approach, and that they did not review the military situation of the empire in the context of what they had learned about other peoples. Indeed, we can detect some degree of rationality and long-term thinking in the changing disposition of the legions.[102] But there are serious objections to the theory of a 'grand strategy', and it is difficult to believe that the Romans ever thought this way.[103] First, they simply lacked the intelligence information required in order to develop such far-sighted or proactive policies – though, as with most governments in charge of a large army, there will have been some strategic planning. They were also defective in adequate and up-to-date geographical knowledge about areas on the periphery of the empire.[104] Second, emperors were usually inexperienced in war, they had no army high command or highly experienced long-term military advisers, and no secretary of state for defence who could coordinate a coherent empire-wide strategy. In addition, there was no permanent mechanism for diplomatic contact or diplomatic representation, no permanent officials charged with foreign policy, and no specialist practitioners in negotiation. It is worth remembering that Augustus' last advice to his successor on military strategy was simple and uncomplicated.[105] Third, in reality Roman frontier zones were not similar in nature or purpose, or seemingly coordinated. Archaeological evidence, which is important because literary evidence is sketchy, is much disputed in respect of the identification and significance of forts, walls and roads.[106] Even in the case of one of the great linear constructions, Hadrian's Wall, there is a school of thought that it was not primarily a defensive barrier, but a means of controlling the movement of peoples and traffic in the vicinity of Roman territory.[107] There is indeed little sign of any concerted attempt to achieve consistent or coordinated long-term objectives in dealing with foreign peoples across the entire empire. As we have seen, decisions on war and peace were taken by individuals often for immediate reasons in the light of local conditions.[108] In the main, emperors were shrewd and rational judges of their self-interest, and tended towards a relatively passive approach, in which they reacted to events and opportunities as they appeared. Finally, it is wrong to assume that the prevailing view in Rome was the need to defend the empire against threats from hostile neighbours. No ancient commentator indicates that the Romans thought in this way; they had no word in Latin for 'frontier' in the sense of a formal barrier or fortified line. Instead, with a self-confident belief in their military superiority, they probably saw no need for long-term planning. Furthermore, the designation of Roman territorial control in no way ruled out the absorption or conquest of peoples beyond.[109]

Finally, the pattern of Roman warfare and the deployment of the legions can shed some light on the causes of war and wider strategic concerns. After the sustained warfare and conquests of the Augustan era there was apparently some fighting in the reign of nearly every emperor who ruled for more than one year, apart from Gaius and Titus. Of course the significance of this warfare varied, but even the quelling of a revolt could require the commitment of large numbers of troops, and the Jewish revolts between 66 and 70 and 132 and 135 amounted to major campaigns.[110] It is clear that until the later third century the Romans were aggressive and militarily self-confident, and this often involved the domination of other peoples and their resources.[111] The success of the army during this period in consolidating and extending Roman power probably made further warfare more likely, since the Romans could not tolerate any disruptive or provocative activity on the periphery of their territory.

Nevertheless, the extent of warfare was relatively limited in geographical terms, and the large majority of Roman soldiers at any one time would not be engaged in serious fighting. The Roman peace was therefore genuine, in that for long periods many provinces saw little military action. Indeed, despite the degree of military activity over three centuries and the Roman emperor's military trappings and complete control of the army, he did not become a warlord or sustain his control by routine warfare. There was no clear-cut imperial dynamic towards war. The Romans were not addicted to warfare and did not seek to sustain their empire by persistent conquering or continual expansion, though its inner logic dictated that no territory be surrendered in order to preserve the integrity of government.

The deployment of the legions at first indicated the main direction of Roman military advance, in Spain, on the Rhine and the Danube, in Britain, and in the east. Later there was an increasingly heavy concentration on the Danubian provinces as Rome tried to deal with turbulent, unpredictable northern tribes. Finally, there was a further shift of resources to the east to extend and then protect Roman interests between the Euphrates and the Tigris in the simmering conflict with the Parthians and their formidable successors, the Sasanids (Figures 1.1 and 1.2).[112] The first significant signs of a changing situation appear in the long wars which Marcus Aurelius fought in the north initially to protect Roman provinces against German tribes invading across the Danube. By the mid-third century the Romans were involved in virtually continuous warfare, but generally not at times or locations of their choosing. They now fought defensive wars to preserve

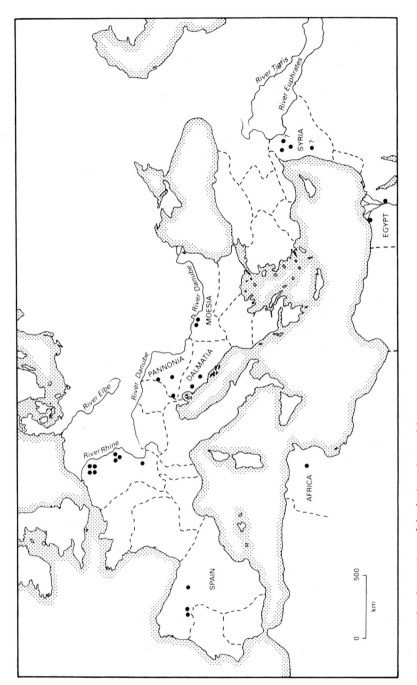

Figure 1.1 The disposition of the legions in AD 14

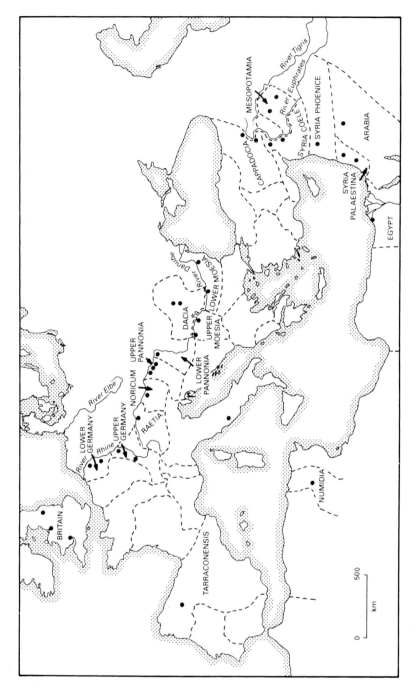

Figure 1.2 The disposition of the legions in AD 200

the status quo and avoid the loss of territory long regarded as Roman. In 260 the emperor Valerian was captured by the Persian king Shapur as he tried to defend Mesopotamia from invasion; he was to die in captivity. Then, probably in 274, the emperor Aurelian decided to abandon the province of Dacia, moving soldiers of the garrison and the civilian administration to the south bank of the Danube. In the later third century, as the empire's strategic position worsened, emperors were committed to fight further wars in order to preserve Roman lands and resources, and the vast cost of this military effort caused even more hardship for the declining body of tax-payers. In the end, wars were fought largely to regenerate imperial power and sustain the memory of Rome's greatness. Even in the fifth century, Rutilius Claudius Namatianus, a poet of Gallo-Roman family and a high-ranking official (he had been Prefect of the City in 414), writing after the sack of Rome by Alaric and the Goths in 410, predicted a return of impe-rial glory: 'Fortune/which is cruel today will be kind tomorrow./Let your law extend to all the known world;/it will not die.'[113]

2

SOLDIERS AND WAR

Who served in the Roman army? This simple question has a wider significance, since the social, economic and legal status of Roman soldiers, and
the nature of the military community, can help us understand what inspired
and motivated these men to fight for Rome under the emperors. The
psychology of men in battle, and the morale and resilience of armies, sometimes against impossible odds, are complex issues. For the ancient world
we usually lack detailed battle descriptions, or the memoirs and letters of
individual soldiers on both sides of the conflict which are so valuable for
vividly bringing to life battle experiences. However, despite obvious differ-
ences in weaponry and military organization, the factors that influence the
morale of soldiers have remained pretty constant, and the methods of
analysing warfare in other ages are therefore relevant.[1]

Recruiting in the Republic

At various stages in its history the Roman army comprised a militia, citizen-
soldiers, mercenaries and professional troops, both conscripts and volunteers,
although there was no clear linear development.[2] The earliest Roman army
will have consisted of the king, his retainers, nobles and whatever clan
members could be organized to fight, largely in raids against neighbouring
communities. This was a citizen militia habituated to seasonal warfare, in
which we may guess that soldiers were motivated by ideas of survival, self-
defence and patriotism. By protecting themselves, their families and their
smallholdings, they also ensured the survival of the Roman state. Of course,
peer pressure will also have been important, as they saw other small farmers
in the ranks with them.

   As Rome developed politically and militarily, the will of the upper classes
usually prevailed in decisions on war and peace, and the government
regularly conscripted its citizens, though preferring those who could equip
themselves.[3] This, however, did not mean that the Roman people were
unwilling soldiers. On the contrary, they were apparently quite belligerent.
The levy for Rome's legionary army around the mid-third century BC

suggests that a large proportion of eligible men with property (*assidui*) were enlisted. Citizens were apparently willing to serve in large numbers at least down to the mid-second century BC. In 225 BC perhaps about 17 per cent of the adult male citizens were in the army, rising to more than 25 per cent at the climax of the war with Hannibal.[4] Furthermore, after 218 BC campaigns were no longer seasonal but could last all year. It is difficult to see how, even with the use of conscription, the senate could have pursued an active foreign policy without a significant measure of popular support and cooperation. The comic playwright Plautus, who was writing between *c.* 205 and 184 BC, certainly assumes that his audience is familiar with war. He often uses specifically Roman military metaphors, puts a famous battle narrative in a Roman context, and, in a stock feature of his work, the Prologues, commonly ends by wishing the audience well in war.[5]

Roman warfare in this period was often brutal. The troops' methods for dealing with captured cities caused the Greek historian Polybius, who had military experience, to comment that they were more violent than Hellenistic armies.[6] Indeed, Roman fighting methods and the ferocity of Roman troops apparently intimidated Macedonian soldiers.[7] It has been suggested that the Romans had a pronounced willingness to use violence against alien peoples, and 'behaved somewhat more ferociously than most of the other politically advanced peoples of the Mediterranean world'.[8] Perhaps therefore in a violent and warlike society men readily accepted the idea of going into battle to kill those whom they saw as enemies.

Nevertheless, hope of personal gain probably had greatest weight in encouraging men to serve. The introduction of a daily cash allowance in the early fourth century shows that the state itself recognized the need to recompense its soldiers for their service. Soldiers in a victorious army expected to acquire booty and slaves, and this is best illustrated by the increasing generosity of donatives distributed at triumphs.[9] Soldiers might therefore have been attracted by the reputation of a previously successful general, under whose command they could expect victory and profit. Thus Scipio Aemilianus was able to raise 4000 volunteers for the siege of Numantia in 137 BC, relying on his prestige and popularity and *clientela* connections.[10]

After *c.* 150 BC enthusiasm for military service declined. The long war in Spain was proving difficult and unpopular; there was little booty, and reports of frequent battles, high casualty rates and the courage of the enemy unnerved many men of military age. Consequently, there were attempts to evade the levy.[11] Moreover, the slave war in Sicily and unprofitable garrison duty in Macedonia created more recruiting problems for the government. Indeed, the property qualification for service had been reduced in 214 and was reduced again in the second century.[12] As men were required to serve for longer or were called up on more occasions, life became harder for small farmers without resources or powerful protectors. Six or more years' continuous absence from Italy could bring the ruin of a farm, and all this was a disincentive to serve which the government would have to overcome or face a crisis of morale among its soldiers.

In 107 BC the consul C. Marius raised additional forces for the troublesome war in Africa against Jugurtha by accepting as volunteers men who did not possess the requisite amount of property (*proletarii*). Given the decline in the property qualification in previous years, it is likely that they were not markedly poorer than the kind of soldier recruited in earlier times, but potentially the way was open for the recruitment of more soldiers who had no land and no means of support other than military life. There was now a more mercenary element, in that eventually more soldiers sought a profitable military career, served for longer periods, and tended to be loyal to commanders who were successful and looked after their interests.[13]

In the political turmoil of the late Republic there was no longer a single army of the Roman state, but individual armies serving under competing leaders. About 250,000 Italians, many of whom will have been conscripts, were under arms.[14] Legions were also raised outside Italy from Roman citizens, and often from non-citizens. Julius Caesar enlisted the legion V Alaudae from Transalpine Gaul, while Pompey and Antony, too, were also active in this way.[15] In addition, Caesar employed non-Romans as mercenary troops in a specialist capacity, notably Gallic and German cavalry. Military leaders probably took what they could get in the way of recruits, and the chief incentives to bravery in battle were donatives, booty, and the allure of individual generals whose record promised continued success. Julius Caesar was famous for his close personal relationship with his men, which he had built up over ten years' successful and lucrative campaigning in Gaul. His troops' loyalty and devotion were undiminished by military setbacks or harsh conditions, and it was said that Pompey, on seeing the bread made from herbs and grass that Caesar's army was living on at the siege of Dyrrachium, ordered that it should be hidden from his men in case the enemy's resolution undermined their own spirit.[16] Soldiers such as these swore their oath of service personally to their commanders, and were in fact virtually mercenaries, supporting their paymaster leaders not because of the compulsion of the law but because of personal inducements, and fighting not against the enemies of Rome but against private adversaries and fellow-citizens.[17] Military service was now a kind of financial package, involving long service in return for regular pay and other benefits. The Roman army therefore did not necessarily have any strong patriotic sentiments or political ideals, or a clear idea of loyalty to the senate or Rome. It had sharpened its skills in warfare against other Romans, and had developed a strong expectation of success. With a professional approach in military preparations, and a tradition of robust leadership from its officers, especially the centurions, it had also developed a strong sense of military community.

Recruiting in the imperial period

After the battle of Actium in 31 BC, Augustus found himself in command of sixty legions, many of which had been recruited by his defeated rivals Antony and Lepidus.[18] There was a legacy of violence and bitterness, and he could hardly expect to be an immediate focus of loyalty. He had to reconstruct and reorganize the army, pensioning off many soldiers in Italy and the provinces. Although he worked as far as possible within existing military traditions, his arrangements were to influence the character of the Roman army at least for the next two centuries, since his successors changed little of what he did. Augustus was restricted by the public façade he had created of the restoration of constitutional government and the maintenance of traditional practices.

The existing legions formed the backbone of the army, and since they consisted largely of Roman citizens, the army in 31 had a predominantly Italian ethos. Indeed, throughout the imperial period it remained a Roman citizen's legal liability to perform military service if required.[19] But Augustus did not set out deliberately to preserve this Italian ethos, and the number of Italians serving as legionaries was eventually to decline sharply. The first signs of this occur under Augustus, since it is clear that the legions in the east soon ceased to receive a significant number of Italian recruits and that little attempt was made to preserve them as an Italian force.[20] Furthermore, Augustus did not insist on conscription in Italy.[21] Italians who wished to serve in the army could join the praetorians, Augustus' bodyguard, established in 27 BC; they had better service conditions, the status of an élite unit, and the likelihood of spending much of their military career in Rome and Italy. Augustus probably realized that the demands on manpower of keeping a large, professional force up to strength meant that an exclusively Italian army was out of the question. He could hardly expect Italy to provide sufficient volunteers, and indeed in the military emergencies of AD 6 and 9, he was forced to recruit freedmen and the urban proletariat.[22] Augustus also encouraged the enlistment as auxiliaries (*auxilia*) of non-Italians living in the less Romanized lands within the empire or on its periphery. Even more importantly, these units of *auxilia* were increasingly arranged and organized in the Roman way, providing regular cavalry and infantry, and were gradually incorporated into the formal military structure. Other specialist groups provided archers and slingers. This was a pragmatic solution to exploit potential reservoirs of manpower, which in its conception, if not in its development, had Republican precedents. Augustus also recruited similar types of men to the permanent fleets, which he established principally to protect the Gallic coast and the shores of Italy.[23] The idea of a property qualification for military service had long since disappeared, and the soldiers in Augustus' army were in the main drawn from the rural lower classes.[24]

After Augustus the government continued to insist that legionaries should in principle be Roman citizens, as the army was supposed to be the Roman people under arms. For a time Italy remained as a central source of potential recruits who were distributed to the western provinces, though it is difficult to say if there was a plan to install a nucleus of Italian recruits in as many areas as possible, or if they were simply sent where they were needed.[25] But the number of recruits from Italy declined steeply throughout the first century AD. From the evidence of inscriptions for the origins of recruits, it seems that by the end of the first century only about 20 per cent of recruits were from Italy, and that by the time of Hadrian virtually no Italians were serving.[26] However, it was apparently traditional practice that, when the Romans were establishing a completely new legion, as far as possible they recruited in Italy; although, when such a legion was on station, fresh recruits were taken from any convenient source.[27]

Against this background of an increasing disinclination to military service among the youth of Italy, the government by the second century had to find approximately between 4000 and 5000 recruits every year.[28] Among the western provinces, Spain and Narbonese Gaul contributed significant numbers of recruits to legions stationed in areas with fewer communities of citizens in the vicinity of the military camps. Then, in a slow and uneven development, which did not necessarily amount to a concerted policy, there was a move towards localization of recruitment, beginning probably with legions that had some Romanized communities nearby, since Roman communities or colonies, and later also military colonies, proved a fruitful source of young men for the army. More recruits could be found in the frontier zones and in the *canabae* or civilian settlements that grew up around military camps.[29] Here soldiers (who were forbidden to marry) often formed liaisons with local women. The children of such unions were usually not Roman citizens but could receive citizenship on enlistment in the legions; their origin was then designated as *castris* (literally 'from' or 'in the camp').[30] For example, in the province of Moesia on the River Danube during the early first century, recruits came from Italy, Narbonese Gaul and Asia Minor, and later from Macedonia, with a few from Moesia itself. But in the second and early third centuries recruiting became more localized, with men designated *castris* and others often being taken from veteran colonies in Moesia and neighbouring provinces.[31] From the second century the legion based in Spain was recruited almost entirely from men born in Spain.[32] It should be emphasized, however, that there was no simple recruiting pattern for the whole empire, and that certain provinces like Britain and Germany had perhaps limited local recruiting.[33]

In Africa in the first century, recruits were sent for distant service in the west, and before Trajan up to 60 per cent of legionaries serving in the province were not of local origin. But gradually recruiting became largely localized, and men from Africa itself came to predominate, from communities with Roman or Latin status in the province, from *canabae*, including sons of soldiers, and from frontier zones, though rarely from African cities. However, although this may be described as local recruitment, in fact most recruits came from the eastern part of Africa, not from Numidia itself, where the legion III Augusta was based. Local loyalty was not necessarily strong, and when in AD 238 the governor of Africa tried to raise support for a rebellion against the emperor Maximinus over the payment of taxes, the legion sided with the emperor.[34]

In the eastern provinces from the early period there was little input from Italy and the west. Recruits came largely from Hellenized areas of Syria and Asia Minor. But there were great variations, and by the third century AD legion III Cyrenaica in Arabia was drawing recruits from less Hellenized and even Semitic-speaking areas round its base at Bostra, and also from Auranitis and Trachonitis.[35] In Egypt the situation is far from clear, since, although there are several important inscriptions and papyri containing lists of recruits at certain times, it is uncertain if they are typical. In the early principate it seems that recruits came mainly from Galatia and Asia Minor, with a few men from the western provinces and a few from Egypt itself.[36] Sons of soldiers designated *castris* gradually became a more important source of fresh manpower, especially in the second century.[37] Although in the eastern provinces localized recruiting probably developed more quickly than in the west, this process was uneven and inconsistent, and came about more through circumstance and local factors than through deliberate policy.

To organize and equip the Roman army was a significant achievement in terms of the ancient world, and it is easy to believe that the army worked with machine-like efficiency and that all units were always kept at their full paper strength. But it is an assumption on our part that the Romans recognized a strong need to maintain precise numbers in each army unit. Doubtless the difficulty of processing recruits, matching them to vacancies created by discharges, death or disability, and transporting them to the relevant unit, caused temporary depletion in the ranks. But it is worth asking if the army was often seriously below normal complement and if, in time of war, the government needed to find large numbers of new recruits. This may have disrupted the usual pattern of recruiting and put additional pressure on recruiting areas.

It is possible to argue that the legions were often well below paper strength, with about 4600 men, and that there was an uneven pattern of recruiting with a large intake in some years and a much smaller one in others. This depends on inscriptions listing soldiers discharged from a particular legion in certain years, and a calculation of the probable lifespan of legionaries. We can therefore work out from the number of discharged veterans the number of original recruits, and estimate the size of the legion.[38] However, the smallness of the statistical sample and the difficulty of calculating mortality rates in the ancient world make these conclusions very uncertain. Furthermore, we do not know what special circumstances may have influenced events in a particular legion, and doubtless some commanders will have been inefficient or even corrupt in recruitment practice.[39] In the case of the auxiliaries, limited evidence from papyri indicates that some mounted cohorts were below strength. On the other hand, the twentieth cohort of Palmyrenes based at Dura Europus in the early third century seems to have been close to or even over normal strength, although there was a rise in recruiting figures in 214–16, perhaps in preparation for Caracalla's campaign against Parthia.[40] This kind of evidence is inconclusive, but it at least suggests that there was significant variation in the complement of units at different times, and that there were sometimes special recruiting efforts in preparation for campaigns, even if only to sharpen up the army and replace sickly or older soldiers. Thus warfare would mean a greater demand on existing recruiting areas and possibly the use of hitherto untapped resources.[41] However, since all men recruited in emergencies were still required to serve for the stipulated twenty-five years, the essential character of the army remained unchanged.

Ancient commentators often talk of special military preparations in emergencies. For example, when hostilities with Parthia threatened in AD 54, Nero ordered that the legions under the command of the governor of Syria, Ummidius Quadratus, should be reinforced by recruiting in the provinces adjacent to Syria.[42] And, in 58, Domitius Corbulo, newly appointed commander against the Parthians, was appalled by the ill-discipline of the Syrian legions, discharging soldiers who were too old or unfit, and ordering recruiting in Galatia and Cappadocia to strengthen them for the campaign.[43] During the civil wars in AD 68 to 69 all contenders recruited soldiers from whatever source they could. Galba raised a new legion (later VII Gemina) entirely from Spanish recruits. Similarly, when Vitellius set out to find reinforcements for his march on Rome, he hurriedly recruited men from Gaul and Germany, some of whom were probably not even Roman citizens.[44] This gave his rival Otho the opportunity to denounce Vitellius' men as foreigners and outsiders.[45] Vespasian in his proclamation as emperor set about recruiting men by recalling veterans and raising levies, presumably throughout Syria,[46] and 6000 men from Dalmatia who appear in the Flavian forces were presumably conscripted.[47] Two irregular legions, I and II Adiutrix, were raised from the fleets based at Misenum and Ravenna, and were eventually incorporated into the army as proper legions.[48]

Heavy war casualties could also play havoc with the normal system of recruitment. There are signs of emergency recruiting to supplement legion X Fretensis, which had suffered severely in the Jewish revolt of AD 66 to 70, in that a number of legionaries recruited in 68 and 69 were Egyptian (Egyptians were not normally recruited to serve outside Egypt).[49] Again, an inscription from Egypt shows the origins of 130 men recruited to legion II Traiana in AD 132 and 133. No recruits came from Egypt, while eighty-eight came from Africa, fifteen from Italy, one from Dalmatia, seven from Asia Minor, and nineteen from Syria and Palestine. This may suggest an attempt to bring the legion up to strength, perhaps after casualties suffered in the Jewish War of 132 to 135; thus men were brought from unusual sources, including three from Rome itself, and none from the usual Italian recruiting ground of the Transpadana.[50] Throughout the first three centuries, in addition to regular supplements for the army, new legions and auxilia were recruited. In the case of legions this sometimes seems to have been associated with major military campaigns or the creation of a new province. This will have imposed an extra burden of finding more than 5000 men at one time. New legions were occasionally and perhaps usually raised in Italy itself, and this was certainly the case with those legions named *Italica*, one raised by Nero and two by Marcus Aurelius.[51]

It is very difficult to judge the effect of changes in the pattern of recruitment on the local economy and society. A small farmer may not have been able to cope with the loss of able-bodied sons to the recruiting officer. On the other hand, the removal of men of employable age might put less pressure on the available pool of casual or seasonal jobs. We may perhaps compare the turmoil caused in Italy by recruitment drives in the wake of military setbacks. The most striking examples are the aftermath of the revolt of the Pannonians in AD 6 and the loss of three legions in Germany in AD 9. Augustus was forced to recruit in Rome itself, which seldom provided men for the army, and even resorted to freedmen.[52] We get an idea of the kind of man recruited from Percennius, one of the leaders of the mutiny in 14, who had been a professional applause-leader in the theatre.[53] The recruiting of freemen in Rome probably in AD 6 is attested by the inscription of C. Fabricius Tuscus, who was 'tribune of the levy of freeborn men which Augustus and Tiberius Caesar held in Rome'.[54] Dio's generalizations about the effect on the youth of Italy of Septimius Severus' initial recruitment of the praetorians from legionaries may be exaggerated, but they do express what an experienced senator thought might happen after a change in recruitment practice. He alleged that the young men turned to banditry and a career as gladiators because there was no employment or any other means of support.[55]

Auxilia units were raised from peoples on the edges of Roman control and throughout the provinces, generally from areas with few communities originally holding Roman citizenship. Spain, for example, contributed cohorts and *alae* to most armies;[56] other important recruiting areas were the Alps, Raetia, Pannonia, Thrace (more than thirty units of Thracians are found in service in the early empire), Syria and Palestine.[57] Gaul, especially parts of Belgica and Lugdunensis, was also very important. Here the Romans used local élites and organizational structures for recruitment, and eight cohorts and one *ala* of Batavians served in Britain before AD 69.[58] In fact Batavian society in the early imperial period was renowned for its military ambience, and one of the social consequences of recruitment was the continuation of the power of the traditional warrior élite, the most prominent of whose members served as prefect commanders in early auxiliary units. By contrast, the importance of martial ideology declined in tribal life in south-west Belgica owing partly to Roman pacification and partly to internal factors, and there were few recruits. However, after the revolt of Julius Civilis in AD 69, when Batavian units then serving on the Rhine defected to his cause,[59] there was a breakdown of the military élite in the Rhineland communities, and other more civilized forms of upper-class competition took over, such as holding administrative posts and financing public buildings.[60] In the long term, areas of recruitment and settlement of soldiers could expect to see changes in social customs and attitudes, burial practices, religious observances and types of building. It is difficult, however, because of the inconsistent availability of reliable comparable evidence (usually archaeological) for these aspects in different areas, to analyse the overall impact of the Roman army and to compare regions where there was little or no recruitment.[61]

In the early period auxiliary units were normally stationed in areas far from where they had been recruited, although this sometimes caused dissension among the troops.[62] The government presumably feared the danger of collaboration and rebellion if large numbers of trained soldiers served among their compatriots. This was borne out by the revolt of Civilis. Gradually, however, units came to be supplemented by recruits from the area where they served, and so their original ethnic character was diluted. By the time of Hadrian, soldiers were usually recruited from the province where a unit was stationed, or from an adjacent province.[63] There was thus an extraordinary mixture of nationalities in the frontier garrisons. Indeed, Tacitus described it as a 'motley agglomeration of nations'.[64] But even with the practice of local recruiting there was always the danger that men could be sent far from their homes in an emergency. Indeed, Britons and Dacians were usually stationed outside their own areas, and this meant that the substantial garrisons in Britain and Dacia had to be supplied by men drawn from other areas. Furthermore, specialist regiments such as archers, especially those enlisted in the east, continued to draw recruits from the original area of recruitment, for example, the first cohort of Hemesene archers stationed in Pannonia.[65] It is also true that since loyalties in the ancient world tended to be parochial, to villages and small communities, for many men even local recruitment will have meant that they served far from their real home and seemed like foreigners to the local population around the legionary bases.

In all sections of the Roman army volunteers would presumably be preferred to conscripts on the grounds that they would make better soldiers. Tiberius, however, had a low opinion of the quality of volunteers from Italy, saying that they lacked the old courage and discipline and were mainly vagrants and down-and-outs.[66] Conditions of service in the early empire did not promise a glittering future; the mutineers in AD 14 complained of low pay, poor land on discharge, and a miserable lifestyle in unpleasant conditions.[67] Furthermore, it is reasonable to suggest that Italians did not wish to serve for twenty-five years far from their homeland, especially at a time when it was not itself in danger. Provincial citizens and recruits to the *auxilia* doubtless had similar sentiments. Therefore in the first two centuries AD the government was probably not slow to resort to conscription in provincial communities to supplement the legions, though usually not in Italy. Non-Romans were liable for conscription into the *auxilia* at all times. It is not possible to say what proportions of volunteers and conscripts served in the army at any one time, but by the late second and early third centuries volunteers were probably more common, in line with the improvement in service conditions under the Severan dynasty, and perhaps the development in local recruiting.[68]

To sum up, by the second century AD at the height of the empire the vast majority of men in the legions were non-Italians. They had a wide variety of racial and local backgrounds, although we cannot determine clearly the relative contributions of particular provinces to the legions. Legions serving in the western part of the empire tended to be filled by men from the west, and those in the eastern part by men from the east. Legionaries were often only recently Roman citizens, or indeed had gained citizenship upon enlistment, and certainly knew little or nothing of Rome itself.[69] Only the praetorians retained a distinctly Italian character up to the reign of Septimius Severus. Interestingly, an inscription from Aquileia probably of the second century AD celebrates an ex-soldier, C. Manlius Valerianus, 'who faithfully commanded a century in a praetorian cohort, not in a barbarian legion'.[70] The auxiliaries were a mixture of men from tribes, nations and cities, some with a long, traditional attachment to Rome, others with no emotional ties. In all sections of the army there was a combination of volunteers and conscripts. By the mid-second century local recruitment was much more common, presumably as the government found it useful and beneficial, but was not consistently applied across the empire. Through this and the increase in the number of volunteers it may be that the government could hope for increased morale and enthusiasm of men fighting for their homelands.[71]

After the death of Severus Alexander in AD 235 there followed a period of significant military and political dislocation accompanied by economic and social upheaval, in which there were revolts and secession and many foreign incursions. The process of recruiting and motivating soldiers presumably went on, though we hear little about it. Diocletian (284–305) resorted to widespread conscription and insisted that the sons of veterans joined up. He made city governments or individual landowners responsible for finding recruits annually, in proportion to the amount of land within their

31

remit. By the fourth century, landowners had begun to group together to meet this obligation. This kind of conscription was so unpopular that men paid money to avoid service, and these funds were then used as a bribe to encourage the enlistment of fighting peoples from outside the empire. It seems improbable that this would produce willing soldiers, especially since military pay had been seriously eroded by inflation, although they now received more payments in kind of meat and salt or corn. Nevertheless, the army in the later empire retained many of its qualities and continued to win battles against foreign enemies, even though its character and composition had changed.

The social background of Roman soldiers

Recruiting practices in the imperial period suggest that soldiers generally continued to come from low social backgrounds, mainly from poorer rural communities. Pay was not generous before the third century, and conditions were sometimes tough. It is unlikely that men of high social standing often volunteered, and they would have been influential enough to avoid conscription.[72] Trajan assumed that recruits would be either volunteers or conscripts or substitutes (*vicarii*).[73] Presumably, better-off people could pay someone to take their place. The evidence that shows soldiers owning property may be explained on the grounds of unexpected inheritance or enrichment through military service. Replies by emperors to legal queries from soldiers show us the routine difficulties of ordinary people who had little influence or standing outside their connection to the military. Indeed, discharge payments in money or land confirm that soldiers were at the lower end of the financial scale. A legionary received 12,000 sesterces on discharge; the property qualification for a man of equestrian rank was 400,000, and for a senator one million sesterces. It is therefore not surprising that so few veterans apparently took up local magistracies, since these had many incidental expenses.

It is true that there is some evidence of letters written by soldiers to their families and others. Furthermore, the sophisticated operation of the Roman military bureaucracy has left a long trail of paperwork and records.[74] But this does not mean that many soldiers were well educated or highly literate, and therefore from a higher social background. The evidence for soldiers' letters is not extensive and may be exceptional. The working of the bureaucracy was very specialized and probably the preserve of only a small number of educated soldiers. Many soldiers probably had only limited literacy skills and social outlook, especially in the east, and in Africa many may not have understood much Latin on joining up. For example, ostraca from the military outpost of Bu Njem in north Africa suggest that soldiers there, many of whom may have been Punic or Libyan in origin, spoke a colloquial Latin and had a low level of literacy.[75] On the other hand, since the centurionate was socially heterogeneous there were varying levels of literacy among centurions.[76] These considerations are relevant to the degree of political awareness and understanding among the soldiers.[77]

The comments of writers like Cassius Dio and Tacitus give us an upper-class view of the military, and this is important since it was men like these who commanded most of Rome's armies. In a speech attributed to Maecenas offering advice to Augustus in 29 BC, Dio expresses his own view that equestrians who had been rank-and-file soldiers should not be promoted to senatorial rank: 'For it is a shameful disgrace that men of this type, who have acted as porters and carried charcoal, should be found among the membership of the Senate.'[78] In the same speech Maecenas recommends that men most in need of a livelihood should be enlisted and trained as soldiers, indicating that in Dio's view men of standing and settled respectability would not normally serve.[79] According to the laws described in the *Digest*, men condemned to the beasts, deported to an island or exiled for a fixed period that was not yet completed were to be discharged and punished if found in the army. Men who joined up in order to avoid prosecution were also to be discharged.[80] The implication of this legislation is that there were men serving with a very dubious background. The praetorians were not necessarily any better. Dio believed that, after Severus had disbanded the existing guard, frustrated Italian recruits brought about increased brigandage and disorder in the countryside.[81] Furthermore, the praetorians enlisted by Severus from his Danubian legionaries were not a reassuring sight: 'He filled the city with a motley crowd of soldiers who were ferocious in appearance, terrifying in manner of speech, and uncultivated in conversation.'[82] Tacitus, in his analysis of the mutinies of AD 14 and the conduct of the soldiers during the civil wars of 68 to 69, paints a gloomy picture of the army and the propensity of the soldiers to plunder and destroy.[83] This apprehensive contempt for soldiers also helps explain Dio's praise of Trajan 'because he did not allow the soldiers to become arrogant during his long campaigns', and his comment that Augustus' organization of the service conditions of the army at least ensured that people would not be deprived of their property.[84] Thus, according to the upper-class view, soldiers were potentially threatening, uneducated men of low degree who should not be allowed to rise above their proper station in life.[85]

In the Roman empire professional soldiers made up a relatively small proportion of the population, and most people, either citizens or subjects, had little direct concern with fighting or the military function. Indeed, throughout the first two centuries AD there was in some respects an increasing distinction between the civil and the military.[86] Soldiers, by their ethnic, legal, social and economic status, had no obvious community of interest with the propertied élite or the urban society and culture they helped to protect. They had no natural connection with the nexus of power and patronage that maintained the rule of the emperors, or interest in the Italian homeland and the centre of imperial power, Rome itself. How, then, were soldiers of this kind inspired and motivated to fight for Rome? What is the basis of the morale of Roman soldiers in battle? Motivation in battle depends partly on personal character, but also on factors deriving from the military community and the soldier's environment, notably peer pressure and unit loyalty, discipline and leadership, and life in the camp.[87] The Roman army was of course a permanent force manned by trained professional soldiers. Now, the professional soldier should look on battle differently; he ought to be imbued with traditional military values and react strongly to the stimulation of unit loyalty and symbols of military camaraderie. Again, we might expect the hardened veteran to have a clearer view of the likelihood of his own survival and the means of achieving it. Out of this should come greater self-confidence and willingness to obey orders. He was also perhaps more remote from the pleasures of life at home, the memory of which might disturb a militia or short-term conscript army.[88] On the other hand, the professional might lack the reckless bravery of the volunteer fighting for a cause.

Morale: personal motivation

The prospect of enrichment through the emoluments of military service, or the likelihood of booty, captives and other handouts, should be an incentive for soldiers.[89] Roman soldiers received regular pay, in three annual instalments. Domitian added a fourth instalment, but there were no further increases until the end of the second century. Rates of pay were not generous, being little more per day than the wages of a labourer, and there were compulsory stoppages for food and clothing.[90] But a labourer could not expect work every day, and the expectation of regular pay-days might well motivate a recruit from a poor background. Furthermore, an annual salary of about 1200 sesterces probably served as a 'living wage' by the early second century AD in Italy.[91] On retirement from the army legionaries received a pension worth more than ten times a year's pay, or a plot of land.[92] Special consideration was given to wounded or sick soldiers who had to be discharged early.[93] In this respect Roman soldiers were better looked after than many soldiers right up to the modern age. What is more, the troops could have confidence in the medical and military hospital facilities available, and could expect that casualties would be speedily treated.[94] All citizen-soldiers had a range of legal privileges in respect of making wills and leaving property,[95] and also marriage rights on discharge, which ensured that their children would be Roman citizens. From the mid-first century onwards those non-citizens serving in the *auxilia* received on discharge Roman citizenship and similar marriage rights that brought citizenship to their children.[96] This practice may have contributed to the integration of such men and their families into the Roman way of life, although it is difficult to judge the level of national patriotism in the Roman army.[97]

Perhaps local patriotism was a more potent influence. As local recruiting became more common, especially in the second century, more men tended to serve in the vicinity of where they were born. More importantly, soldiers perhaps came to build up stronger relationships in the military community and beyond because of the practice of housing legions in permanent bases in a fixed location. If troops were needed elsewhere, a detachment (*vexillatio*) was transferred, while the bulk of the legion and its command and infrastructure remained. Some legions came to develop a long association with the communities that existed or grew up around their barracks. The legion III Augusta was established in Africa from 30 BC, and from the reign of Trajan was stationed at Lambaesis for 140 years until it was temporarily cashiered in AD 238. In the province of Upper Pannonia on the Danube, the legion XIV Gemina was based at Carnuntum from about AD 114 up to the end of Roman control in the area, and a sizeable civilian community developed beside the camp.[98] In Spain (Hispania Tarraconensis) the legion VII Gemina, which had originally been raised by Galba from Roman citizens in the province, returned in AD 75 and was based until the late fourth century at Legio (modern León), which took its name from the legion.[99] The link between the Romans and the locality is nicely illustrated by the dedication set up by the commander of the legion to the nymphs of a local spring.[100] In general, many soldiers had a wife and family in neighbouring settlements, and veteran soldiers often settled in the vicinity.[101] There is therefore some reason to suppose that the troops came to have strong emotional attachments to the local area, and might fight more enthusiastically for land and people they considered to be their own.[102] There is little clear evidence for this, but in AD 69 the Syrian legions were stirred up by reports that they were to be moved to Germany: 'the troops felt at home in the camp where they had served so long and for which they had acquired a real affection.'[103] Again, it is significant that the soldiers who accompanied Severus Alexander from the Danube to the east for his campaign against the Parthians were desperate to return when they heard that the Germans had overrun Roman territory and threatened their families in their absence.[104]

By the end of the third century AD a gradual change in the army's organization had come about, with the development of a field army (*comitatenses*) which was independent of any territorial or provincial attachment, and could attend on the person of the emperor. The *comitatenses* by definition were expected to move around the empire at relatively short notice, and it may be that men recruited or transferred into them were younger men who had no family ties. This perhaps undermined the bonds that had sometimes developed between soldiers and the area in which they served. On the other hand, there were also soldiers (*limitanei*) who were permanently stationed in provinces deemed to need a military presence, and there is no reason to believe that in this period the *limitanei* were of a significantly inferior quality to the troops of the field army.[105]

Morale: the military community

The Roman commander Lucius Aemilius Paulus described the military camp as the soldier's second homeland: 'its rampart serves as his city walls, and his tent is the soldier's hearth and home.'[106] The closed military community of the Roman army will have played an important part in sustaining not only discipline but also the spirit of military comradeship and mutual respect and reliance that are seemingly crucial in keeping soldiers together during campaigns and battles. In this environment the soldier will ideally have felt a high sense of duty; he will have been eager not to disgrace himself in front of his comrades in his unit, and in particular not to let them down. This is important in military psychology, and military service could engender a feeling of excitement, or even of irresponsibility, in that soldiers were carrying out actions that they would not otherwise be allowed to do or would not dream of doing.[107] The self-confident, soldierly enthusiasm of the military community and its concerns are vividly expressed by an inscription set up in Africa by an anonymous chief centurion:

> I wanted to hold slaughtered Dacians. I held them.
> I wanted to sit on a chair of peace. I sat on it.
> I wanted to take part in famous triumphs. It was done.
> I wanted the full benefits of the chief centurionate. I have had them.
> I wanted to see naked nymphs. I saw them.[108]

In military life unit loyalty and the accompanying symbols are very important, especially colours or standards, badges and other insignia. The Roman army was highly structured, and had a well-developed idea of comradeship, expressed in the words *commilitium* and *commilito*, which as the address 'fellow-soldier' or 'comrade' was used not only by soldiers but also by emperors to inspire and flatter their men.[109] The legion had a complement of about 5240 men divided into ten cohorts, nine of which consisted of six centuries with eighty men in each, while the other, the first or leading cohort, had five centuries of double size (800 men). There were also 120 legionary cavalry. Each century was further divided into ten *contubernia*.

Therefore the smallest unit in the Roman army was the *contubernium*; eight comrades shared the same tent and the use of a mule in the field, and in a permanent military camp shared two rooms: one for storage, the other for sleeping. So, each soldier performed military chores, messed and fought in the company of the same small group of people. Illustration comes from the Roman siege camp at the Jewish fortress of Masada, where the hearths have been identified where each *contubernium* cooked its meals.[110] Close proximity to his colleagues might well encourage a soldier to put on a brave show in battle.[111]

The century was a self-contained unit under the command of a centurion, and was sometimes identified by his name. The tents of the ten *contubernia* making up a century were grouped together, and in permanent camps each century had its own accommodation of rectangular barrack blocks containing at least ten double rooms; the centuries were arranged in groups of six according to their cohort. Each cohort was commanded by its senior centurion, and with 480 men was small enough to give the soldiers a sense of personal identity, and also large enough to operate independently when required; it probably had its own standard to instil loyalty and act as a rallying point.[112]

The legion, however, was the backbone of the Roman army. Large units are important because they very clearly have a permanent existence and identity, and embody tradition and the history of the army. They can help develop military ideology and inculcate *esprit de corps* and rivalry, inspiring the soldier to make his unit do better than other units.[113] A long-established unit such as the legion, or the regiment in a modern army, provided for new recruits a ready-made framework shored up by an attractive mystique, and of course was also the spiritual home of the veteran professional soldier.

In the Roman army each legion had a number and a name, based on the circumstances of its foundation, the location of its early service, a famous exploit or some kind of imperial favour. For example, legion V Alaudae ('Larks') was originally raised by Caesar in Transalpine Gaul and took its name from the crest of bird feathers on the soldiers' helmets. Legion I Minervia was formed by Domitian in AD 83 and named after the goddess Minerva whom he specially favoured. Legion XXX Ulpia Victrix ('Ulpian Victorious') was named after its founder Trajan and its distinguished conduct in the Second Dacian War. The legion XIV Gemina won the titles *Martia Victrix* ('Martial and Victorious') for its part in the defeat of Boudicca in Britain in AD 60 to 61. Legionary names remained unchanged, and most legions were distinguished by their longevity. Of the twenty-five legions in service in AD 14, twenty were still in service in the second century with the same numerals and usually the same name.[114] The identifying numbers of legions that had been disgraced or destroyed were not used again; for example, the numerals XVII, XVIII, XIX, which had belonged to the three legions lost in Germany under Quinctilius Varus.

The supreme symbol of each legion was its eagle standard, which represented in gold or gilt an eagle with outspread wings. This symbolized the continuity of the legion's existence. The eagle was moved from the base only when the whole legion was on the march, and was planted in the ground first when camp was pitched. It was kept in the camp shrine and received

religious observances.[115] The importance of the eagle standard in military
ideology may be judged from the many references to it in literature and art.
Indeed, it was used tactically, in that a commander, by deliberately putting
the standard at risk, could force the soldiers of the legion to advance to the
rescue. To lose the standard to the enemy in battle was considered the ultimate disgrace. Augustus arranged great celebrations when he obtained the
return of the military standard lost by Crassus in Parthia over thirty years
before.[116] No effort was spared to find the eagles lost with Varus' three legions.
Some legions also displayed their own emblem, often associated with signs
of the Zodiac. For example, legion II Augusta, which had been founded
or reorganized by Augustus, had a capricorn, which symbolized his good-
luck. Even detachments of legions (*vexillationes*) had their own standards, a
decorated banner carried on a pole, and therefore their own identity.[117] There
was therefore strong group identity and cohesion in the Roman army. During the mutiny of AD 14 proposals to merge the three Pannonian legions
failed because all parties insisted on retaining the identity of each legion;
eventually they put all the standards side by side on a platform.[118] The same
kind of loyalty applied to units of *auxilia*, which had a number and a name
(although the ethnic significance of the names was eventually diluted), and
standards for each cohort and cavalry *ala*. These units numbered either
about 500 or, from the end of the first century AD, sometimes between
800 and 1000. Again the cohorts were subdivided into centuries and *contubernia*, and the *alae* into squadrons (*turmae*) with thirty-two men in each.[119]

Unit identity was built up and maintained by military training and
day-to-day life in the camp. The troops' common purpose and identity were
expressed by the oath (*sacramentum*) they swore on enlistment and renewed
annually, 'to carry out all the emperor's commands energetically, never desert
their military service or shirk death on behalf of the Roman state')[120] Then
there was a common training routine, which was aimed at physical fitness,
proficiency in marching, unit manoeuvres, and weapons drill in throwing
the *pilum* and using a two-edged sword.[121] The new recruit, trained along
with his comrades, would receive his uniform, which also served to bind
him into the military hierarchy, since legionaries had a distinctive outfit,
marking them out from auxiliaries, while praetorians had a uniform that
indicated their élite status. When Otho ordered the arsenal in the praetorian
camp to be opened as he organized the overthrow of Galba, normal dis-
tinctions and niceties were ignored: 'Weapons were hastily snatched up
without tradition and military discipline, which laid down that praetorians
and legionaries should be distinguished by their equipment. In confusion
they seized helmets and shields meant for auxiliaries.'[122]

The routine of camp life sustained and bound together the military
community. The drudgery of chores and minor duties will have served to
remind soldiers of their common purpose and identity, which marked them

out from civilians even when there was no war in prospect. The records of military bureaucrats preserved on papyri or wooden tablets reveal the daily life of an enclosed community. For example, the record of a detachment of the legion III Augusta stationed at Bu-Njem in north Africa in the third century AD indicates that, of fifty-seven soldiers on 24 December, there were present one clerk, one orderly, one scout, eight cavalry; twenty-two were possibly on exercises, one man was on the watchtower, one at the gate, one at the commanding officer's, one possibly doing building work, three were sick, one was being flogged, seventeen had no specific task of whom fifteen were at the bakehouse (?) and two at the bath.[123] The clubs (*collegia*) that certain groups of soldiers and officers were permitted to form will also have contributed to the comradeship and team spirit of military life. These clubs met to honour military divinities and the achievements of the imperial family, and had an active social role in providing mutual assistance for their members.[124] Soldiers' gravestones also demonstrate a close-knit military environment. It became common practice for soldiers who had died in service to be commemorated by an epitaph, often set up under the terms of their will by relatives or by their comrades. The better-off had elaborate memorials depicting them in uniform, as in a famous example from Colchester: 'Marcus Favonius Facilis, of the tribe Pollia, centurion of legion XX. The freedmen Vercundus and Novicius erected [it]. He lies here.'[125]

Battle imposes its own restraints on soldiers, most of whom probably feel compelled to carry out orders and do their duty with their comrades in the fighting. In a well-disciplined army the habit of obedience is important, and in the Roman army this was enforced by military law, which regulated daily relations between comrades, ensuring proper and responsible behaviour in the confined life of the barracks. Clear rules also defined the soldier's responsibilities in battle to his unit, comrades and officers. The most important aspect of this concerned desertion, loss of weapons and cowardice. Those guilty of desertion and cowardice in the face of the enemy in time of war were liable to the death penalty. But offenders could be much more leniently treated outside campaigns, with a sensible scale of punishment depending on the circumstances and length of desertion. Emperors sometimes intervened to reduce the penalties inflicted,[126] but on other occasions commanders made an example of certain individuals or units that had disgraced themselves in combat. The emperor Augustus, so the story goes, inflicted the traditional punishment of decimation on units that gave way in battle.[127] This meant that one in ten soldiers was selected by lot and executed. Although much depended on individual commanders, in the main the Roman army was well organized and responsive to orders in battle, and there are few accounts of serious indiscipline or collapse of morale.[128] Josephus, who had seen Roman troops at first hand during the Jewish revolt of AD 66 to 70, particularly admired their seemingly unbreakable discipline in battle, though it may have been in his interests to exaggerate: 'Therefore they sustain the shock of combat very easily. For their usual well-ordered ranks are not disrupted by any confusion, or numbed by fear, or exhausted by toil; so, certain victory inevitably follows since the enemy cannot match this.'[129]

Soldiers need to feel that conspicuous acts of courage in battle will be rewarded. The Roman army had a highly developed system of military decorations that suited different acts of bravery, according to the rank and status of the recipient. These decorations took the form of gold and silver necklaces and armlets, and inscribed discs that could be worn on armour for dress parades. There were also crowns representing a wall for the first man to scale a city wall or storm a camp, and any soldier could also win the 'civic crown' (*civica corona*) for saving a comrade's life.[130] Soldiers took these decorations seriously, and recorded them on their career inscriptions or funeral monuments, usually indicating that they had received them from the emperor himself. This shows how the soldiers valued the idea that the emperor knew of their exploits. A legionary from Cremona had his military decorations buried next to his ashes.[131] It is of course unlikely that emperors distributed decorations in person except when on campaign. However, after the fall of Jerusalem in AD 70, Titus, who ranked as a prince, held a public ceremony in which he decorated soldiers personally in the presence of the whole army.[132] Special money payments and promotions were also made.[133] In a few cases we hear how an entire unit was decorated for its bravery in battle. Thus the first cohort of Britons acquired from Trajan the titles 'Ulpian Decorated Loyal and Faithful' because 'they performed dutifully and loyally in the Dacian campaign'. They also received a special grant of Roman citizenship.[134]

The morale of soldiers in the battle line has much to do with their officers. Those who earned the trust and respect of their men for their technical competence, which helped protect the soldiers' lives, for their consistent discipline, for their conspicuous presence in the camp and on the battlefield, for their courage and for the example they set, and even for honourable wounds, could get the best out of the troops even when the battle was going badly. The senior command of the Roman army was recruited from the upper classes. There were six military tribunes (five equestrians and one senator)[135] in each legion, which was commanded by the *legatus legionis*, usually a senator of praetorian rank. Larger military forces, consisting of several legions and auxiliary regiments, which were stationed in certain provinces, were commanded by a senator of consular rank, the *legatus Augusti*, who was also the provincial governor. There was no military academy or formal training for any of these military officers, who had differing levels of interest, aptitude and experience of army command. Tacitus in his biography of his father-in-law, Agricola, a distinguished commander, neatly sums up the different approaches of young Romans to military life:

But Agricola did not behave extravagantly like those young men who turn their military service into an unruly party; he did not use his military tribunate and his inexperience as an excuse to seek long leave and a good time. Instead he got to know the province and to be known by the army.[136]

But, whatever their shortcomings in training and preparation, Roman officers seem to have taken their responsibilities seriously, both to the men they commanded and in the conduct of warfare. There was a clear and consistent command structure, and Roman senators, even if they produced few really inspiring commanders, like a Pompey or a Caesar, were not armchair generals; they wore the traditional military dress of a Roman general, commanded in person and took real military decisions. They seem in general to have been proud of their role with the army. Some even died fighting, like Claudius Fronto: 'after successful battles against the Germans and the Iazyges he fell fighting bravely to the end for the Fatherland.'[137] Even Quinctilius Varus achieved a dignified end by committing suicide.

However enthusiastic they were, Roman officers could rarely expect more than three years in command of a legion or an army, and had only a limited chance to build up a rapport with their men.[138] Here the senior officers were effectively supported by the centurions, who had charge of eighty men.[139] They are often seen as the equivalent of non-commissioned officers in a modern army, but this does not do them justice. They were in the main very experienced, well-tried soldiers often serving for twenty years or more, many of whom were destined to go on to more senior posts in the army and then in civilian administration.[140] They had a crucial position between military tribunes and the ordinary soldiers, and were certainly responsible for much of the day-to-day discipline, organization and training of the army.[141] In battle they ensured that the constituent units of the legion carried out their orders. The centurions of the first cohort and the chief centurion (*primus pilus*) of the legion were very senior and would have useful advice to offer at councils of war.

Ancient writers seemingly endorse the accepted truism that the presence of a supreme commander or king or emperor on the battlefield brings special encouragement to the troops. Dio commented that Tiberius sat on a high, conspicuous platform to watch an attack on Seretium in Dalmatia in AD 9 not only so that he could provide help if he had to, but also to encourage his men to fight with more spirit.[142] Similarly, during Septimius Severus' march on Rome in AD 193, 'the soldiers carried out all their duties enthusiastically because they respected him for sharing their work and the leading role he took in all their hardships'.[143] The Roman emperor was at all times a focus of loyalty in the army. In the ideal relationship he was someone with whom the soldiers could identify. We see this in the letter of a recruit in Egypt seeking service in an auxiliary cohort 'so that I may

41

be able . . . to serve under the standards of the Emperor, our Lord'.[144] From the late first century AD onwards, the Roman emperor accompanied his army on major campaigns and often directed the troops personally on the battlefield. Indeed, some emperors while on campaign tried to lead the life of a true fellow-soldier.[145] In a tradition that went back to the early Republic, a Roman commander usually made a speech to his army before battle. Emperors followed this practice, and in the right setting could probably make themselves heard to groups of several thousand. Ancient writers tell us (probably rightly) that they had a simple message, and encouraged the troops by emphasizing their abilities and denigrating the enemy (see Plate 2.1).[146] At the siege of Jerusalem, Titus believed that hope and encouraging words best-roused the fervour of troops in battle, and that exhortations and promises often made men forget danger.[147] It was not, however, until the third century that a Roman emperor actually fought in battle. Maximinus, campaigning against the Germans, plunged into a swamp on horseback in pursuit of the enemy and shamed the rest of the army into following his example.[148]

It was also the commander's job to boost his army's confidence by performing appropriate religious observances. In the Republic magistrates normally tried to discover the will of the gods before major state undertakings. Therefore, before joining battle, commanders took the auspices in various ways, for example, by sacrificing animal victims and examining their entrails for appropriate signs. Indeed, the right of command was often expressed as the right to take the *auspicia*. Anecdotal evidence suggests that this was important. We can enjoy the story of the Roman admiral who threw the sacred chickens into the sea because they were reluctant to eat, and lost the battle. It is, however, difficult to tell how seriously the troops took divine support in battle, or how often signs and auguries were invented, as they often were in political life. But we might think that the poor men from rural Italy who made up the army would tend to be superstitious.

In the imperial period inscriptions set up by soldiers indicate that many of them privately worshipped gods with apparent sincerity and feeling.[149] A soldier of legion I Minervia set up an altar at Cologne in honour of local mother goddesses (*Matronae Aufanae*) to celebrate his return from duty with a detachment of his legion, which had travelled from Bonn to the east; he says that he had been at 'the river Alutus beyond the Caucasus mountain'.[150] Furthermore, the great military rituals were continued, not surprisingly, since the emperor was also chief priest. The army had specialists to kill animals (*victimarii*), and to examine their entrails (*haruspices*). Campaigns and victories were accompanied by sacrifices, offerings, vows and religious festivals. This is spectacularly illustrated by the representations on Trajan's monumental column, which show the emperor making an offering at an altar and presiding over the formal purification (*lustratio*) of the army before the invasion of Dacia (see Plate 2.2).[151] On a more humble

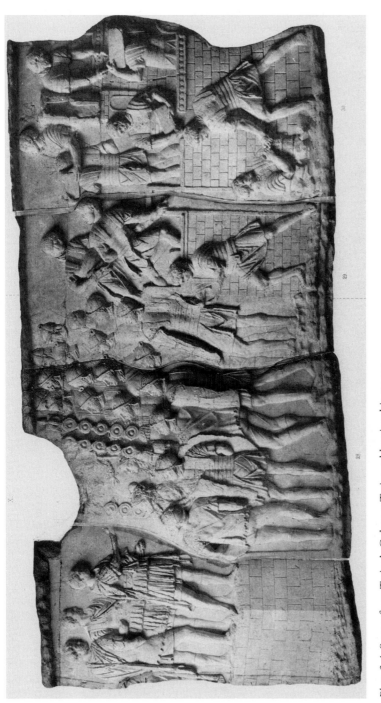

Plate 2.1 Scene from Trajan's Column: Trajan addressing his troops

Source: Lepper and Frere (1988), by permission of Mr Frank Lepper and Professor Sheppard Frere

Plate 2.2 Scene from Trajan's Column: Trajan conducting a sacrifice

Source: Lepper and Frere (1988), by permission of Mr Frank Lepper and Professor Sheppard Frere

level a distance slab from Bridgeness in Scotland depicts the officers of the legion II Augusta looking on while their commander pours a liquid offering at an altar.[152] In AD 213 when the emperor Caracalla set out on campaign against German tribes, the college of the Arval Brethren duly offered prayers for his good fortune and victory.[153] Augustus tried to channel religious interest and personal emotions by establishing a calendar of military festivals and celebrations that was still being used (with suitable additions) in the third century AD) by the twentieth cohort of Palmyrenes stationed at Dura-Europus on the river Euphrates. The calendar was written in Latin and had obviously been heavily used.[154] It contained major Roman festivals, but also emphasized the imperial family, with many celebrations of the reigning emperor and other imperial luminaries. There was a close link to military life with observances for military divinities, pay-day and the military standards.[155] The calendar, a variation of which was probably to be found in all military camps, will have helped to confirm a common identity and loyalty in the army, based around the rituals and observances of the traditional Roman religious system. The shrine in every army camp contained the military standards and statues of the emperor, and served as a further emotional focus of loyalty and worship in an organized, professional environment. Thus Turranius Firminus, veteran of legion II Adiutrix based at Aquincum (Budapest), put up his own money to repair the sentry-box 'for the safeguarding of the standards and sacred statues'.[156] Modern army life has been described as a 'total institution', in that a barrier is built between the institution and the outside world to restrict interaction between them, so that the purposes for which the institution exists may be most effectively pursued without external interference.[157] In some ways the Roman army prepared for war in this way, and, like a modern army with its chaplains, also had the emotional seal of its own religious mechanisms.

In the ancient world at certain times and places violence was commonplace in society. What men were asked to do in battle was possibly not so different from what they saw around them in day-to-day life, and battlefield weaponry was not much more formidable than that available in the streets. Therefore, the ordeal of hand-to-hand fighting and bloodshed was not necessarily alien to those who joined up, and the thought of it might not be a deterrent. Recruits might hope to encounter little fighting, and those from a poor and disadvantaged background could readily see the army as a means of social advancement not otherwise available to men of their class, and therefore worth the risk. Since the rewards of military service included admittance to Roman citizenship and absorption into the Roman way of life, soldiers could identify with the idea of 'Roman'. Therefore it was not a lofty ideology but the army itself, with its unique identity, discipline, routine and comradeship, that sustained their loyalty in a way of life for which they would fight, and seasoned them to customary displays of courage. Well equipped and prepared, the army could give a soldier

confidence that he was part of a seemingly invincible structure that dominated the contemporary environment and looked after his interests. An
inscription from Novae in Lower Moesia (base of legion I Italica) illustrates
not only long service in the military community but also the opportunities
available to ordinary recruits, expressed through simple piety and respect
for the emperor:

> For the safety of the Emperor, the vow that I Lucius Maximus
> Gaetulicus, son of Lucius, of the tribe Voltinia, from Vienne, made
> as a new recruit in legion XX Valeria Victrix to Imperial Victory,
> All-Divine and Most Reverend, I have now fulfilled as chief
> centurion in legion I Italica after fifty-seven years' service, in the
> consulship of Marullus and Aelianus (AD 184).[158]

3

THE NATURE OF WAR

What great courage is revealed! The sword [is red from killing the enemy] and worn away with slaughter. The [spear by
which the fierce] barbarians were pierced and fell completes
[the trophy].[1]

In these bloodthirsty verses the son of L. Apronius (governor of Africa
AD 18–21) gives one view of battle. It is, however, difficult to get close
to the experience of ordinary soldiers in the battle line. The evidence of
inscriptions and papyri is mainly concerned with the army's detailed administrative procedures and has led some to define it as a 'bureaucratic army'.[2]
But the army existed to fight battles and to extend and safeguard the
interests of Rome by killing sufficient numbers of the enemy. As for literary
sources, manuals on ancient warfare and military science tend to be technical
or concerned with the ploys of famous generals, and remote from the
crush of battle.[3] Battle descriptions are plentiful in the works of historians
or other writers, but bring their own problems of interpretation for the
reader. They are often brief and lacking in detail, deal only with certain
incidents, and do not treat soldiers as individuals. They are inevitably
composed from the point of view of upper-class writers, who are not in
the main interested in what happened to the ordinary soldier, just as they
ignored the lower classes generally.[4] Still less is there any direct evidence
for the feelings of those who faced the Romans in battle.[5] In some cases
battle accounts are emotional and rhetorical, though here we should distinguish between embellishment of a factual account and a literary construct
that is entirely a work of imagination. It has been argued that the Roman
narrative tradition rather than the Greek came to dominate later European
literature and military history, simplifying characterization and motivation,
and portraying legionaries as pliant automatons.[6]

Yet it would be unwise to exclude ancient accounts of battles entirely
from an enquiry into the nature of battle. This is especially true if for
literary accounts of battle we substitute individual items abstracted from
the descriptions of different authors relating to battles in different periods,
in order to illustrate a modern reconstruction of what an ancient battle
'must have been' like. Ancient battle narratives do have an important contribution to make, not least because some of the authors were prominent in
Roman life and administration. Tacitus had held high office and had an

47

excellent potential source of military information in his father-in-law, Agricola. Dio had at least commanded soldiers while governor of Pannonia, though not on active service, while Josephus had been a commander of the Jewish forces in Galilee during the revolt of AD 66. Writers of this background in my view expressed what articulate contemporaries thought about the nature, character and psychology of battle in imperial Rome. It is important how they chose to define battle and report the incidents they thought significant. This is part of the complex cultural and intellectual background of the kind of men in ancient society who commanded soldiers in battle. I consider battle narratives to be valuable evidence and use them cautiously with other available material to re-create realistically the experience of the Roman soldier in battle, although the dividing line between fact and literary embellishment may sometimes be blurred.[7] In this way we may also understand more about how the army worked, since the nature of battle depends partly on the kind of units in the army and their deployment, and appreciate the factors in Rome's military success.[8]

The structure of the army; types of war

In the second century AD the army contained between 170,000 and 180,000 legionary troops and perhaps 220,000 auxiliaries.[9] But there were no more than three legions in any one province, and Britain had one of the largest provincial armies with a combined strength of about 50,000 legionaries and *auxilia*. The legions operated essentially as heavy infantry. The *auxilia* provided cavalry, various specialist missile-throwers, and also infantry, though sometimes equipped in a distinctive way. In the army of the Republic, cavalry had often been a weak point; for example, Roman defeats at the hands of Hannibal owed something to the Carthaginians' significant superiority in this arm. Part of the problem was the expense and difficulty of maintaining large numbers of horses in Italy. In the early Republic the constitution provided for only 1800 cavalry at public expense. Rome therefore recruited cavalry from her Italian allies, but experience taught enterprising Roman commanders to look for more efficient cavalry forces elsewhere. Numidians were popular, and Julius Caesar made particular use of units of Gallic and German cavalry, often under the command of native princes. In the imperial period, these troops were gradually incorporated into the formal structure of the army in *alae*, equipped with spear, sword and shield.[10] Occasionally special cavalry was still employed; for example, the famous Moorish cavalry under the command of Lusius Quietus, who served Trajan and rose to become consul and governor of Judaea.[11] The total number of cavalry in the Roman army is difficult to recover since it is impossible to trace all the *auxilia* units in service at any one time. However, there were cavalry *alae* stationed in all provinces with legionary troops, and in Mauretania Caesariensis, which had no legionary troops, there were substantial cavalry forces of around

4000 men. The army had perhaps up to 50,000 cavalry serving in the second century AD.[12] The praetorians, the emperor's personal bodyguard, were 10,000 strong, grouped in cohorts, and a detachment usually accompanied the emperor on campaign. However, although they were equipped as élite heavy infantry, there is little sign that they made any specific tactical impact on the battlefield. Each legion had a number of siege engines,[13] and more siege equipment could be built on campaign. The structure of the army permitted it to achieve typical Roman war objectives, namely to bring major enemy forces to a set battle, defeat them, and make further resistance impossible by investing and capturing their strongholds or cities.

In general the Romans did not use diplomacy to recruit military allies for their wars. They did not regard other peoples to be of sufficient standing and military capability. However, the Romans did sometimes require foreign peoples by the terms of a peace settlement to supply troops. When Marcus Aurelius negotiated terms with the Iazyges they were obliged to supply 8000 cavalry, some of whom were immediately sent to Britain.[14] In the later empire, however, it became increasingly common for the Romans to employ barbarians, even former enemies, to fight for them. These people, who presumably used their own fighting methods, were then settled in the empire.[15]

In all periods emperors expected friendly kings theoretically independent but within the orbit of Roman influence to supply troops on demand for campaigns.[16] The most striking example in the early empire was the creation by Augustus *c.* 25 BC of the legion XXII Deiotariana from the army of King Deiotarus of Galatia, which he had equipped and trained on the Roman model.[17] On a more limited level, when, in 25 BC, Augustus ordered the invasion of Arabia under the prefect of Egypt, Aelius Gallus, the force consisted of legionaries, *auxilia*, 500 men from King Herod and 1000 from Obodas, king of the Nabataeans.[18] Similarly, *c.* AD 135 when Arrian the governor of Cappadocia organized resistance to the invasion of the Alani, his force as well as regular Roman troops comprised allied forces from Lesser Armenia and Trapezus, and spearmen from Colchis and Rhizion.[19] Because of the scarcity of our evidence it is possible that the Romans had this kind of support on many more occasions than we know about. Nevertheless, it seems unlikely that such support was ever decisive in achieving the Roman army's objectives. The Romans in the main relied on their own military resources.

Augustus finally won control of the Roman world in 31 BC at the naval battle of Actium, and he went on to establish Rome's first permanent navy, which was based eventually at Misenum and Ravenna, guarding the western and eastern coastlines of Italy. Subsequently, more squadrons were based on rivers and coasts where the Romans were militarily active, principally in Germany, Britain, on the Danube and on the Pontic sea. The total force rose to about 30,000, recruited from non-citizens in the provinces. The fleet conveyed officials and dignitaries, and also supplies for the army. It assisted in the suppression of piracy and could also act as troop transports.[20] For example, in AD 66, Cestius Gallus sent a detachment of his troops by ship to take by surprise the coastal city of Joppa.[21] Occasionally the fleet acted as an integral part of combined operations, as when Germanicus launched a campaign against the German tribes beyond the Rhine, and sailed part of his force through the North Sea and then up the river Ems. But this was not a complete success because of poor weather and storms.[22] Campaigns against Parthia, which usually involved an attack on the capital Ctesiphon, were sometimes assisted by naval operations on the Euphrates or Tigris, with the ships serving presumably as troop transports and carriers of supplies.[23] Normally the Roman navy did not spearhead military operations, was not an integral part of military strategy, and did not contribute to decisive victories. In the first three centuries AD there is no record of any significant naval battle, or any account of what life was like at sea in a warship. The Romans' control of the Mediterranean area depended on the power of their army and their domination of the territory around its shores.

A soldier's experience in battle depends on the nature of warfare. Roman troops would normally be engaged in external campaigns, that is, traditional warfare against militarily inferior peoples outside the empire or on its periphery, with the object of punishing or conquering them. Here the Romans often faced tribesmen who relied on a single headlong assault, or in the east highly skilled Parthian cavalry and archers. The Roman army could normally be expected to win these battles, though sometimes such encounters might create new tactical problems. Civil war by contrast set skilled Roman armies against each other armed with the same kinds of weapon and using the same tactics and stratagems. There might be higher casualties and destruction and devastation within the empire itself. Wars fought among fellow-soldiers also brought a questionable moral dimension, and perhaps also problems of motivation. Tacitus illustrates this with an anecdote from the civil wars in Italy in AD 68 to 69. A son unwittingly fatally wounded his own father, and they recognized each other as the son was searching his semi-conscious victim. When other soldiers noticed what had happened, 'throughout the battle lines ran a current of amazement and complaint, and men cursed this most cruel of all wars. However, this did not stop them from killing and robbing relatives, kinsmen and brothers.'[24] The Roman army also fought internal wars as a virtual army of occupation, in which it put down bandits and local rebellions, conducted police operations, and in some cases consolidated recently conquered areas. In certain parts of the Roman world it might indeed be difficult to distinguish between a state of war and peace. For example, in Judaea there was endemic violence and ideological resistance to Roman rule, and the Jewish rebellions in 66 to 70, 115 to 117 and 132 to 135 amounted to full-scale war.[25]

Battle tactics

Tactics dictate how a battle develops and therefore help to shape the experience of individual soldiers. Roman tactics tended to be straightforward, based on the structure of the army, traditional military practices, and a restricted range of manoeuvres and stratagems, in which the exploits of earlier generals were an important influence.[26] Each legion contained about 5240 men, and it was probably unnecessary for the Romans to employ a larger formation since most wars against foreign enemies were fought with relatively small armies. The subdivision of the legion into ten cohorts[27] combined flexibility with strength, as the cohorts could operate independently and be moved around the battlefield as needed, but could also be rapidly manoeuvred to concentrate the entire strength of the legion at one particular point. The legionary standards served as important rallying points. Commanders normally drew up the legion in two or (more commonly) three lines, one behind the other; the third line was often employed as a kind of tactical reserve. They seemingly deployed four cohorts in the first line and three in each of the next two. A cohort of 480 men, if deployed in three ranks, would have covered an area of approximately 146 × 6.4m. The leading cohort was probably up to double the size of the others; 800 men would take up about 247 × 6.4m.[28] It is, however, unlikely that the legion advanced in one continuous battle line. The cohorts possibly had spaces between them at least up to the moment of contact with the enemy. The spaces could be closed up by the cohorts in the second rank moving forward to fill the spaces in the line in front, or by each cohort in the first rank extending its frontage, which would have allowed individual soldiers more space to use their weapons (see Figure 3.1).[29]

The commander had to decide whether to deploy the legion on a broad or shallow front, taking into account the numbers and disposition of the enemy. Since the Roman soldiers were trained swordsmen, it will have been important to get as many as possible to engage the enemy. That would mean a shallow formation on a broad front. But it has often proved difficult to keep troops in order when advancing across a broad front, especially in uneven terrain. If a narrow, deeper formation was used, this will have limited the number of soldiers in contact with the enemy.[30] Auxiliary infantry, cavalry and specialist fighters were grouped in substantial cohorts or *alae*, units of about 480 or sometimes about 800 men, which could be manoeuvred in the same way as the legionary cohorts.[31] In certain cases the commander could use a temporary battle group consisting of units of infantry and cavalry for special operations, as Arrian arranged in his battle preparations against the Alani.[32]

Roman soldiers were often deployed in a battle order that placed legionary and auxiliary infantry in a central position while cavalry was stationed on the flanks to protect the infantry and to drive opposing forces away. Reserves of infantry or cavalry could be committed to act as an

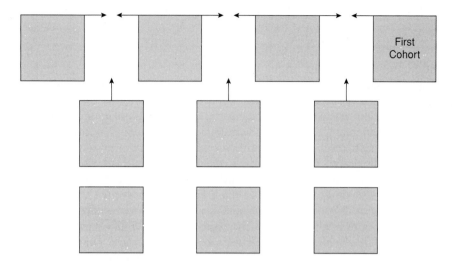

Figure 3.1 Possible formations of legionary cohorts

ambushing or outflanking force, or to repel breakthroughs. Terrain and fortifications offered further protection, but commanders normally aimed to go on the offensive and the infantry usually decided the battle.[33] In AD 60, Suetonius Paulinus brought Boudicca and the British rebels to battle using this classic formation, with all his infantry in the centre and cavalry on both wings.[34] Germanicus imaginatively adapted this kind of formation in AD 16 during his expedition across the Rhine against a German tribe, the Cherusci. He dispersed their impetuous charge by a simultaneous cavalry attack in the flank, an incursion by another force of cavalry in their rear, and an infantry engagement head-on.[35] At the civil war battle of Issus in 194, Cornelius Anullinus, commander of the Severan forces, placed his light-armed soldiers and archers behind the legionary line to shoot over the legionaries' heads in a concerted barrage; a cavalry force was dispatched to make a surprise attack on the enemy's rear. But again it was the clash of the infantry that decided the battle.[36]

The commander was personally in charge of battlefield tactics. He often took up a stationary position behind the main battle line where he could be seen by at least some of the soldiers and could be reached easily by messengers.[37] Alternatively, he could ride round to different parts of the battlefield and make his dispositions from personal observation or on advice from commanders on the spot.[38] He would normally take advice from his officers in a council of war and ensure that there was an effective chain of battlefield command.[39] For example, Arrian organized his battle line against the Alani so that Valens, legate of legion XV Apollinaris, had overall command of the right wing, while the tribunes of legion XII Fulminata (in the absence of the legate) commanded the left wing. There were also subordinate commanders of the cavalry and light-armed troops.[40]

Most battles started with a barrage of spears and other available missiles in order to disrupt the enemy formation; then the infantry drew their swords and advanced to close quarters, at which point it would degenerate into a series of hand-to-hand single combats.[41] There was little opportunity for changing this kind of tactic. Occasionally, however, commanders deployed what may be described as field artillery; that is, small, mobile, bolt-firing catapults that were pulled by mules and worked on the same principle as siege guns (see Plate 3.1).[42] In the second battle of Bedriacum during the civil war of AD 69, the Vitellian forces managed to concentrate their artillery (including large catapults) on a raised roadway, with a clear field of fire over the open land and vineyards around. Tacitus describes the scene: 'Their shooting had at first been sporadic, and their shots had struck the vine-props without hurting the enemy. The Sixteenth Legion had an enormous field-piece, which hurled massive stones. These were now mowing down the opposing front line and would have inflicted extensive defeat but for an act of heroism by two soldiers.' These men managed to sneak up using shields from fallen enemy soldiers to conceal their identity and cut the ropes that worked the engine. They were immediately killed, but the catapult was knocked out of action.[43]

Despite the conservative nature of Roman tactics, commanders proved capable of adapting and developing their methods to suit new or unusual types of warfare. In AD 22, Blaesus, the governor of Africa, had to deal with Tacfarinas, who had waged a successful guerrilla campaign using small groups of soldiers with repeated attacks and rapid withdrawals. Blaesus divided his army into small, independent formations under experienced officers which were highly mobile and became expert in desert fighting. Forts were built to hem in the enemy and the troops were kept in continual battle readiness to harry Tacfarinas throughout the winter.[44]

Against the Parthians the Romans faced a more persistent threat since they employed mounted archers and formidable cavalry forces, some of which were armoured. At first, Roman commanders resorted to a defensive hollow square with the baggage train in the middle, but this was over-whelmed at the battle of Carrhae in 53 BC. Subsequently the Romans used archers and slingers to keep the cavalry at bay, and also developed the use of the tortoise (*testudo*) in open battle. Here the first rank of legionaries knelt holding their shields in front of them, while succeeding ranks held their shields over the rank in front of them, producing a barrier like a tiled roof. Subsequently, *c.* AD 135, Arrian, defending Cappadocia against the Alani, who used armoured cavalry, drew up his legionaries in a defensive formation like the Greek phalanx, in which those in the first ranks carried a long thrusting spear. He backed this up with strong cavalry forces and a concentrated barrage of missiles to open the battle (Figure 3.2).[45] In this story we see the importance of a square defensive formation to resist enemy

Plate 3.1 Scene from Trajan's Column: mobile field artillery

Source: Lepper and Frere (1988), by permission of Mr Frank Lepper and Professor Sheppard Frere

attack. Right up until modern times this formation has had great psychological significance for soldiers because of its impression of strength and safety and the proximity of comrades.[46]

Of course, by careful dispositions before and by sound tactics during battle a general aimed to sustain morale and build on confidence that should have been instilled by training and life in the military community.[47] Writers on military stratagems frequently emphasize the importance of the general's skill in understanding the psychology of warfare. It was part of the tactical preparation for battle to deceive the enemy into thinking that matters on their side were worse, and in a classic ploy to convince them that your forces were more numerous than they were in reality.[48] Thus a Roman general might distinguish himself not so much by innovative tactics as by his detailed preparations for battle and organization of the units of his army.[49] In the preparations for battle, by his personal conduct and cheerful, confident demeanour and valour (*virtus*), he could display strong moral leadership and encouragement, and build up the determination of his men, dispelling fears and emphasizing their strengths and achievements.[50] Onasander, in his textbook on generalship, summed up the qualities needed:

> For the appearance of the leaders has a corresponding effect on the minds of the commanded, and if the general is cheerful and looks happy, the army also is encouraged, believing that there is no danger. But if he looks frightened and worried, the spirits of the soldiers fall along with his, in the belief that disaster is about to strike.[51]

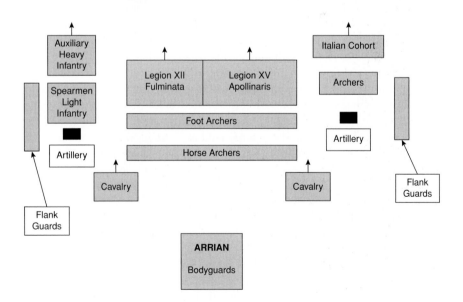

Figure 3.2 Arrian's battle formation against the Alani.

Battle experience

The great commander Gaius Marius in the campaign against the invading Gauls in 102 BC made his soldiers observe the enemy closely from the fortifications of the camp. 'In this way he gradually accustomed them to seeing them [the enemy] without fear and to listening without terror to the amazing and animal-like noises that they made. He urged them to study their equipment and how they moved, so that eventually what had at first seemed terrible became familiar and obvious as they got used to the sight'.[52] Sight and noise were the two most important factors in an ancient battle. Tacitus, in a comment that may owe something to the military experience of his father-in-law Agricola, famously noted that 'in all battles defeat begins with the eyes'.[53] Similarly, Julius Caesar found that his soldiers were being frightened by stories from traders and others about the size and skill of the German warriors, whose facial expressions and fierce gaze could not be endured in battle. He had to call a meeting to dispel the fears.[54] As the Parthians advanced on the Romans at Carrhae in 53 BC they simultaneously in many different parts of the field beat on drums fitted with bronze bells, making an eerie and terrifying noise. 'Apparently they have correctly noted that of all our senses the sense of hearing has the most disturbing effect on us, most quickly stirs our emotions, and most effectively destroys our judgement.'[55] These anecdotes usefully portray the sights and sounds of the ancient battlefield and the importance of psychology in warfare.[56]

Fighting in the Roman army was a personal experience, involving face-to-face combat, in which men used muscular force and cutting weapons to inflict highly visible, bloody wounds. The throwing-spear (*pilum*) was the traditional weapon of the legionaries and had a long tapering iron head (about 60 mm long) with a pyramid-shaped, barbed point. This weapon was constructed so as to bend on impact with armour or flesh and bone, so that it could not be thrown back. Any shield in which it lodged would be unusable. Since its weight was concentrated behind its point, it had the strength to penetrate a shield or armour, and its long, tapering head was able to reach the body of the enemy soldier.[57] At its maximum range of about 30m or 100 feet, its penetrating power will have been less.

After throwing their spears the legionaries came to close quarters using a two-edged sword, with a blade length of between 40 and 55cm, and a sharp, triangular point between 9.6 and 20cm long. This sword was designed for cutting and thrusting, in which the legionaries were trained, rather than for slashing. It is likely that the legionary crouched behind his shield with left foot forward, and then, while shoving his shield into the chest or face of his opponent, swivelled to thrust forward moving his weight on to his right foot.[58] Although this amounted to single combat, the soldier needed to know that his comrades on his left and right were performing a similar manoeuvre to keep the enemy occupied. Therefore, this kind of fighting required a disciplined battle line. If a soldier killed his opponent, ideally he should push forward into his space in the battle line, which would begin the break-up of the enemy formation, or perhaps attack the enemy soldier on either side.

According to Vegetius, the space allowed for each legionary to fight in the battle line amounted to a frontage of 90cm, and a depth of 2m, including 30cm occupied by the man himself. This allowed him to draw back and throw his *pilum* without striking the man behind and also to stab and cut with his sword.[59] The troops would also be close enough to their comrades in the battle line to feel confident of their support. Soldiers in a second rank behind the leading rank could throw their *pila* over the heads of those in front.

For protection, legionaries were equipped with a helmet made of iron with a deep neck guard and flaps to protect the cheeks. Developments in design later provided greater protection on the front and top of the helmet through the addition of a crossbar and a wider neck guard.[60] From the mid-first century the soldier wore articulated plate armour (*lorica segmentata*) on a base of leather straps, which covered the chest, back and shoulders (weight *c.* 9kg) and allowed the arms and legs freedom of movement.[61] There was added protection on the shoulders to guard against scything downward strokes and perhaps those deflected off the helmet. The most important piece of defensive equipment was a rectangular curving shield, about 125cm long by 60cm wide, made of wood and leather, often with an iron rim and an iron boss in the centre protecting the grip. The shield would normally have been held with a straight arm, was very effective for deflecting weapons, and was also comparatively light, weighing *c.* 7.5kg. It could be used in battle for long periods and also carried easily on the march.[62]

The equipment of auxiliary soldiers presumably at first reflected the differing fighting styles of the native peoples recruited into the army but later became more standardized. Infantrymen usually carried a flat shield, a stabbing sword and spears, and could fight in open order as skirmishers or in formation like the legions.[63] Specialist troops such as archers would inflict penetrating and cutting injuries with their missiles, while the impact of a sling shot even on a head protected by a helmet could leave a man dazed or concussed.[64]

Tacitus cleverly explains the benefits of Roman arms and fighting styles in contrast to those of foreign peoples in the advice that he has Germanicus give to his troops before battle against the Germans in AD 16:

> The natives' huge shields and long spears are not so manageable among tree-trunks and scrub as Roman spears and swords and tight-fitting armour. You must strike repeated blows and aim your sword points at their faces. The Germans do not wear breastplates or helmets, and even their shields are not reinforced with iron or

leather, but are merely plaited wickerwork or flimsy painted wooden sheets. The front rank alone has some kind of spear. The rest have nothing but clubs burnt at the end, or with short metal tips. Physically they look tough and are good for a short charge. But they cannot stand being wounded. They quit and run away unashamedly, ignoring their commanders.[65]

Despite the increased numbers and importance of the cavalry in the Roman army of the imperial period, we do not hear much about cavalry actions in battle. However, Arrian, who had commanded troops as governor of Cappadocia, describes cavalry-training exercises in a military textbook (*Ars Tactica*).[66] This work helps us to see how, at least in theory, cavalrymen engaged in battle. The exercises were principally designed to test the accuracy of the soldiers in throwing:

> good horsemanship is especially needed to be able to throw at those who are charging in and at the same time to give one's right hand side the protection of the shield. When riding parallel to his target, the rider must swivel himself to the right in order to throw. When making a complete about turn . . . he must turn right round as far as the tenderness of the sides allow, to face the horse's tail, so as to throw backwards as straight as possible . . . and he must quickly turn forwards again and bring his shield to cover his back.[67]

Then Arrian describes more manoeuvres:

> They advance first with spears levelled in defensive style, then as though they were overtaking a fleeing enemy. Others, as if against another enemy, as their horses turn, swing their shields over their heads to a position behind them and turn their spears as though meeting an enemy's assault. . . . Also they draw their swords and make a variety of strokes, best calculated to overtake an enemy in flight, to kill a man already down, or to achieve any success by a quick movement from the flanks.[68]

Hadrian, addressing the first *ala* of Pannonians at Lambaesis in Africa, congratulated his troops: 'You did everything in order. You filled the plain with your exercises, you threw your javelins with a certain degree of style, although you were using rather short and stiff javelins'.[69]

Cavalry is most effective as an attacking force. Heavy (armoured) cavalry has a shock effect, while light cavalry can try to wear the enemy down by harassment. Several formations of light cavalry were employed; cavalrymen were normally drawn up so that the lines were wider than they were deep. But a deep or sometimes a wedge formation could be used to break through the enemy line.[70] Cavalry attacking infantry could hope to cause the line to break by the fearsome impression of their gallop, or they could throw spears, while horse archers used arrows shooting from horseback. Although it is difficult to make horses charge into an immovable line, if the cavalry got close enough they could slash with their swords at the heads and shoulders of the enemy, but would themselves be vulnerable to leg wounds. A battle with other cavalry would be different. Again it is unusual for two lines of cavalry to charge at full speed into each other since the impact could immobilize both sides; thus a cavalry battle would often result in a mêlée using swords and shields in a confined space. This is why cavalrymen had defensive armour, and helmets with deep neck guards and ear protectors designed to protect them from blows coming from different directions.[71] Josephus describes one encounter between cavalry and infantry. A Jewish infantry force was attempting to storm the town of Ascalon, but was repulsed by a single Roman cavalry unit. The Jews were inexperienced and advanced in disorder, while the Romans presented orderly disciplined ranks that responded perfectly to their commander's signal. The Jews were routed and fled across the plain, which was suited to cavalry manoeuvres. 'The cavalry headed off and made the fugitives turn, smashed through the crowds huddled together in flight, slaughtering them in throngs, and, wherever groups of them fled, the Romans surrounded them and, galloping round them, easily shot them down with their javelins.'[72]

It is probable that from the second century AD the Romans began to use relatively heavily armoured cavalry, whose entire role was to intimidate the enemy by the expected shock of their charge. Under Trajan appears the First Ulpian thousand-man *ala* of lance-carriers (*ala I Ulpia contariorum milliaria*). This must have been equipped with a long lance (*kontos*), which was held in two hands along one side of the horse's neck.[73] In the reign of Hadrian an *ala cataphracta* first appeared in which both rider and horse may have been armoured. The value of armoured cavalry was probably in the visual shock of their slow and steady advance (it would be tiring for the horses to move at more than a trot) and their ability to wound from a distance with their long lances. However, there is only limited flexibility in the deployment of this kind of cavalry because horses and riders tire quickly, especially in a warm climate, if clad in heavy armour.

Battles fought with even the limited technology of the ancient world will have been noisy affairs. In battle both sides tried to sustain their own courage and to undermine the enemy's by creating as much noise as possible. The Parthians as we have seen used drums,[74] while some German tribes emitted a roaring battle cry called the *baritus*, which they amplified by holding their shields in front of their mouths.[75] Roman commanders liked to make sure that fighting began with a rousing war cry, which was organized and taken up in unison as the enemy approached. This was important in the psychology of battle. Arrian's final orders for battle against the Alani were: 'When the troops have been drawn up like this there should be silence until the enemy come within weapon range. When they have come within range, everyone should utter a huge and ferocious war cry.'[76] It seems that the normal Roman practice was to advance silently until the moment of charge, as Dio describes in the defeat of Boudicca. 'The armies approached each other, the barbarians with much shouting mingled with menacing battle songs, but the Romans silently and in order until they came within a javelin throw of the enemy'.[77]

A trumpet or horn often gave the signal for hostilities, and in the thick of battle signals were best given by these instruments, which attracted the men's attention to the standards.[78] They also added to the din and could serve to disconcert the enemy. Battle began with the sound of spears being thrown and arrows and other missiles fired, and the noise of impact on armour or flesh and bone. Then came the clash of steel as the armies met with swords and shields, and the groans of the wounded and dying. New recruits were terrified by this din, according to the anonymous account of Caesar's victory in the civil war in Spain. 'So, when the uproar of groans mingled with the clang of swords fell on their ears, inexperienced soldiers were paralysed with terror.'[79]

For men in armour carrying shields, a prolonged infantry battle fought in southern Mediterranean lands will have been hot and dusty. In Rome's campaigns against Parthia flies were sometimes a further hazard. Some battles went on all day, or were resumed the next day, as in the battle of the River Medway during the conquest of Britain.[80] Yet it is reckoned that a man wielding weapons can fight effectively for about fifteen or twenty minutes before he needs a rest.[81] In the second battle of Bedriacum, which dragged on into the night, soldiers apparently withdrew from the battle line and even sat down for a rest and carried on conversations with their opponents.[82] Lulls in the battle were probably common and would allow wounded men to withdraw or be carried away, and fresh troops moved in.

Skilful generalship could make the best use of atmospheric conditions, so that the enemy had the sun in their eyes or showers of hail blowing into their faces. At the battle of Issus in 194 in the civil war between Septimius Severus and Pescennius Niger, Severus' forces found a sudden thunderstorm at their back helped them overcome their opponents, who were directly facing it and who felt that even heaven was against them.[83] In the second battle of Bedriacum in AD 69 the moon shone in the faces of the Vitellian soldiers, making them an easy target. At the same time, since it was behind the Flavians it exaggerated their shadows and made the enemy gunners shoot short.[84] Elsewhere, the troops fighting under Caecina in Germany in AD 15 were caught in marshy conditions and suffered badly from cold and damp and their inability to get a firm grip; they could not throw their *pila* while standing in water.[85]

The inability of our sources to give a clear picture of battle in Roman times may in part reflect the fact that they were often confused, blood-thirsty mêlées, even though the actual fighting might be confined to relatively small numbers of the first ranks who could get to grips. Of course, those in the rear ranks would be moving forward and in a way pressing the combatants together. In Greek phalanx warfare, when one side eventually gave way it was difficult for the slow-moving phalanx to pursue the enemy rapidly while keeping its formation. By contrast, the commander of a Roman army could rapidly detach cohorts for independent work, and had at his disposal reserves, lightly armed troops and cavalry who could pursue defeated enemies ruthlessly. For example, at Mons Graupius, when the defeated British fled into woods, Agricola ordered his troops to ring them like hunters.

> He ordered strong, lightly armed infantry cohorts to scour the woods like a cordon, and where they were thicker dismounted cavalry and where they were thinner mounted cavalry to do the same. But the Britons turned tail when they saw our troops resuming the pursuit in good order with steady ranks.[86]

Despite the difficulties in distinguishing fact from literary exaggeration and invention in ancient battle descriptions, in my view we must take account of what ancient writers had to say about entire sequences of combat.[87] I am interested in what they thought were the crucial features of battle and how the Roman army operated. Therefore I have decided to set out the firsthand accounts of Josephus and Tacitus, describing respectively the Roman army in defeat at Jerusalem in AD 66 and in victory at Mons Graupius in AD 84 (Figure 3.3).

In AD 66, Cestius Gallus, the governor of Syria, marched against the Jewish rebels in Jerusalem, taking legion XII Fulminata and detachments from the other three legions in Syria, six auxiliary infantry cohorts and four cavalry *alae*, as well as soldiers supplied by friendly kings.[88] But, unable to press home his attack, he decided to withdraw to Syria.

> On the following day, by continuing with his retreat, Cestius encour-aged the enemy to further opposition, and pressing closely round the rearguard they killed many men; they also advanced along both sides of the road and pelted the flanks with spears. The rearguard did not dare to turn to face the men who were wounding them from behind, since they thought that an immense throng was on their heels, and they did not try to repel those who were attacking them in the flanks since they themselves were heavily armed and were afraid to break up their ranks since they saw that the Jews were lightly equipped and ready for sudden incursions. Consequently, the

Romans suffered a lot of damage without being able to strike back against their enemies. For the entire journey, men were being hit, or dislodged from the ranks, and falling to the ground. After many had been killed, including Priscus, commander of the sixth legion, Longinus, a tribune, and a prefect of an *ala* called Aemilius Jucundus, with great difficulty the army reached Gabao, the site of their earlier camp, after abandoning much of their baggage. . . . To speed up the retreat he [Cestius] ordered the disposal of everything that hampered the army. They therefore killed the mules and asses and all the draught animals except those that carried missiles and artillery pieces, which they kept because they needed them and also because they were afraid that the Jews might capture them and use them against themselves. Cestius then led the army towards Beth-horon. The Jews made fewer attacks on the open ground, but when the Romans were packed together in the narrow defile of the descending road-way some of the Jews got in front and prevented them from emerging, while others drove the rearguard down into the ravine, and the main body positioned above the narrowest part of the road pelted the column with missiles. In this position even the infantry had great difficulty in defending themselves, and the cavalry's situation was even more dangerous and precarious, since under the bombardment of missiles they could not advance in order down the road, and it was impossible for horses to charge the enemy up the steep slope. On both sides there were cliffs and ravines down which they fell to their death. Since no one could discover a means of escape or of self-defence, they were reduced in their helplessness to lamentation and groans of despair, to which the Jews responded with war cries and yells of intermingled delight and rage. Indeed, Cestius and his entire army would almost certainly have been overwhelmed if night had not fallen, during which the Romans were able to escape to Beth-horon, while the Jews encircled them and watched for them to come out.

Cestius now gave up hope of continuing on the march openly and planned to run away. Having selected about four hundred of his most courageous soldiers, he stationed them on the roofs of houses with orders to shout out the watchwords of the camp sentries so that the Jews would think that the entire army was still there. He himself with the rest of the army advanced silently for three and a half miles. At dawn when the Jews saw that the Romans' quarters were deserted, they charged the four hundred men who had deceived them, quickly killed them with their javelins, and then went after Cestius. He had got a considerable start on them during the night and after daybreak quickened the pace of his retreat with the result that in a terrified panic they abandoned their artillery and catapults and most of the other war engines, which the Jews then captured and then subsequently used against the men who had left them behind. . . .They [the Jews] had suffered only a few casualties, while the Romans and their allies had lost 5300 infantry, and 480 cavalry.

This is one of the best accounts of an ancient battle, from a man experienced in military affairs.[89] Josephus carefully describes the different units in operation and the particular problems of the cavalry in this battle, as they struggle with the terrain and the lightly armed Jews. He explains the motivation and decisions of Gallus, noting where correct military procedures were followed (including even a classic stratagem to conceal a retreat) before complete panic set in. He also vividly evokes the combination of terrain, weaponry, noise and confusion, and produces a convincing psychological portrait of a battle where the legion was unable to use its skills to their best effect. He is meticulous in recording casualty figures and naming the senior officers killed.

In AD 84 Agricola aimed to lure the tribes of the Scottish Highlands to battle by threatening the populated, fertile areas bordering the Moray Firth, sometimes using sea-borne raids.[90] The British gathered under the leadership of one Calgacus and took up position on higher ground with the first ranks on the plain and the rest rising in tiers up the slope of a hill. There were also war chariots on the plain. Agricola placed 8000 auxiliary infantry in the centre of his line, with 3000 cavalry guarding the flanks. The legions formed a line in front of the camp wall ready to intervene when required. He also had four cavalry *alae* in reserve for emergencies.

> The battle began with an exchange of missiles, and the Britons displayed both valour and skill in parrying our soldiers' javelins with their enormous swords or deflecting them with their little shields, while they themselves poured volleys on us. Then Agricola ordered the four cohorts of Batavians and the two of Tungrians to come to close quarters and fight it out at sword point. This was a well-practised manoeuvre for those veteran soldiers, but very difficult for the enemy, who were armed with their small shields and large swords. British swords lack a thrusting point, and are therefore unsuited to swordplay in fighting at close quarters. The Batavians began to rain blow after blow, shove with the bosses of their shields and stab at the faces of their enemies. They annihilated the soldiers on the plain and began to advance up the hill. This provoked the rest of our units to smash in to their nearest opponents and massacre them. Many Britons were left behind half dead or even unwounded, because of the speed of our victorious advance. Meanwhile our cavalry squadrons, after the rout of the

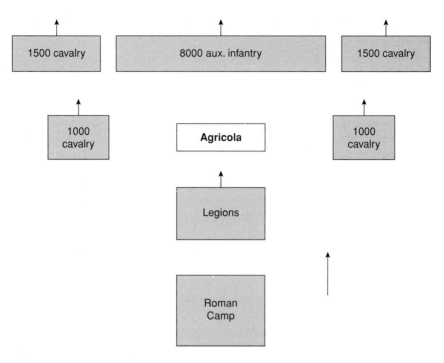

Figure 3.3 Agricola's battle formation at Mons Graupius

war chariots, now plunged right into the infantry battle. By their attack they brought new terror, but the closely packed enemy ranks and the uneven ground soon brought them to a halt. The battle now looked anything but a cavalry engagement, while our infantry struggling for a foothold on the slope was jostled by the flanks of the horses.[91] And stray chariots, with their horses panic-stricken without a driver, often went plunging into the flanks or front.

The Britons who had taken up position on the hilltops had so far taken no part in the battle and, being unengaged, contemptuously noted the smallness of our numbers. They now began to descend slowly and surround the rear of our victorious troops. But Agricola had been concerned about precisely this move, and placed in the path of their advance the four *alae* of cavalry, which he was keeping back for emergencies. He therefore crushed and scattered them in a rout as severe as their assault had been spirited. So the tactics of the Britons were turned against themselves. The Roman cavalry squadrons, on the orders of the general, rode round from the front of the battle and fell on the enemy in the rear. Then followed an awe-inspiring and terrible spectacle over the open country. Our troops pursued, took prisoners and then killed them when more of the enemy appeared. Among the enemy each man now followed his own inclination. Some groups, though fully armed, fled before smaller numbers, while some men, though unarmed, charged forward and met their death. Weapons, bodies, and severed limbs were scattered everywhere and the earth was stained with blood.[92]

The aftermath of the battle was grim. During the night, while the Romans plundered, the Britons wandered through the countryside trying to recover their wounded and shouting for survivors. Many abandoned and set fire to their homes, and there was no longer any concerted resistance. In the morning the land was silent and deserted, and the enemy had dispersed in indiscriminate flight.[93]

Although Tacitus is more interested in the psychology than in the detail of the battle, this is useful, and doubtless Agricola could supply an account of the crucial incidents. We see how the general is in command of the battle, adapts his tactics, and gives the orders on the deployment of reserves and the conduct of the pursuit. We also see how the infantry and the cavalry had specific tasks to perform in relation to the terrain and the state of the battle, and we learn of the fighting methods and skill of the experienced veterans, who know how to use their swords in a confined space, stabbing at the face while shoving with their shield boss. The attack of the reserve cavalry was the turning point of the battle, and as the British lines broke their army disintegrated in the face of ruthless and well-organized pursuit, which witnessed the killing of prisoners. If Tacitus' casualty figures are right, his unforgettable picture of the bloodstained battlefield is probably true enough.

These battle accounts dwell on the psychology of battle and the human drama of courage and fear. In popular opinion ancient hand-to-hand warfare was fragmented, and much depended on the courage and initiative of small groups or even of individual soldiers, and the fighting techniques and skill of the veterans. The personal leadership of the commander, the use of basic military procedures, and the organized deployment of cavalry and infantry to perform specific roles were all thought to be crucial.

Wounds

Now they [the soldiers of Philip V of Macedon] saw bodies dismembered by the Spanish sword, arms cut off with the shoulder attached, or heads severed from bodies, with the necks completely sliced through, internal organs exposed, and other terrible wounds, and a general panic followed when they realised the kind of weapon and the kind of men they had to fight against.[94]

These Greek troops had previously seen only wounds inflicted by spears and arrows, and were shocked by the distinctive wounds caused by the stabbing and cutting of Roman sword-play. The skeletons recovered from Maiden Castle in Dorset, which probably belong to the men who defended the fort against Vespasian and the Roman invaders in AD 43, show evidence of several cutting wounds to the head, and in one case many wounds had been inflicted. But *pila* and arrows also inflicted penetrating wounds, and at Maiden Castle Roman artillery did a lot of damage. High-velocity bolts penetrated skulls, and in one case a catapult bolt had lodged in the victim's spinal column (Plates 3.2 and 3.3).[95]

Despite their armour, Roman troops will have suffered both cutting and penetrative wounds and fractures, especially fractures of arms and legs, head wounds and fractures of the skull where the helmet had split, and also damage to the eyes, which were largely unprotected. Cornelius Celsus, who probably lived in the early first century AD and wrote on many topics including medicine, leaves a vivid and detailed account of the treatment of war wounds.[96] Although he was strongly influenced by the work of Hippocrates and Greek medicine in general, he refers to his own experience in surgery. He mentions wounds caused by arrows, by other pointed weapon heads, and also by lead balls and stones, presumably fired by slingers. The doctor had to decide whether to extract the weapon, or to make an incision on the other side of the body and push it through while not causing any more damage. Celsus gives precise instructions on how to avoid damage

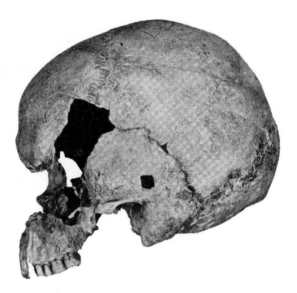

Plate 3.2 Skull from Maiden Castle

Source: Wheeler (1943), by permission of the Society of Antiquaries of London

Plate 3.3 Skeleton from Maiden Castle
Source: Wheeler (1943), by permission of the Society of Antiquaries of London

to blood-vessels and sinews, and recommends that in dealing with a barbed point reed sleeves should be put over the barbs to make extraction less hazardous. The doctor faced a special difficulty if the weapon had lodged in a bone; he might have to cut a triangular incision to aid release, and even give it a sharp knock. We can only imagine the pain of soldiers being treated in this way without anaesthetics, though some natural drugs were available. Celsus also describes a special implement for removing arrow-heads, which seems rather complicated, and Paul of Aegina in his description of the removal of weapon points mentions a special kind of forceps.[97] However, although surgical instruments of the Roman period have been discovered, there is no clear evidence of any special instruments for treating war wounds. It is interesting that in a Pompeian wall painting, which may reflect contemporary practice in the early empire, we see a figure removing an arrowhead from the thigh of Aeneas using a pair of pincers.[98]

Celsus presumably discussed all these techniques in detail because they were likely to be used, but it is not clear that there was any specialist training or a corps of military doctors. Men appear on inscriptions described as *medici*, and there is great debate about whether these are real doctors or what we would describe as medical orderlies.[99] However, much of this is based on a misunderstanding. In the Roman world, in the absence of professional qualifications or accreditation, there was no such thing as a 'qualified' doctor. A man practising medicine (*medicus*) was either more or less experienced, and his reputation depended on the confidence he inspired in his patients. It is likely that there were skilled practitioners, often of Greek origin, who were attached to various units, and in the course of time they presumably acquired experience in dealing with wounds. During major campaigns commanders probably recruited more doctors skilled in surgery from wherever they could be found. It is clear that other soldiers acted in a lesser capacity, applying bandages and dressings on the battlefield, as in the famous depiction on Trajan's column.[100] The Roman imperial army certainly tried to look after its men. Trajan set the example by tearing up his own clothing to make bandages during his Dacian campaigns,[101] and it was a sign of a perilous military situation if wounded troops had no dressings.[102] There were presumably field hospitals or temporary treatment areas. In a story again from the Dacian campaigns, we hear how a badly wounded cavalryman was carried from the battlefield to a tent for treatment, and when he found that his wound was fatal rejoined the battle.[103]

There were of course military hospitals in the legionary camps, and these were carefully laid out with attention to the comfort of the patients and good sanitation. In hygienic conditions, properly set fractures and even deep wounds could heal.[104] However, there is no doubt that in ancient warfare many wounds will have been fatal, through infection and lack of proper techniques.[105] So, according to Paul of Aegina, if the weapon is lodged in a vital spot, 'and if fatal symptoms have already shown themselves, as the extraction would cause much laceration, we must decline the attempt'. But he emphasizes that if there is a chance of saving the patient the doctor must go ahead, after first warning of the danger.[106]

Casualties

According to Strabo, in a battle fought during the Roman invasion of Arabia under Augustus the Arabs lost 10,000 men, the Romans 2.[107] We naturally incline to be sceptical about the disparity in these figures, partly because the transmission of numbers in ancient texts was notoriously subject to error, and also because battle casualties were sometimes manipulated by writers seeking to emphasize the scale of a Roman victory or to play down a defeat. However, Appian, writing about the civil wars at the end of the Republic, but apparently referring to his own day in the second century AD, notes that an acclamation as imperator required 10,000 enemy soldiers to have been killed.[108] This may be useful, since we often know the number of imperator acclamations received by emperors, but it is very unlikely that this rule, even if accurately reported, was scrupulously observed by emperors. In some specific cases we can expect greater accuracy from our sources. Josephus, appointed by the Jews to command in Galilee, reports a disastrous Jewish attack on the Roman garrison at Ascalon, in which 10,000 Jews including two generals were killed, with only a few Roman casualties. In a second assault they lost 8000 men.[109] More precisely, he notes that during Cestius Gallus' retreat from Jerusalem in AD 66 he lost 5300 infantry and 480 cavalry.[110] Tacitus gives the casualty figures from the battle of Mons Graupius – at which his father-in-law Agricola commanded – as 10,000 British dead and 360 Roman, which represents less than 3 per cent of the troops used by Agricola in the battle.[111] He presumably could get reliable figures from Agricola, although 10,000 seems a suspiciously round figure. Tacitus in fact rarely gives casualty figures for the Romans, and his detailed account of the defeat of Boudicca by Suetonius Paulinus in Britain may be based on genuine figures, although he does not personally endorse them. There were 80,000 British and 400 Roman dead with rather more wounded. This represents about 8 per cent of the Roman fighting strength, and the British losses are credible where one side has been completely routed.[112] Dio in a sombre passage comments on the extent of Roman losses at the civil war battle of Issus, in which Septimius Severus defeated Pescennius Niger, who had 20,000 dead.[113] This would amount to three or four legions and may be an exaggeration.[114] Dio must certainly be wrong in his assessment of 50,000 Roman casualties for Severus' campaign in Scotland, and in his claim that 40,000 died on each side at the first battle of Cremona in AD 69.[115]

We are on safer ground with other evidence. The notorious defeat of Quinctilius Varus in the Teutoburg Forest at the hands of the German leader Arminius brought the destruction of three legions (XVII, XVIII, XIX), six auxiliary infantry cohorts and three cavalry *alae*, with a loss of probably more than 20,000 men.[116] After the reign of Augustus at least four legions were lost on active service. Legions V Alaudae, IX Hispana, XXI Rapax and XXII Deiotariana all disappear from the army lists, and we must assume that they were annihilated, although we cannot say precisely when and where in each case. This would amount to a loss of more than 20,000 legionaries.[117]

The Romans set up elaborate war memorials, usually to celebrate military victory and the destruction of their enemies. However, they also remembered fallen comrades. Germanicus buried the remains of the dead of Varus' disaster and constructed a funeral mound.[118] The most famous Roman war memorial discovered is at Adamklissi in the Dobrudja plain in southern Romania. There are three monuments, including a mausoleum and an altar, which records the names of 3800 legionary and auxiliary soldiers killed in what had clearly been a substantial Roman defeat: 'In memory of the courageous men who gave their lives for the State.'[119] This is the only precise and detailed enumeration of Roman casualties we have. Trajan also established a monument and annual funeral rites to commemorate soldiers killed in battle against the Dacians, possibly at Tapae.[120] It was normal to bury the dead at the scene of the battle,[121] and it was considered disgraceful to leave fallen soldiers unburied. This was usually a sign of a great Roman defeat or the depravity of civil war.[122]

It is impossible to know what proportion of serving legionaries died in battle, still less the numbers who died of disease, or the losses suffered by the *auxilia*. Tacitus, describing Agricola's disposition of his forces for the battle of Mons Graupius, notes that the auxiliaries were positioned in front of the legions and that 'there would be great glory in the victory if it cost no Roman blood'.[123] This may be a rhetorical flourish to emphasize the supposedly Roman character of the legionaries in contrast to the non-citizen *auxilia*, but, if Agricola was following an established military practice, it might follow that the *auxilia* suffered a relatively high percentage of casualties in battle. Of course, competent commanders usually made it their priority not to sacrifice the lives of their soldiers needlessly. Thus the future emperor Tiberius had an excellent rapport with the troops under his command, which was at least partly due to his cautious approach and concern for his army.[124]

We cannot estimate the proportion of Roman soldiers lost in battle in relation to enemy killed, but the Romans were entirely ruthless in achieving their objectives. They conducted military campaigns to achieve the complete destruction of the enemy's ability to resist, and this included anyone who got in their way. There is no doubt that up to the late third century AD Roman military activity caused enormous loss of life and suffering, although we can only guess at the extent of this. However, Dio's account of the Jewish rebellion of AD 132 to 135 may not be far from the truth:

> Fifty of their [the Jews'] most important strongholds and 985 of their most famous villages were utterly destroyed. Five hundred and eighty thousand men were killed in the raids and battles, and the number of those who died by famine, disease, and fire was beyond calculation. So nearly the whole of Judaea was made desolate. . . . Many Romans also were killed in this war.[125]

'The Romans always win'

A recent discovery has brought us a splendid message scratched on a rock face in southern Jordan: 'The Romans always win. I, Lauricius write this, Zeno.'[126] Whoever wrote this, either a boastful Roman or a disgruntled native, was convinced of the inevitability of Roman victory. Indeed, despite occasional defeats the Roman army in the main fought successful campaigns to protect and extend the empire over a period of 300 years. Of course, it is easy to suggest possible reasons for Roman success in battle, such as superior resources, organization, manpower, discipline, weapons, leadership, and even a physical superiority that goes with long training, regular food and good sanitation. These factors may have contributed to success on some occasions, but they are variable.[127]

Thus, for example, the Romans could not match the potential manpower of the tribes beyond the Rhine and the Danube, and Tacitus noted not only that the Germans had very fine physiques, but also that the Chatti had mastered even that special Roman quality of discipline in battle.[128] As for command, Roman officers were essentially non-specialist, with no formal training, although the centurions could provide consistency and experience.[129] It was only in the later third and early fourth centuries that members of the equestrian order took over most military responsibilities from senators and a more professional ethos emerged, and it was precisely in this period that Roman superiority in battle began to disappear. Although Roman troops were certainly better-armed and -protected than their opponents, they had no overwhelming superiority, as in the use of guns against swords. Furthermore, the empire did not develop a strategic or diplomatic initiative for total security. It remained a string of provinces based in the Mediterranean, dealt with individual military problems on an *ad hoc* basis in different areas, and was vulnerable to simultaneous attacks on several fronts. The main tactical development in the army up to AD 300 amounted to the creation of stronger cavalry forces (though it is by no means clear how much impact this had in battle), and the field army, which in theory could travel with the emperor to any troubled area. Roman discipline was usually very effective and was sometimes rigorously enforced. Therefore, in Africa in AD 20 when a legionary cohort turned tail and abandoned its commander to his fate, the provincial governor applied the traditional punishment by which, after a drawing of lots, every tenth man was flogged to death.[130] Yet it is likely that discipline was not uniformly or consistently enforced, and was probably applied more toughly during campaigns.[131]

More important perhaps was a factor that operated consistently in Rome's favour. The Roman army was a professional standing army with a trained ruthlessness and the resources necessary to wear down all opposition in a long campaign. Opponents who could not stay in the field for long might be forced to seek a quick battle.[132] Roman soldiers had confidence in their superiority and their ultimate victory because they were part of an army whose successful record had been demonstrated over generations. They had the psychological boost of generally being on the attack. This is demonstrated by the offensive tactics usually adopted by Roman commanders, confirming the idea of innate Roman superiority. All this was supported by a thoroughly professional and meticulous preparation for campaigns, seen in effective scouting, the use of marching columns deployed to suit the terrain and the likelihood of imminent attack, and well-organized temporary and permanent camping techniques.[133] If things did go wrong, as the experienced officer Velleius Paterculus pointed out, the almost routine valour of the Roman soldier, his obedience to military practice and his loyalty to his comrades could win the day, even when his commander had failed him. In a dangerous moment during the war in Pannonia, when several officers and centurions had been wounded and the army was hard-pressed, 'the legions, shouting encouragement to each other, charged the enemy, and not content with repelling their onslaught broke through their battle line and won victory from a desperate situation'.[134]

Once the legions had defeated the enemy in battle, the follow-up was determined, violent and unrelenting. As there were no clear rules for ending a battle, when the opposition disintegrated the Romans had free disposition of material, people and land if they so chose.[135] In the reign of Augustus, for example, Marcus Crassus hounded a Thracian tribe (the Bastarnae) almost to complete annihilation,[136] and the revolt of the Pannonians in AD 6 was crushed with extreme ferocity.[137] After the short-lived mutiny of AD 14, Germanicus led the legions across the Rhine to redeem themselves: '[They] devastated the country with fire and sword for fifty miles around. No pity was shown to age or sex. Religious as well as secular buildings were razed to the ground.'[138] The following year Germanicus advanced unexpectedly on the Chatti: 'Helpless women, children, and old people were immediately captured or massacred.'[139] Then, in AD 16, also under Germanicus' command, the Romans crushed the Cherusci:

> The rest were indiscriminately massacred. Many tried to swim the Weser. They were bombarded with javelins, or swept away by the current, or finally overwhelmed by the press of fugitives and the collapse of the river banks. Some shamefully tried to escape by climbing up trees. As they concealed themselves among the branches, bowmen had fun by shooting them down. Others were brought down by felling the trees. It was a great victory and we had few casualties. The massacre of the enemy continued from midday until dusk, and their bodies and weapons were scattered for ten miles around.[140]

When, under Domitian, the Nasamones, a Numidian tribe, revolted, the governor of Numidia obliterated them, including non-combatants. The emperor commented: 'I have forbidden the Nasamones to exist.'[141]

Defeat in battle against the Romans was often accompanied by the extermination or deportation of the men of military age, like that perpetrated by Tiberius and Drusus in Raetia in 15 BC: 'Because the country had a large population and seemed likely to rebel, they deported most of the strongest men who were of military age, leaving only enough to populate the land but not enough to start a revolt.'[142] Similarly, in Pannonia, Tiberius enslaved and deported all men of military age and ravaged the land.[143] Plautius Silvanus Aelianus celebrated among his exploits as governor of Moesia in the reign of Nero the fact that he 'brought across more than 100,000 of the number of Transdanubians for the payment of taxes, together with their wives and children and leaders or kings'.[144] The Romans occasionally resorted to mutilation. The historian Florus, writing in the second century AD, despised foreign peoples and thought that savage enemies could only be tamed by using their own methods against them. Referring to the war against the Thracians, he comments, 'captives were savagely treated by fire and sword, but the barbarians thought that nothing was more awful than that they should be left alive with their hands cut off and be forced to survive their punishment'.[145] Leaders of peoples that opposed the Romans who did not die or commit suicide (like Decebalus) during the campaign were often brought back to Rome to be paraded in the emperor's triumphal procession, after which they were ceremonially executed.

> The triumphal procession [of Vespasian and Titus] reached its conclusion at the temple of Jupiter Capitolinus where they came to a halt. It was an ancient custom to wait here until the death of the general of the enemy should be announced. This man was Simon, son of Gioras, who had just taken part in the procession with the prisoners; then a noose was placed round his neck and he was whipped by his escort as he was dragged to the place near the forum where Roman law demands that those condemned to death for villainy should be executed. When it was announced that Simon was dead there was a roar of approval and they began the sacrifices.[146]

Enemies of Rome who took refuge behind walls found no respite, for the ruthless cruelty displayed by the Romans in finishing off a defeated foe was matched by the determination, skill and extreme violence with which they conducted sieges and made a cruel example of those who continued to resist. In the Republic, Polybius the Greek historian noted the violence with which the Romans sometimes behaved during sieges. When they stormed New Carthage in 209 BC, Scipio Africanus

> directed most of them, according to the Roman custom, against the people in the city, telling them to kill everyone they met and to spare no one, and not to start looting until the order was given to do so. The purpose of this custom is to strike terror. You can often see in cities captured by the Romans not only human beings who have been massacred, but even dogs sliced in two and the limbs of other animals cut off.[147]

Of course the Romans were technically very well equipped, with powerful siege weapons, including battering-rams, wicker and hide screens, scaling towers, stone-throwing catapults and machines for firing bolts like arrow heads, and were particularly skilled in the building of extensive earthworks.[148] In most respects Roman siege methods were not much more advanced than those employed in the Hellenistic period, but the Roman army was distinguished by its determination, persistence and professional competence, and of course its ability to stay in the field almost indefinitely.

73

Thanks to the writing of Josephus we are well informed about the spectacular five-month siege at Jerusalem in AD 70, and the six-month siege of Masada by Flavius Silva, which ended in 73 or 74.[149] At Masada it is still possible to see the Roman circumvallation, eight siege camps, and the siege mound, which was built up to the base of the walls as a platform for artillery. The Roman main camp, though on lower ground, is built on a slope so that it seems to loom up towards the defenders on the rampart above. On a smaller scale, it is interesting to look at the siege of Jotapata early in the same Jewish revolt, in which Josephus himself defended the town against Vespasian. Here the Jews penned up in the city faced three Roman legions supported by auxiliaries and 160 catapults. Vespasian used an artillery barrage to drive the defenders from the walls and prevent them from dropping boulders, so that a siege mound could be built. Josephus describes how a stone from one of the catapults knocked off a man's head and allegedly carried it for about 550 metres. The defenders tried to build their walls higher and lowered sacks of chaff to break the force of the battering-ram. Eventually the Romans got a ram up to the walls, made a breach and put gangways in place. Then, while the Jews were occupied by a general assault on the walls, the legionaries, using the tortoise (*testudo*) formation, in which they interlocked their shields above their heads, forced their way through the breach, although the Jews poured boiling oil over them and oily liquid on to the gangway to make it slippery.[150] The end was characteristic:

> On that day the Romans massacred all the people who showed themselves. On the following days they searched the hiding places and took their vengeance on those who hid in underground vaults and caverns. They spared no one whatever their age, except for children and women. One thousand two hundred prisoners were collected, and the total number of the dead, both during the final capture and in earlier battles, was calculated at 40,000. Vespasian ordered the city to be razed to the ground and all the forts to be burnt.[151]

Although Josephus may have exaggerated some of the damage done by Roman catapults, this is probably a good indication of the panic created among the inexperienced by these weapons.

The Romans clearly felt few restraints in dealing with people they felt were obstinate in their resistance. Frontinus, the distinguished Roman senator, who held several military commands and was governor of Britain (AD 73/4–77), in his collection of military stratagems, cites several methods for bringing a war to a close after a successful battle. The three examples he cites from Roman history show the use of severed enemy heads to intimidate the survivors. Thus he describes how the famous general Domitius

Corbulo, when besieging Tigranocerta in Armenia, reckoned that the
defenders would hold out obstinately. He therefore

> executed Vadandus, one of the noblemen he had captured, shot his
> head out of a catapult, and sent it flying inside the fortifications
> of the enemy. It happened to fall right in the middle of a council
> meeting that the barbarians were holding just at that moment, and
> the sight of it (like some portent) so terrorised them that they
> hurriedly surrendered.[152]

The Romans of course had other ways of inspiring terror, in many smaller-
scale incidents that we probably only rarely hear about. When the people
of the town of Uspe in the Crimea offered to surrender, 'the victorious
Romans rejected this because it was cruel to slaughter men who had
surrendered, but difficult to provide guards for such large numbers (about
10,000). It was better that they should meet their death in proper warfare.
So the soldiers, who had scaled the walls on ladders, were ordered to kill
them.'[153] The thorough elimination by the Roman army of those who
took refuge behind walls contributed to an impression of overwhelming
power that could not be stopped, and in the case of Uspe had a devastating psychological effect on neighbouring peoples. 'The destruction of
Uspe instilled terror into the others. Weapons, fortifications, mountains
and obstacles, rivers, and cities had all equally been overcome.'[154] Indeed,
the economic and social consequences of defeat by Rome were incalcu-
lable. This idea was forcibly expressed by Josephus when he condemned
the futility of the Jewish revolt of AD 66 in a speech given to king
Agrippa II. 'Are you really going to close your eyes to the Roman empire,
and are you not going to recognize your own weakness? Is it not the case
that our troops have often been defeated even by neighbouring peoples,
while their army is undefeated throughout the entire world?'[155] In the
end the Jews saw their historic capital city and the great temple destroyed,
and a Roman legion permanently quartered there. The money previously
contributed by Jews for the upkeep of the temple was now collected by
a special Roman treasury.[156]

The final link in the chain of Roman success was the competent organization of ordnance and logistics to support the army on campaign. Given
the technological limits of the ancient world, the Romans certainly seem
to have been far ahead of other peoples whom they encountered. For
example, Tacitus, while noting that the Parthian forces had certain qualities, also criticized them for their inability to press sieges and for their
incompetent commissariat.[157] There is unfortunately very little evidence for
how the Romans organized the logistics of their campaigns. The army
could carry all its own supplies and equipment, which would have made
it very cumbersome and slow-moving, or use a supply dump and supply

columns, which were vulnerable and needed troops deployed to protect them. Both of these options involved the use of huge numbers of wagons, carts and draught animals. Food and fodder would also have to be carried, although in the right season an army could live off the land by sending out foraging parties.[158] In keeping the army supplied, the impressive network of roads was an important feature, ensuring the effective movement of supplies and provisions.[159] Furthermore, Roman domination of the Mediterranean and the main rivers of Europe allowed water transport by the imperial fleets.[160]

Emperors tried to keep soldiers comfortable and reasonably contented while they were inflicting massive devastation and deprivation on the enemy. This meant not only keeping them supplied but also well protected in proper camps or forts, and looking after their material comforts. On one level we can see the future emperor Tiberius trying hard to please his officers and make military campaigns rather more pleasant by offering them the use of his doctor, litter, kitchen and private bath.[161] For the ordinary soldier, apart from food and clothing, an efficient medical service was probably of greatest psychological importance. Traditionally, it was important to look after wounded soldiers and the Romans took this seriously.[162] The good commander shared the hardships of his men, and it was considered disgraceful if he abandoned his wounded. Tacitus directly criticizes Caesennius Paetus who surrendered to the Parthians at Rhandeia and then beat an undignified retreat. 'In one day Paetus marched forty miles, abandoning the wounded all along the way. This panic-striken flight was no less disgraceful than running away in battle.'[163] Finally, if a soldier had to be invalided out because of wounds or illness, he received his discharge benefits in proportion to the nature of his disability and the number of years he had served in the army.[164] Therefore soldiers were protected against destitution as far as possible, and it is worth pointing out that this kind of provision was not common practice in armies until comparatively recent times.

However, soldiers in all ages must face up to the fate of death in battle. One striking story of personal tragedy, and also of compassion and remembrance, appears in the inscription of Marcus Caelius from Bologna in northern Italy, a centurion who died in Germany in the military disaster of Quinctilius Varus in AD 9. His body was never identified, and his remains were probably buried on the battlefield by Germanicus' army in 15. His monument, set up by his brother at Vetera (Xanten) in Lower Germany, has a carving of Caelius in full uniform holding his centurion's staff and displaying his military decorations:

> Marcus Caelius, son of Titus of the tribe Lemonia, from Bononia, centurion of legion XVIII, fifty-three and a half years old, fell in the Varian war. Permission is granted to place his bones within [the monument]. Publius Caelius, son of Titus, of the tribe Lemonia, his brother, set this up.[165]

4

WAR AND THE
COMMUNITY

Dio of Prusa, a wealthy Greek orator, compared Roman soldiers to shep-
herds, who, with the emperor, guarded the flock of empire.[1] Aelius Aristides,
another rich Greek man of letters, praised the wonderful efficiency of the
army spread around the frontiers guarding the grateful peoples. The soldiers
'lived day by day in good order and never failed to do what they had
been commanded'.[2] Now, both men were influential enough not to have
to come into contact with soldiers, and the ideal situation they imagined,
in which the army did its noble duty largely sealed off from provincial life
and society, was probably far from reality. A standing army meant that the
empire was virtually in a constant state of military readiness;[3] some areas
had a permanent army presence, while others faced the coming and going
of soldiers along main roads. Naturally this situation had a sharper edge in
wartime, not least because the army was not always successful in its primary
duty of protecting Roman territory and maintaining order. However, even
in peacetime the army was a feature of provincial life, and local communities paid the taxes that funded it and supplied the recruits that replenished
its numbers. The continuous military presence spawned a complex interrelation between army and society, and even after service was over veterans
remained as reminders of war, settlement and Rome's pervasive influence.[4]

The effects of war

The Romans usually talked in terms of conquest and defined their power
as stretching potentially without limit, so that no peoples were truly independent. Nevertheless they occasionally recognized the idea of the army
acting as a shield protecting the subject peoples under their charge, and
the territorial integrity of the areas they ruled.[5] Even if this view is wishful
thinking, it does express an ideal that apparently could be endorsed and
appreciated by contemporaries, and when provincial communities celebrated deliverance from physical danger they usually honoured the emperor,
sometimes indeed mentioning a military unit.[6] By contrast, it was a serious
criticism sometimes directed against unpopular emperors that they had
failed to protect Roman territory. Suetonius denounced Tiberius for his
negligent foreign policy, claiming (quite falsely) that the emperor had

permitted Roman provinces to be overrun 'to the great dishonour of the empire and no less to its danger'.[7]

In the first two centuries AD if the army suffered a serious defeat there was no strategic reserve immediately available and no system of linear defence. Once an invader had crossed the Rhine or the Danube or the Euphrates then the communities in the remoter provinces would be the first to suffer. Many cities had no defences or military forces of their own, and had to rely on the legions for protection. The shock of defeat brought unexpected fears even to the Romans themselves. In the brief memoir of his achievements, the *Res Gestae*, Augustus makes no mention of the disastrous defeat of Quinctilius Varus in Germany.[8] But public business was suspended, there was a period of national mourning, and the emperor resorted to emergency recruitment since he feared that Italy itself might be under threat. 'Augustus . . . mourned greatly . . . also because of his fear for the German and Gallic provinces, and especially because he expected that the enemy would march against Italy and against Rome itself.'[9]

Domitian's reign brought a flurry of military activity, including the extension of Roman control in the valley of the River Neckar between the Rhine and the Danube, and two imperial triumphs; but there were also serious incursions into Roman territory. In 84/5 the Dacians swept into Moesia, defeating and killing the governor Oppius Sabinus, while in 86 the praetorian prefect Cornelius Fuscus and his army were lost. Then in 92 the Marcomanni and Quadi attacked Pannonia, and in the fighting an entire legion was wiped out along with its commander.[10] Tacitus speaks of armies lost through the rashness or cowardice of their leaders, and officers and their cohorts stormed and captured; he goes on: 'It was no longer the frontier of Roman power and the river bank that were in jeopardy, but the bases of the legions and the preservation of the Empire'.[11] He is certainly exaggerating because of his hostility to Domitian, but these were clearly substantial military setbacks, and we may guess at the loss and devastation among provincial communities.

The most serious and prolonged crisis and threat to Roman military power occurred in the reign of Marcus Aurelius, when tribes on the Rhine and the Danube repeatedly threatened Roman territory. Dio observed: 'I admire him particularly for the very reason that amid unparalleled and extraordinary difficulties he both himself survived and saved the empire.'[12] After a Roman defeat in 170 the Marcomanni and Quadi crossed the Julian Alps and swept into Italy, destroying Opitergium (Oderzo) and putting Aquileia under siege.[13] The provinces of Noricum, Pannonia and Upper Moesia will have suffered most heavily in this incursion, and then there was a further invasion by the Costoboci into Lower Moesia, Thrace and Macedonia, which penetrated to central Greece (Achaea). To make matters worse, in 171, Baetica was pillaged by Moorish rebels who crossed the Straits of Gibraltar.[14] Although there is little detailed evidence, it is likely that many towns and communities in the provinces were destroyed, damaged or threatened before the invaders were repulsed. In Pannonia there are signs of widespread devastation; perhaps up to 150,000 people were taken into captivity, while cattle and movable possessions were seized; there are coin hoards and burnt layers in forts and civil settlements, indicating panic and violent conflict.[15] In Noricum there is evidence of the destruction of civilian and military sites, particularly in the east of the province in 170 to 171, and there are also coin hoards from this period. Even after partial recovery the province continued to be afflicted by the plague.[16] There are also signs of the turmoil in a legal decision by Marcus: 'In respect of work which is carried out on city walls or gates or public areas, or if city walls are to be constructed, the divine Marcus replied that when the governor of a province is approached he must consult the emperor.'[17] This suggests a widespread building of emergency defences by communities who felt themselves to be in imminent danger. For example, Salonae, chief city in Dalmatia and an important link on the sea route from the Danube area to Italy, was fortified in AD 170 by detachments from the II and III Italica legions, recently recruited by Marcus.[18] Work was also going on to strengthen the defences at Philippopolis in Thrace.[19] Some building work was confused and disorganized, as we see from the wall built to defend part of Athens after the invasion of the Heruli in AD 268, which incorporated substantial fragments from other destroyed buildings.[20]

On other less well documented occasions it is likely that the physical and psychological effects of warfare and foreign invasion were experienced by Roman provincial communities, not to mention the depredations of civil wars, internal rebellions and banditry. At any time the movement of peoples over whom the Romans had no control could upset the settled security of the provinces. Arrian, who was governor of Cappadocia c. AD 135, had to mobilize his forces to confront the Alani, a nomadic people from the northern Pontic region who tried to cross the Caucasus.[21] A brief comment in Dio reveals that during the reign of Commodus tribesmen stormed across Hadrian's Wall, annihilated a Roman force and caused a great deal of damage in the province.[22] Under Severus Alexander in AD 230, the newly established Persian monarchy overran Mesopotamia and threatened Cappadocia and Syria. The emperor launched a major campaign in 232, which, although inconclusive, enabled the Romans to recover Mesopotamia. There was, however, little time to celebrate before news arrived that German tribes had crossed the Rhine and the Danube and were devastating the empire, overrunning the garrisons on the river banks, and also the cities and villages, and threatening the Illyrians, who were next door to Italy.[23] Once again, albeit briefly, we see how quickly the apparently secure territorial control of Rome could be disrupted, with dire consequences for ordinary people.

In the third century for a time Rome's authority was severely challenged by persistent political instability, frequent civil wars, a series of invasions by foreign peoples, and the virtual secession of part of the empire in Gaul and Palmyra.[24] In these years the emperor Gordian III may have died of his wounds in AD 244 after defeat in the war against Persia,[25] the emperor Decius was killed in battle against the Goths in AD 251, while Valerian was captured as the Persian king Shapur overran Mesopotamia in AD 260. He was to die in captivity. It is difficult to discover how far these turbulent events affected local communities. Spain suffered invasions from the Moors and from people across the Rhine, and in Pannonia there is the evidence of coin hoarding, suggesting violence and perhaps panic, and also the emergence of fortified villas and estates. In Noricum the important town of Lauriacum (Lorsch), the base of legion II Italica, was burnt in AD 235/236, and there was further serious trouble later. In Gaul there are coin hoards and the evidence of burnt layers, but these are apparently sited largely along main roads.[26]

Civil wars conducted entirely within Roman territory by trained Roman soldiers could be especially destructive, not least because there was often an additional motive of revenge, and sometimes of inter-city rivalry as communities supported their own favourite contenders for the purple. Sometimes they had no choice. Tacitus gives a masterly description of the social, economic and psychological effects of the civil wars of 68 to 69 on the people of Italy and the provinces. He notes the greed and licence of the soldiers once the normal restraints of discipline were removed, and the ambitious men of note who lurked in the background unscrupulously exploiting them.[27] The hostility of the troops to local communities increased as they dreamed of sacking cities, plundering the countryside and ransacking private homes.[28] At Divodurum (Metz) the army of Vitellius massacred 4000 of the population for no good reason. After this, as the column of soldiers approached, the whole population of cities came out to meet it begging for mercy, as women and children grovelled before the soldiers along the way, securing peace in the absence of war, as Tacitus puts it.[29] Othonian troops on a raiding mission in Liguria in north-west Italy 'behaved as if they were dealing with enemy territory and cities, and burned, devastated and plundered them with a ferocity made more awful by the total lack of precautions everywhere against such a threat'. During the sack of the town of Albintimilium and the surrounding countryside, the mother of Agricola, Tacitus' father-in-law, was murdered on her estate.[30] This kind of destruction was repeated throughout Italy during the victorious Vitellian march on Rome, as soldiers with local knowledge picked out prosperous farms and rich landowners for plunder. There were over 60,000 soldiers with Vitellius as well as many camp followers, and the land was stripped bare.[31] Not even Rome itself was spared. The conflict between the Vitellians and Flavians saw the Capitoline temple of Jupiter burned to the ground, and when the Flavian forces eventually captured the city there was fierce fighting cheered on by some of the plebs.[32]

There were other rebellions, notably those of L. Arruntius Camillus Scribonianus, governor of Dalmatia under Claudius (AD 42), L. Antonius Saturninus, governor of Upper Germany under Domitian (AD 89), and C. Avidius Cassius, governor of Syria under Marcus Aurelius (AD 175). These did not lead to a general conflagration, and the effects were probably confined to the immediate vicinity. However, the prolonged conflict that lasted from 193 to 197 involving Septimius Severus, governor of Pannonia, Pescennius Niger, governor of Syria, and Clodius Albinus, governor of Britain, was particularly destructive because all three men commanded large armies in important provinces and because the war went on for so long. Those who supported the wrong side incurred the winner's displeasure, and some communities were heavily fined. The intensity of the campaign and its effect on local communities are best seen in the case of Byzantium, which obstinately continued to support Niger long after his cause had been defeated, and sustained a siege of three years in which the defenders were reduced by privation to desperate measures, apparently including cannibalism. On the surrender of the city, soldiers and magistrates were executed, many citizens had their property confiscated, the great walls were demolished, and the whole community was humiliated by being reduced to the status of a village and included under the jurisdiction of its great rival, Perinthus.[33] The civil war ended in AD 197 with the defeat of Albinus at Lugdunum, the sacking and burning of the city, and a series of reprisals against his supporters.[34] But the case of Perinthus demonstrates that some communities profited from civil war – a period of instability during which the normal restraints of diplomacy, established prestige and the status quo were removed. Similarly there were rewards for soldiers, both money and promotions, and honours and advancement for their commanders in the political repercussions of military conflict.

Internal revolts by subdued peoples may have been relatively common. They were not necessarily recognized or reported as wars, or were perhaps concealed by an emperor.[35] For example, under Tiberius the Frisii, a people on the east bank of the Rhine outside the Roman province, who had been paying a kind of taxation to Rome, revolted because of the rapacity of the collectors. An attempt to chastise the tribe did not go well, and 'rather than appoint a commander for the war, Tiberius suppressed the losses'.[36] But some native revolts developed into full-scale warfare that required substantial military action by Rome and attracted the attention of historians. So, in the early first century, the province of Africa was threatened by the daring raids of Tacfarinas, who had deserted from a Roman auxiliary unit. Local communities suffered social and economic disruption from the campaign of burning and pillage, which brought the destruction of villages and enormous loot. It took seven years of intermittent warfare before he was finally suppressed.[37] We have already seen the appalling cost in life and property of the rebellion of Boudicca in Britain in AD 60 to

61.[38] Elsewhere there is sometimes only a tantalizingly brief account of a potentially serious uprising. For example, there was a disturbance in Egypt in 172 instigated by the so-called Boukoloi, probably in fact the population of the Nile Delta. Under the leadership of a priest their revolt spread to the rest of Egypt and might well have brought the capture of Alexandria if the governor of Syria had not intervened.[39]

These revolts, though significant, cannot match the Jewish insurrections, sustained by a highly resilient racial, cultural and religious identity. There were two serious attempts to re-establish Jewish independence in AD 66 to 70 and 132 to 135, and Rome had to make a huge commitment in men and resources to suppress them. The consequences for Judaea were disastrous, with enormous loss of life and destruction of property. Furthermore, in the aftermath of Trajan's campaigns against Parthia the Jews of the Diaspora rose in revolt, first in Egypt and north Africa in AD 115, and then in Mesopotamia in 116. There were sectarian massacres by Jews and Greeks, and possibly over one million people died; in Cyprus the Greeks were massacred by the victorious Jews, and the city of Salamis was annihilated with the loss of 250,000 lives. The prefect of Egypt, M. Rutilius Lupus, was for a time besieged in Alexandria.[40]

The jurist Ulpian, writing in the third century, said: 'Enemies (hostes) are those against whom the Roman people have formally declared war, or who themselves have declared war against the Roman people; others are called robbers or bandits.'[41] Brigandage, which was often associated with piracy, was seemingly more or less endemic in the Roman world throughout the first three centuries AD. Often the effects of banditry could be limited, in that bandits tended to make rapid raids in order to steal cattle, movable possessions, liquor and stored food. But in some areas banditry was a persistent scourge, notably in Cilicia and Isauria, Judaea, Gaul at times, Sardinia and Egypt.[42] There were also serious problems in Numidia and Mauretania in the reign of Antoninus Pius.[43] Even Italy was not immune. In the reign of Septimius Severus the notorious bandit Bulla was at large for two years with his robber band of about 600 men, even though the emperor himself took an interest and sent large numbers of soldiers to hunt him down. Eventually he was betrayed by his mistress and was thrown to the beasts in the arena.[44]

In general, brigandage was not specifically nationalistic or anti-Roman, but embraced men disaffected with the greed and oppression of Roman officials, the destitute, escaped slaves, fugitives, people displaced by enemy incursions, and also army deserters. For example, the serious disturbances faced by Commodus in Gaul were apparently instigated by Maternus, a deserter who led a band of similar renegade soldiers.[45] Whole communities suffered, especially travellers, since roads were vulnerable, and probably most often the poor since they were least able to protect themselves.[46] Only in Judaea does the persistent banditry described by the abundant literary sources seem to be exceptional, in that to some extent it was ideologically motivated by Jewish religious and nationalistic beliefs, and sometimes Romans were specifically the targets.[47]

The government took vigorous steps to repress bandits. Sometimes local forces were used, such as village guards under the command of the irenarch, a local official with minor responsibility for law and order, and border or mountain guards.[48] But often the Roman army was deployed to deal with bandits, supported if necessary by the imperial navy. These full-scale military operations were sometimes accompanied by the building of watchtowers and guard posts to supervise main roads.[49] An inscription from Intercisa in Pannonia records the site of an army watchtower constructed in the reign of Commodus for surveillance over 'places liable to clandestine forays by bandits'.[50] Although tough military measures might be effective in the short term, the problem was that brigands could often retreat to mountain strongholds, which would have required a disproportionate effort to storm. Doubtless they had sympathizers among the local people who could help them to slip away. Thus military action had to be repeated, and this in itself also involved disruption and probably expense for local communities. It needs to be emphasized that for ordinary people in some regions day-to-day life remained perilous despite the presence of the Roman army. Of the numerous inscriptions attesting the fate of individuals who encountered brigands, one from Viminacium (Kostolac) must stand as an example. It tells how a civilian 'died a horrible death at the hands of brigands'.[51]

Paying for the army

In his famous analysis of Roman government set in a fictional debate in the reign of Augustus, Dio expressed the dilemma: 'We cannot survive without soldiers, and men will not serve as soldiers without pay.' However, he also argued that a standing army could at least be funded in an organized and planned way, avoiding the chaos and disruption of special levies.[52] Augustus himself was deeply concerned about these matters. On his death he left a memorandum for his successor in which he set out the numbers and dispositions of the armed forces as well as all the tax revenues of the provinces.[53] Augustus arranged service conditions for soldiers in 13 BC and again in AD 6, including rates of pay and discharge gratuities. Writing about this, Dio reveals the real anxiety of the upper classes, and notes that 'in the rest of the population the measures aroused confident expectations that they would not in future be robbed of their property'.[54] Of course, in his own day in the early third century, some of his fears had been realized. The emperor Caracalla was fond of spending money on his soldiers, 'many of whom he kept in attendance upon him, alleging one excuse after another and one war after another. But he made it his job to strip, rob, and wear down all the rest of mankind, and most of all the senators.'[55] According to Dio, he said that no one in the world should have money but him, and that he would give it to the soldiers.[56] Caracalla's successor Macrinus lamented that he found it impossible to give the soldiers their full pay, which Caracalla had dramatically increased, as well as the hand-outs they expected.[57] The succeeding emperor Elagabalus was heard to complain how he had failed to find favour with the praetorians 'to whom I am giving so much'.[58] The spiralling cost of the army under the Severan emperors is also picked up by Dio's contemporary Herodian, who alleges with some exaggeration that 'in one day he [Caracalla] extravagantly squandered all the monies that Severus had accumulated in eighteen years and confiscated as a result of the calamity of other people'.[59] The last member of the Severan dynasty, Severus Alexander, was overthrown partly because of his perceived miserliness towards the soldiers.[60]

The pressure of army expenditure remained inexorable. The emperor needed the soldiers' support first of all to sustain himself in power, and therefore he had to ensure that they were content. The admittedly short-lived mutiny after the death of Augustus in AD 14 was a warning because some of the soldiers' complaints concentrated on low rates of pay.[61] It is in this context that we need to examine the day-to-day annual cost of the army. By his decision to create a professional standing army which was at least in theory ready to meet any military eventuality, Augustus committed his successors to enormous annual expenditure, which would be hard to curtail except by reducing the number of soldiers. That, of course, could make a bad impression. It was alleged (probably falsely) that Domitian regretted the cost of his increase in military pay (see below) and was forced to reduce the number of soldiers, bringing great danger to Rome 'because he made its defenders too few'.[62]

The cost of the army cannot be calculated accurately since we do not know clearly the total number of soldiers, their proportions in various pay grades, the pay rates of officers, the rate of auxiliary pay, and the rate of legionary pay in the late second century.[63] With allowance for this we may estimate that in the reign of Augustus the annual cost of the army and fleet was in the order of 370 million sesterces.[64] This is a conservative view and takes no account of irregular payments (donatives), the cost of ordnance and transport, payments to higher officers, and is based on the assumption that discharge payments (*praemia*) were not extended to auxiliaries and the fleet.[65] On the other hand, military units were probably not always kept at full strength, and the government retrieved some money in compulsory deductions from soldiers' pay to cover costs such as food, clothing and weapons.

Domitian increased military pay by one-third, from 900 to 1200 sesterces. Since by the end of the second century AD the legions numbered thirty, and the *auxilia* had probably increased at a higher rate than the legions, the annual cost of the army will now have been around 600 million sesterces.[66] From this alone we see how difficult it was for the Roman emperor to consider raising army pay. Yet at the end of the second century there were substantial pay increases, first by Septimius Severus and then by his son, Caracalla. This surely indicates the political difficulties of these times.[67] We do not know the exact amount of Severus' increase, and unfortunately later increases are expressed by our sources as a percentage of the earlier sum. Therefore there are widely differing modern estimates of military pay at the end of the second century. However, even on a conservative view, it seems that in the reign of Caracalla the wage bill of the legions alone amounted to more than 370 million sesterces annually.[68] The pay rises in the Severan period probably outstripped inflation and represented a significant improvement in the conditions of military service that perhaps encouraged more volunteers.[69]

Emperors also made irregular payments (donatives) to the troops, and these became increasingly frequent, representing an important addition to military pay and the annual cost of the army. The donative soon lost much of its original association with military campaigns and visits to the troops, and was more commonly used to mark the accession of an emperor, or his birthday, or the crushing of a conspiracy.[70] Although Augustus avoided large donatives, other emperors were less restrained. For example, Claudius paid out 15,000 sesterces per man to the praetorians at his troubled accession, at a cost of 135 million sesterces, to say nothing of the additional expenditure if the donative was awarded in proportion to the legions.[71] Marcus Aurelius, respected by senators and praised for his prudent conduct of affairs, paid 20,000 sesterces per man to the praetorians at his accession, at a cost of about 240 million sesterces for the troops in Rome alone.[72]

We can put into context the scale of the sums expended on the army by observing that at the end of the Republic about 4.8 million sesterces would have been enough to feed around 10,000 families at subsistence level for one year.[73] Furthermore, if the annual revenue of the empire in the early first century AD was between 800 and 1000 million sesterces,[74] up to 40 per cent of the disposable income of the state was being spent on military affairs. This burden must have been sustained by the empire's regular taxes, the poll tax (*tributum capitis*) and the land tax (*tributum soli*), levied on the population of the provinces but not in Italy. We do not, however, have enough information to understand precisely how they correlate, or how accounts were kept, and how far calculations of requirements were made. Roman citizens in Italy had been exempt from direct taxes from 167 BC, until Augustus introduced two new taxes in AD 6/7 to help fund the new military treasury (*aerarium militare*), which he set up to deal with soldiers' discharge payments. These taxes, a 5 per cent death duty on the estates of Roman citizens (except for near relatives and the very poor), and a 1 per cent tax on auctions, were resented at the time, and Augustus had to smooth the way by asking the senate if it could put forward a better suggestion.[75] He also contributed 170 million sesterces of his own funds. Senatorial resentment at taxes for military expenditure continued. Dio complained about Caracalla's generosity to the army because it led to new taxes, or tax increases; death duty was increased to 10 per cent, and all exemptions were removed.[76]

Since most military expenditure was recurrent it would be unaffected by the need to fight a major campaign; but war must have put some extra pressure on the system. For example, the recruitment of extra troops to bring the legions up to strength will have added to the cost of the army, while enemy incursions into Roman territory or serious revolts might cause devastation and reduce the number of available taxpayers. More directly, Dio's complaints about extra taxes were directed against Caracalla's military expeditions, which he considered unnecessary. Of course, the extra cost of war might rather unpredictably be recouped by booty, as in Augustus' conquest of Egypt or Trajan's victory over Dacia. On the other hand, during Marcus Aurelius' long wars against the marauding German tribes on the Danube, he refused the soldiers' request for a donative, on the grounds that whatever they got beyond their normal pay 'would be wrung from the blood of their parents and kinsmen'.[77] This suggests that the emperor had few funds for additional military expenditure. Later, when Marcus again ran short of money, rather than impose a new tax he sold off imperial furniture and his wife's jewellery.[78] The proceeds were immediately given to the troops. The sale was presumably a gesture to encourage public support, but there is a clear connection between major wars and a need to find extra sources of revenue.

Apart from the burden of direct taxation, the army had to be supplied, fed and moved around the provinces. The provision of grain, weaponry and clothing could be part of a tax requirement on individual communities.[79] Indeed, cities in the east may have minted coins to pay troops marching through their territory.[80] Soldiers and other government officers also had the right to demand hospitality and accommodation (*hospitium*) while on official business, and to requisition the necessary means of transport, including draught animals, carts and guides (*angaria*). Responsibility for the maintenance of the extensive road network, which was so important for the movement of troops within the empire, was often placed on individuals or adjacent communities.[81] Obviously those living close to main roads or military bases and camps suffered most, and demands from soldiers will have been extremely burdensome even if the rules concerning exactions were properly followed; unfortunately soldiers were frequently violent and grasping, and oppressed the local population.[82]

The pressure on local communities would, of course, be much worse during a military campaign when an entire army was on the move. The presence of extra troops in an area meant the provision of additional supplies, and this will in part have involved the extension of the usual supply mechanisms. Nevertheless, a significant burden will have fallen on local communities, in particular to make up any shortfall.[83] An inscription from Tridentum in Raetia records how C. Valerius Marianus, a citizen and magistrate of the town, was placed in charge of the corn supply for legion III Italica, stationed in Raetia.[84] The context of this is uncertain, but it seems that the government had pressed Marianus, who apparently had no military experience, into the job of finding supplies for the legion. By doing this he was perhaps able to take the pressure away from his own community. A community faced with the appearance of an army on its doorstep would certainly be eager for a rich citizen to help out. We hear how Julius Severus received Trajan's army in winter quarters at Ancyra on its way to fight the Parthians.[85]

As well as the need to billet thousands of soldiers, important officers had to be looked after, and perhaps even the emperor himself. The effects of the visit of a high-ranking person can be seen from the edict issued by Germanicus, grandson of Augustus, in an attempt to deal with abuses concerning the provisions of animals, transport and hospitality during his visit to Egypt in AD 19.[86] The presence of the emperor himself was of course a great honour, but it was Antoninus Pius who reportedly said that even the entourage of a frugal emperor was a burden to local communities.[87] He would normally expect an official welcome. This is represented on Trajan's column, where several scenes show the emperor passing through towns on the way to the front in the Dacian Wars. He is received by the magistrates and crowds of joyful women and children while sacrificial animals stand ready.[88]

To accommodate, feed and entertain the emperor was doubtless expensive and demanding. When Hadrian and his army visited Palmyra, one rich citizen made himself personally responsible for his entertainment, and also provided for the soldiers.[89] The same emperor and his military entourage, while on the way through Lete in Macedonia, found that a local benefactor, Manius Salarius Sabinus, official in charge of the Gymnasium, had 'provided for the supplies of 400 *medimnoi* of wheat, 100 of barley, and 60 of beans, with 100 *metretae* of wine at a much cheaper rate than the current price'.[90] Inscriptions set up in Ephesus recording the visit of Lucius Verus probably on his return from the Parthian war in 166 provide the most detailed evidence for the reception of an emperor on campaign. The city was decorated for the imperial arrival, and individuals were appointed to organize the provision of food. Verus stayed for several days; and one citizen, Vedius Antoninus, took responsibility for his entertainment every day, sparing no expense and dealing with everything meticulously. The scale of Antoninus' personal generosity may be judged by the fact that the men assigned to provide food gratefully set up a statue to him. His father-in-law, the sophist Damianus, who was also secretary of the city council, provided food for all the soldiers passing through the city over a period of thirteen months.[91] Local dignitaries who took on the responsibility of looking after an emperor could find themselves called upon again, as in the case of Claudius Asclepiodotus who assisted the passage of Elagabalus and his army, as he had done with Septimius Severus and Caracalla.[92]

Whatever kind of gratification the emperor wished on his travels had to be provided. Lucius Verus, before he arrived in Ephesus, had visited Athens and expressed a wish to be initiated into the mysteries at Eleusis. The ceremony had to be repeated for him since it had been completed already.[93] On the other hand, the city regarded it as a great honour to have the emperor take part in the rites, as we know from another inscription honouring a priest who mentions with pride the emperors whom he had initiated into the mysteries.[94] Thus the presence of the emperor with his army was two-edged. Not only did individuals who entertained him have the opportunity to win imperial favour, but also whole communities could benefit, receiving buildings, gifts, privileges and the opportunity to present requests personally. When Trajan stopped in Antioch on his Parthian campaign in AD 115, people flocked from the surrounding areas with petitions and requests or just to sightsee. When an earthquake struck there was enormous loss of life in the crowded city.[95] Indeed, Pizus in Thrace owed its existence to the personal initiative of the emperor Septimius Severus, who ordered the foundation of a small trading community with 171 settlers as he passed through the area on his return from the eastern campaigns.[96]

In the third century warfare became more intrusive, with frequent civil wars, rebellions and invasions of Roman territory. Life in the provinces was more precarious, and the government made ever greater demands on local communities. By the end of the third century army numbers had risen to about half a million, and more local resources were channelled towards the troops. A military subsistence allowance (*annona militaris*) established the collection of foodstuffs, wine, clothing and animals for the army. This was originally an extraordinary imposition but eventually became a regular tax, and stood in lieu of payment in cash to the troops (inflation having undermined the value of cash payments). The exploitation of the local population was made worse by the brutality and illegality that often accompanied the collection of the tax,[97] and the army seemed less effective now in its crucial role of defending Roman interests and territorial integrity. At a time when the tax base was declining and the burden of tax was greater, some of the links between soldiers and civilians in local areas were breaking down, and the army seemed to feed off city states and their territory, while politically ambitious generals and warlords pursued their own ends. Eventually the state had to face the economic cost of reorganizing the professional army when it was defeated or forced to retreat in disorder, and this had further consequences for the tax-paying classes, and also for the army itself, which naturally wished to reassert its privileged position. Throughout the first three centuries AD it was the inevitable outcome of the existence of a professional standing army permanently based in the provinces that the provincial communities made by far the greatest contribution to the support of the military. They also suffered the greatest devastation, since most wars were fought far from the Italian homeland.

The military presence: internal control and policing

By AD 200 there were thirty-three legions in service, permanently stationed in nineteen of the thirty-eight provinces of the empire.[98] Furthermore, in those provinces that escaped a legionary presence, there were often small detachments of auxiliary troops based in forts whose job it was to keep order and supervise roads and other installations. There were also troops in attendance on the governor, acting as bodyguards and messengers. Some provinces were closer to a permanent war footing. Britain had to find room for three legions, and around AD 210 there were legionary bases at Caerleon (Isca), Chester (Deva) and York (Eburacum), as well as many smaller forts for auxiliary troops in its garrison of some 50,000 men.[99] Throughout the empire legionary bases were sited where it suited the Roman army's require-ments, often at important road junctions and river crossings in areas with potential for commerce and trade. Most of these locations have been more or less continuously occupied thereafter, and many have remained or become important centres in the modern world, like Ara Ubiorum (Cologne) and Bonna (Bonn) in Lower Germany, Moguntiacum (Mainz) and Argentorate (Strasbourg) in Upper Germany, Castra Regina (Regensburg) in Raetia, Vindobona (Vienna) in Upper Pannonia, Acquincum (Budapest) in Lower Pannonia, Singidunum (Belgrade) in Upper Moesia, Melitene (Malatya) in Cappadocia, Aelia Capitolina (Jerusalem) in Syria Palaestina, Legio (León) in Spain. In the west, legionary troops were generally quartered in purpose-built camps (normally containing a single legion, sometimes with auxiliary troops), and garrison towns grew up with the legions. In the east, garrisons tended to be based in existing, long-established cities, such as Cyrrhus, Zeugma and Samosata, though some bases did influence the development of towns (e.g. Melitene and Satala in Cappadocia).[100]

The siting and development of legionary bases mark the ebb and flow of Roman military activity, and changes in the balance of power. At these army centres there will have been constant excitement and activity with the coming and going of troops, and a definite military ambience about life and culture. In time of war this will have been much more dramatic. During the northern wars, Marcus Aurelius made his headquarters from AD 171 to 173 at Carnuntum on the Danube, the legionary base of legion

XIV Gemina and the residence of the governor of Upper Pannonia, and later at Sirmium on the River Save. Imperial business with all its panoply of officials and administration and numerous petitioners followed him.[101]

The army had the job of consolidating Roman control after conquest. This was often a violent process that could go on for many years, as the government established a framework of administration and taxation and set about recruiting the local population. There may have been revolts and dislocation, and it is likely that the Romans built the legionary base at Nijmegen in Germany in response to the revolt of the Batavi in AD 69. Simmering discontent with Roman rule in Judaea ended in the revolt of AD 66 to 70, which was suppressed only after a full-scale war and the stationing of legion X Fretensis in Jerusalem itself.[102]

After consolidation had been completed and major opposition suppressed, the army remained as an army of occupation. The troops had a significant role as peacekeepers within the provinces, both in maintaining internal security and in putting down the kind of low-intensity violence that the Romans usually ascribed to banditry.[103] In many provinces soldiers were widely dispersed in a large number of relatively small detachments in forts and small camps. For example, in Egypt soldiers were stationed in many towns and villages, with a substantial concentration at Alexandria, the seat of the governor, making the important political point of a highly visible Roman presence on the ground.[104] In general, the troops aimed to supervise and control movement of people and to protect roads and other lines of communication. Small forts perhaps temporarily garrisoned as the situation required could guarantee communications and also provide intelligence information. In the eastern provinces, as noted above, detachments of legions were often stationed in small towns, involving the army more closely in everyday activities. The army of occupation operated in the first instance to protect the rulers, not the ruled, and it was the army that enforced the political domination of Rome and, if necessary, ensured by whatever means necessary that government decisions were carried out.[105]

Therefore the army's presence, whether or not external war was threatening, was likely to intrude in the lives of the local provincial population. Because of the inadequacy of local control of law and order, a state of affairs for which the Romans themselves were partly responsible, soldiers frequently acted in a police role. This evolved easily from their duties in guarding roads and tollhouses. In fact the *stationarii* (a kind of seconded road guard) expanded their role and acquired a doubtful reputation as tax collectors and supervisors of the imperial post.[106] At the local level soldiers supported government officials and became enforcers of their decisions, in some cases quite improperly. Lucilius Capito, rascally procurator of Asia under Tiberius, had used soldiers to enforce his commands.[107] Trajan, in reply to a request from Pliny, the governor of Bithynia, for permission to carry on using soldiers to guard public prisons, said that as few soldiers as possible should be called away from their usual military duties. But it is clear that soldiers were likely to be used in this kind of police job.[108]

From this it was a short step to a situation where soldiers detained or arrested small-time criminals and hoodlums at the behest of those in authority. It made sense for the military authorities to try such men, and in practice the case would be delegated to the man in charge of a detachment of soldiers, often a centurion. A number of legal cases recorded on papyri in Egypt suggest that at least in this province – and there is no reason to suppose that the same was not true in other provinces – centurions informally exercised an effective legal authority and arrived at *de facto* remedies for litigants. The cases deal with, among other things, assault, theft, tax collecting and the criminal activities of administrators. Centurions were asked to bring individuals to justice, to carry out searches, or to provide some kind of protection.[109] The litigants were presumably unable or unwilling to exercise their full legal rights, and hoped for a quick settlement. It is interesting that they or their legal advisers humbly supplicated Roman centurions as figures of power and authority, the representatives of a mighty army. Clearly local people would want to keep on the right side of them. In practice, centurions, backed up by the soldiers they commanded, administered a kind of rough justice. They brought the operation of the central government right into village life, and emphasized the apparently all-seeing presence of the Roman army. In this, as in so many activities, the army was both a source of potential benefits and also a threat.

The military presence: soldiers and subjects

The power of the Roman army, both in terms of the political subjection of an entire province and in the daily life of local communities, was seemingly all-pervasive, and much of provincial administration appeared to have a military aspect. Local people, unless rich and eminent, were protected only by luck or by the government's ability to enforce rules of proper conduct among its troops. Despite the good intentions of many emperors and governors, there is no doubt that the permanent presence of soldiers near provincial communities or in transit along the roads that linked the military infrastructure greatly contributed to the oppression and brutalization of the local population. This was a feature of life in the empire irrespective of whether wars were actually being fought, because of the nature of the standing army and its dispositions. Thus a senior official offered routine advice to provincial governors: 'Take care that nothing is done by individual soldiers exploiting their position and claiming unjust advantages for themselves, which does not pertain to the communal benefit of the army.'[110] Trajan, when informed by Pliny about the problems experienced by the town of Juliopolis in Bithynia because of crowds of people passing though on official business, assumed that soldiers might be the main culprits in demanding facilities from the townspeople.[111] Indeed, the evidence suggests that the oppression of ordinary civilians by soldiers both acting on their own responsibility and sometimes on the orders of corrupt officials was commonplace and frequently repeated, despite the attempts by the government to deal with it.[112] Soldiers abused procedures that permitted them to demand travel facilities and hospitality when they were on official business. They took animals and sustenance beyond their legal entitlement, often using violence. They robbed and assaulted local people, confident in their membership of the largest and most important state-run organization in the ancient world.

To live close to a main road or army camp could be particularly dangerous. Epictetus, a writer on philosophy of the first century AD, who incidentally tells us much about life in the early empire, offers some striking advice: 'If a requisition is taking place and a soldier takes your mule, let it go, do not hold on to it and do not complain. For if you do, you will get a beating and lose your mule all the same.'[113] Columella, also of the first century and writing about agriculture, advised against the purchase of an estate close to a military road because of the 'depredations of passing travellers and the endless hospitality required for those who turn aside from it'.[114] The villagers of Scaptopara in Thrace would have agreed. Their community not only had hot springs and was close to the site of a famous festival, but was also situated between two military camps. They complained that soldiers had repeatedly ignored the instructions of the governor of Thrace that they were to be left undisturbed, and had left their proper routes to come and demand hospitality for which they paid nothing.[115] The government was frequently unable to enforce its will, and there is a note of despair in the edict of Marcus Petronius Mamertinus, prefect of Egypt (AD 133 to 137), about the improper requisition of boats, animals and guides by soldiers travelling through the province. 'Because of this private persons are subjected to arrogance and abuse and the army has come to be censured for greed and injustice.'[116]

The military presence: economic effects

The presence of so many soldiers across such a wide geographical area of the empire provided opportunities and may have encouraged economic developments. In the second century AD in the Roman Empire an army of 300,000 soldiers might well consume annually about 100,000 tonnes of wheat at one kilogram of grain per person each day. With a larger army, this would have risen to 150,000 tonnes by the early third century.[117] In Britain in the late second century the large complement of troops would also have needed large numbers of replacement horses and mules, and about 2000 calves a year for the replacement of leather tents and clothing, and possibly more than 2000 animals a year for religious sacrifice.[118] Large supplies of animals and foodstuffs could not be obtained from the lands (*prata legionis*) normally attached to the camp for the use of soldiers. The soldiers would also need various kinds of meat, fruit, vegetables, oil and wine. The government normally supplied soldiers with food, clothing and weapons but made a fixed deduction from their salary to defray costs. Cavalrymen were supplied with horses at a set rate and then became responsible for their upkeep.

In the early phase after conquest the army might have to rely on imported goods for many of its needs. There is evidence for long-distance supply in the remains of wheat discovered at the legionary base at Caerleon, which contained Mediterranean weeds, suggesting import possibly from southern France.[119] At the legionary base at York remains of grain pests also indicate that grain was transported at least from southern Britain; the type of grain was also different from that grown in the countryside round York.[120] After the army had consolidated its position and settled down into an army of occupation, it could seek to organize local suppliers as best it could. Obviously it would be more convenient and less expensive to obtain as many supplies as possible from local sources. For example, Plautius Silvanus, governor of Moesia on the Danube under Nero around AD 60 to 67, was able to send a large amount of grain to Rome, which suggests that his army had adequate provisions in the frontier zone.[121]

Eventually the local economy might become fully integrated into the Roman system, so that military requirements were met by local markets and the exchange of goods, as suppliers nearby became more numerous. There was not necessarily a strict chronological development in these various stages of organizing supplies for the army.[122] In any event, it is possible that in the long run the presence of the Roman army encouraged local agriculture and cattle-rearing in the vicinity of camps and forts and across the whole frontier zone. Cereal and cattle or hides could be supplied in the form of taxes in kind or compulsory purchase, but there will have been opportunities for local people to sell for profit.[123] Although it remains very difficult to demonstrate that the arrival of a large army had an expansionist effect in the economy of north Britain, for example, in the development of arable production,[124] nevertheless there are some indications that in Northumberland, beyond Hadrian's Wall, grain and cattle culture increased after Roman occupation.[125] It has also been suggested that the presence of large Roman forces in Germany in the early years of Augustus led to an intensification of agricultural production in Gaul and gave a boost to Gallic pottery-making. In the longer term supplying the army continued to stimulate economic activity in Gaul, as did an ordered communication system based on the Roman roads built initially to facilitate military movements and the development of centres able to exploit the new 'commercial tides'.[126] Naturally, supplying the army with foodstuffs placed an unequal burden on the provinces. The army in the Danubian provinces would rely heavily on all the Balkan provinces, while the army on the Rhine relied on Gaul, and the British garrison looked to Britain and Gaul or further afield. However, the evidence for material culture is fragmented and often chronologically imprecise, and it is impossible to quantify how the pressures of military supply intensified in time of warfare.

In the case of manufactured goods, such as arms, armour, clothing, tools, equipment, tiles, pots, metalwork and building materials, the army would naturally prefer to make as much as possible for itself. Commenting on the duties of the prefect of engineers, Vegetius said that his main responsibility was to ensure that 'nothing that the army was thought to require should be lacking in the camp'.[127] An extract from the *Digest* on military affairs contains a list of soldiers exempt from certain military duties, including dressers, ditchers, farriers, architects, helmsmen, shipwrights, glass-makers, smiths, arrow-makers, coppersmiths, helmet-makers, cartwrights, roof-makers, sword-makers, waterpipe-makers, trumpet-makers, horn-makers, bow-makers, plumbers, metalworkers, stone-cutters, lime-burners, wood-choppers, choppers and burners of charcoal.[128] There is extensive evidence for soldiers as artisans, craftsmen and engineers, and some military camps seem to have been a hive of manufacturing activity.[129] Indeed, it is possible that the legionary brickworks at Vetera (Xanten) may have turned out over one million bricks a year, and that bricks made by the legionaries could even be exchanged for other goods.[130]

However, the army was not self-sufficient, and the government would have to try to manage local resources and encourage local production to make up the shortfall or seek goods from further afield, either by requisition or by compulsory purchase, or by normal dealing in the marketplace. Evidence is limited, but, for example, we find Egyptian villagers in the Fayum supplying spear shafts and receiving payment from public funds.[131] Similarly in AD 138 the weavers of Philadelphia in Egypt were required to produce blankets of a specified quality for the army in Cappadocia, for which they received payment in advance.[132] As the army settled into a province and the local population got used to its presence, the army bases could become a great attraction for people with goods to trade or sell; indeed, goodwill on the part of local people might assist the ready avail-ability of supplies in the immediate area. A letter to his father from Julius Apollinarius of legion III Cyrenaica based at Bostra in Arabia in AD 107 refers to merchants coming every day to the camp.[133] The long-serving legion VII Gemina in Spain virtually became a provincial institution like a small town, and served as a significant market.[134]

If the army had to resort to the importation of supplies over long distances, this might serve to stimulate trade and produce profits for traders. Goods being transported for military use travelled tax-free, as we learn from a legal reply of Hadrian.[135] The text also suggests that some goods arrived on government order, and it is likely that some traders operated with quasi-official backing. Indeed, the army issued contracts to certain traders to arrange and transport essential military supplies. A waxed tablet from Frisia, dating to the first or second century AD, records the purchase of a cow by Gargilius Secundus, with two legionary centurions acting as witnesses.[136] It may be that Secundus was a contractor acting on behalf of the army. Furthermore, as we have seen, when army commanders came to build military camps, they were not necessarily influenced only by the defensive capabilities of a site or by wider strategic concerns. It is interesting that what seems to be a small fort (burgus) on the Danube was called 'trading post' (commercium) by contemporaries 'because it had been constructed for that purpose'.[137] Communities along the great river routes in the western provinces, the Rhône and the Rhine, are likely to have benefited from the movement of goods, and there will have been a trickle-down effect from the military economy as other goods were brought in along with military supplies. Increased trade in the wake of the army also reached frontier zones and in some cases reinforced the power of the native élites on the other side of the frontier.[138] Warfare meant that the army would need even more supplies, though trade might be disrupted by military activity beyond the frontiers.

Finally, the army also brought with it a range of activities and facilities associated with a settled urban environment: piped water-supply, baths, amphitheatres, hospitals and other carefully planned buildings. Army units had the experts and manpower to design and build what they needed, although in the first instance such buildings would be for the troops' own benefit, but there is evidence that they contributed expertise and muscle to local projects.[139] For example, we hear how a soldier who was an expert in surveying was seconded by the Legate of legion III Augusta to help the town of Saldae in Mauretania to sort out a persistent problem with the construction of a tunnel for a water-pipeline.[140]

To sum up, soldiers were paid regularly in coins and therefore made up one of the largest groups near frontier zones with considerable potential spending power for goods and services. For example, in Numidia it is possible that the army diffused a money economy throughout the immediate region and remained as the principal source of coined money.[141] It is also likely that individual soldiers would seek to supplement their rations by purchasing special items.[142] However, the economic effects of the army's presence should not be exaggerated. Soldiers were often widely dispersed and based in small groups. Even a legionary base might contain between only 5000 to 6000 men, and many could be on duty or on secondment elsewhere.[143] It is likely that many soldiers would often have little or no money to spend, or spend it rapidly in the wine shop. Since much military supply was based on a command economy, the economic impact of the army may have been significant only in relatively small local areas, and much more limited in terms of a whole province. Furthermore, the impact of the army's presence varied from province to province. For example, in Egypt, since society was already highly monetized and urbanized, the army had limited economic influence.[144] In any case, any beneficial effects from the presence of Roman soldiers were accidental. The army was sent where it was first and foremost in the military interests of Rome.

The military presence: social effects

In 171 BC a deputation arrived in Rome from Spain representing the children of legionaries who had settled down with Spanish wives, with whom they had no right of marriage. There were more than 4000 of them, and the senate decided they should be allowed to form a Latin colony at Carteia in Spain.[145] An army of at least two legions was based permanently in Spain from the end of the second Punic War, and the soldiers could hardly be expected to remain celibate. In the imperial period, professional soldiers who were permanently based near civilian communities and often had no fighting in prospect will have tended to move outside the military environment and to establish relationships with the local population. Furthermore, the practice of local recruiting in some provinces meant that soldiers might have other kin in the vicinity, or at least within a few days' journey.[146] It is interesting to note the high level of commemorations among military populations by the nuclear family in provinces like Africa, Pannonia and Spain, where there was a significant degree of local recruitment.[147] Then, again, the permanent movement of entire legions from one province to another became increasingly rare as the government preferred to send a detachment (*vexillatio*) of a legion if reinforcements were required; this would have had less impact on the local communities close to military bases.[148]

Now, Augustus had forbidden soldiers to contract a marriage during military service. It is not clear what his motive was. He perhaps thought that the army would be more efficient without ties, or that the government should be free of responsibility for dependants, or that there should be no distractions from loyalty to him. As it was, the rule was virtually unenforceable, since soldiers sought the comforts of family life. Many did form unofficial unions (there is no way of telling what proportion), and lived with women whom they regarded as 'wives' and fathered children whom they thought legitimate. The government was ambivalent and tended to turn a blind eye, while the children of unofficial unions with local women were often enlisted into the army and given Roman citizenship.[149] However, officials continued to enforce the consequences of a ban that remained in place until Septimius Severus swept it away at the end of the second century. For example, since the children of these unions were illegitimate they could not inherit their father's property in intestate succession and were subject to other legal restrictions. Furthermore, since illegitimate children could not be entered in the record of births, a soldier's children might find it hard to prove their identity for claims in a will even if stated as heirs. Indeed, evidence from court cases shows that soldiers did not understand why their children should be disadvantaged. One soldier pleading his case before the prefect of Egypt asks: 'What have the children done wrong?'[150]

Over the first two centuries AD, therefore, soldiers' families emerged as a significant aspect of military life. Clearly wives and children could not live in the military camps or in military establishments in towns. Indeed, even after the ban on marriage had been removed there is little sign of the provision of married quarters in camps.[151] Therefore families settled as close as possible to the camps, where soldiers presumably tried to visit them when they could (it may be that in peaceful conditions soldiers were not expected to sleep in the camp every night).[152] These settlements were originally temporary, but in time others were attracted to them – traders, innkeepers, entertainers, craftsmen, women, hangers-on – all those who had something to gain from an area where soldiers and civilians could mix. And some veteran soldiers after discharge preferred to settle locally with their families, close to the comrades with whom they had served, rather than be part of a military colony in a distant region or live individually in villages.[153] These communities that emerged adjacent to some legionary camps were known as *canabae*, while similar settlements called *vici* appeared on a smaller scale around camps and forts housing auxiliary soldiers. *Auxilia* often occupied outposts where larger concentrations of troops were either unnecessary or impracticable and presumably formed the same kind of relationships as legionaries.

As the *canabae*, which were under the jurisdiction of the local legionary commander, gradually acquired a more permanent structure and better amenities, and began to have the air of fully fledged communities, they began to attract more Roman citizens. Eventually some developed into independent communities with their own magistrates. For example, at Carnuntum on the Danube, in the province of Pannonia, a military camp had been built in the reign of Tiberius. On the division of Pannonia into two provinces under Trajan, Carnuntum became the seat of the governor of Upper Pannonia. The *canabae* grew up in an unsystematic fashion on three sides of the military camp of legion XIV Gemina, which was stationed here from the end of Trajan's reign to the end of Roman control in the area. Close by, an amphitheatre and a forum were built. Then a separate civilian settlement was established to the west of the camp, with several large buildings including a new amphitheatre with a capacity of about 13,000. In AD 124 during a visit to Pannonia, Hadrian granted municipal status to Carnuntum, and in AD 194 Septimius Severus, who as governor of Upper Pannonia had launched his successful bid for power from here, granted colonial status with the title *Septimia Carnuntum*. This illustrates how the social, economic and political development of communities could be bound up with the army, warfare and the careers of powerful governors (see Figure 4.1).[154]

At Chester the *canabae* were established close to the legionary camp, with some civilian buildings grouped along the road from the east gate, others on the west side between the defences and the river Dee, with a limited settlement on the southern side. The amphitheatre outside the camp could accommodate 7000 spectators, and clearly served the legion and most of the civilian population, who also shared the water supply by tapping into the camp aqueduct. By the end of the second century there was a significant improvement in living conditions in the civilian sector as timber buildings were gradually replaced by stone and more elaborate houses were built.[155]

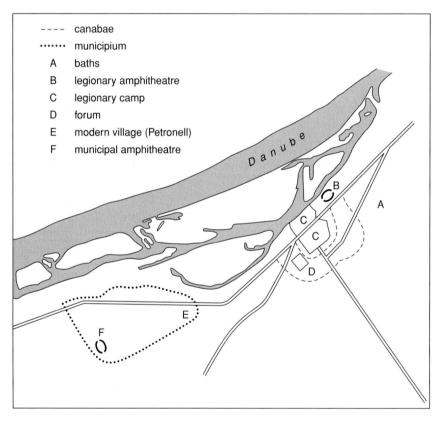

Figure 4.1 Carnuntum (legionary base and settlement)

Source: Raaflaub and Rosenstein (1999, 225), by permission of the Center for Hellenic Studies, Washington, DC

The auxiliary fort at Rapidum (Sour Djouab) in Mauretania Caesariensis, where from AD 122 the second cohort of Sardians was based, was sited in a fertile depression on an important route for east–west communications in the province. Here a civilian settlement grew up just a few feet away from two sides of the camp and was subsequently expanded. In about AD 167 the veterans and civilians dwelling in Rapidum built at their own expense a rampart around the settlement. Rapidum acquired municipal status in the third century, but in about 250 the cohort was withdrawn and the camp and the part of the town closest to it were abandoned. Subsequently more of the town was abandoned before it was eventually destroyed *c.* 275, and it had only partially been reoccupied by 300 (see Figure 4.2).[156] Again we see the close relationship between the presence of the army, military policy and the success of adjacent civilian communities.

It is difficult to say what impact the proximity of soldiers had on local cultural and social practices. In some areas where troops were kept fairly much together and based in camps, and where recruits generally came from outside the province, as in the case of Britain, military contact with civilians

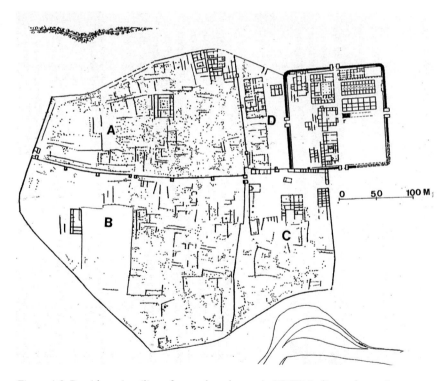

Figure 4.2 Rapidum (auxiliary fort and settlement). ABCD indicate the various stages of settlement and abandonment

Source: Laporte (1989, 26), by permission of the author

ht have been restricted to an area around the *canabae* and *vici*. Elsewhere,
; familiarity with the locals, little active service and the dispersal of the
troops into smaller units could provide opportunities for a considerable
degree of integration as the soldiers lived and worked side by side with
the local population. There is, however, little clear sign of this except in
Egypt, where the unique evidence of papyri offers an insight into the
personal lives of ordinary people.[157] Although they were probably not particularly literate in the Latin language,[158] soldiers naturally brought the images
and authority of Rome, and demonstrated the advantages of the Roman
way of life through the practices and rituals of the military camps: baths,
amphitheatres, medical care. They also brought new deities, such as Jupiter
Doliche and Mithras in Noricum, Pannonia and Moesia.[159] On the other
hand, Mithras tended to remain as a military cult with only limited impact
on local élites. And at Dura on the Euphrates while the garrison officially
followed the Roman military calendar, the community nearby worshipped
a mixture of local gods and other deities.[160]

Of course, in everyday life soldiers were often comparatively well off
compared to ordinary people, and they used their status and wealth to act
on behalf of others in legal cases, or to present petitions to the emperor on
behalf of local people.[161] They also took part in business, owning and buying
and selling property, contracting debts and lending money.[162] There is a
striking example of this in the archive of documents from the Judaean desert
belonging to a Jewish lady, Babatha, showing how a Roman centurion in
the camp at En Gedi had lent money to a local Jew named Judah, who
owned a neighbouring palm grove.[163] For many people in the Roman world,
either in war or in peace soldiers were simply an unavoidable part of life.

Veterans

In early Rome victorious warfare brought the confiscation of land from
defeated enemies and its distribution to the veteran soldiers who had helped
conquer it: 'Wars created the motive for dividing up land. For land captured
from the enemy was allocated to the victorious soldiery and veterans, and,
after the defeat of the enemy, was granted in equal amount in proportion
to the [military] unit.'[164] Land distribution and the foundation of colonies
(that is, the establishment of settlers in an urban centre with surrounding
agricultural land) continued to be a demonstration of Roman power and
control. Symmetrical rows of fields, often marked by *limites* (roadways or
balks) or by ditches, trees and irrigation channels, showed an order imposed
by Rome. Indeed, this process left great physical remains, still apparent
in the topography of Europe and north Africa to this day, in the division
of the land into large squares or rectangles (*centuriae*), often 706m × 706m,
containing 200 *iugera* (124.6 acres = 50.4ha).[165] But, more than this,
some of the most striking examples of social upheaval and changes in the

pattern of landholding in the Roman world were brought about by the settlement of veteran soldiers in military colonies.

In the fourth century BC small groups of Roman citizens were set up in Roman territory in colonies (*coloniae maritimae*) whose likely purpose was to defend the coastline of Italy where Rome had a vested interest. Others were set up outside Roman territory with ostensible strategic intent, like Alba Fucens, established with 6000 settlers in 303 BC at a crossroads on the route to the Adriatic. The Romans continued to found colonies, though from the late second century BC there were also social and political motives, and a further need to provide for veteran soldiers discharged by the political dynasts. Between 47 and 14 BC more than 130,000 soldiers were allocated land in Italy in about fifty colonial settlements.[166] This influx of ex-soldiers, many of whom had been recruited in different parts of Italy, had significant social effects, some of which may be traced in changes in local burial practices.[167] Even the appearance of the land was changed; large estates were divided up into a number of smallholdings, or small plots grouped together to make one holding. Eviction and confiscation often accompanied these changes, at least before 31 BC.[168]

The government had not abandoned the military function of colonies of veterans. Augusta Taurinorum (Turin) established near where the M. Genève Pass comes down into the Po Valley, and Augusta Praetoria Salassorum (Aosta) on the ascent from the Po at the road junction to the Greater and Lesser St Bernard passes, both had a strategic purpose. Aosta was set up probably in 25 BC with 3000 veterans of the praetorian guard after the defeat of the Celtic Salassi by M. Terentius Varro Murena, and served to observe the Alpine routes and act as a secure base of operations and a focus of loyalty in the area.[169]

Between AD 14 and 117 we know of the foundation of about fifty colonies, mainly outside Italy.[170] These usually catered for discharged soldiers, and Vespasian was particularly active with many settlements in areas where Roman control was insecure, as in Africa, or where, as in Italy, existing foundations needed reinforcement.[171] Such settlements were often expensive and sophisticated new towns, offering more facilities and attracting new people to the area, who saw the arrival of Roman citizens with money in their pockets as a good opportunity for profit. For example, at Timgad, founded by Trajan in AD 100 for veterans of the legion III Augusta, which was stationed nearby at Lambaesis, the planners created a sophisticated urban environment in a desert setting. The town is laid out like a military camp, square in shape, with rounded corners and one gate in each side. Straight roads intersect at right-angles, and there are regimented barrack-like squares for the houses, which would make the soldiers feel at home. Within the walls were all the amenities of civilized urban life, including baths, a theatre, and even a library (see Figure 4.3).[172] Despite their sophistication, veteran settlements were a sign of Roman warfare, political control and the subjugation of the native population, whose land the settlers had occupied.

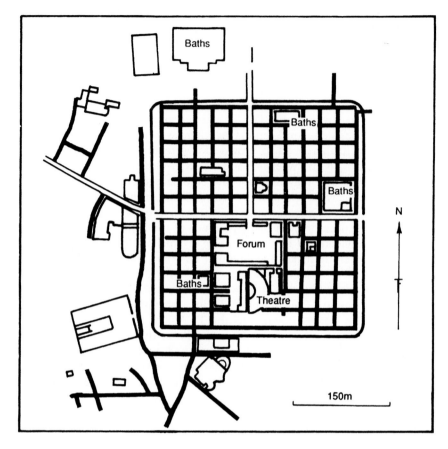

Figure 4.3 Timgad (veteran settlement)
Source: Owens (1991, 135)

However, during this period around 300 colonies would have been needed to cope with the likely number of veterans discharged.[173] Presumably, then, more soldiers received a monetary discharge payment and found their own place to settle than were planted in colonies; indeed, many seem to have settled in the province where they had served.[174] Augustus had established payments for veterans (at least for legionaries) as a burden on the state and set up a treasury in AD 6/7 to deal with them.[175] These monetary rewards continued through the second century; we find veterans of the legion II Adiutrix, who had settled in Trajan's colony at Poetovio, one with a double portion of land, two others with a 'cash discharge grant'.[176] One of them, Gargilius Felix, originally came from Tacapae in Africa. Some soldiers drifted to Rome, as we see in the poignant gravestone set up by a veteran for his young wife, who was apparently a native of Carnuntum

102

in Pannonia: 'To the Spirits of the Departed. Julia Carnuntilla from the province of Upper Pannonia lived nineteen years two months five days. Julius Lupianus, veteran, set this up for his matchless, admirable wife.'[177]

Veterans, both those settled in a colony and individual settlers, were a privileged group and were probably well off compared to most of the local population. A veteran in Egypt could have used his discharge gratuity to buy about thirty-six *arourai* of grain land as well as a house and other essentials. This would have been a substantial holding in terms of the villages in Egypt where veterans settled.[178] The elaborate funeral monument erected at Colonia Agrippina (Cologne) in the first century AD by Lucius Poblicius, veteran of legion V Alaudae, shows not only his wealth but also his willingness to settle in the province where he had served, Lower Germany (Plate 4.1).[179] Centurions, who in the early first century AD may have earned about fifteen times the salary of a legionary, will have been particularly well provided for on retirement.[180] For example, an inscription from Varia near Tivoli tells how Marcus Helvius Rufus Civica, a retired chief centurion, erected baths for his fellow citizens and visitors. As an ordinary soldier he had won the *civica corona* from the emperor Tiberius for saving a comrade's life, hence his extra name Civica. Clearly he had made good and was an important person in his home town.[181]

In addition to an influx of capital, veterans brought other potential advantages. They had legal privileges (notably being exempt from certain punishments and some taxes and customs dues), provided a nucleus of Roman citizens, were self-sufficient, and had plenty of know-how from years spent in the army, which doubtless helped small communities to function. They could act as a channel of contact between the government, the army and local people. They could attract the emperor's attention, and that could bring funding for public buildings, for which there is some evidence in the early colonies of Augustus in Italy.[182]

Outside Italy, an example of a colony that worked well in terms of Roman government policy was Berytus (modern Beirut). After the destruction of the existing town, Berytus was settled by Augustus soon after Actium, and Agrippa established more soldiers from two legions in 14 BC. The colony therefore rewarded veterans without disturbance of Italian landholders, planted a symbol and focus of Roman control amid conquered peoples, and provided a possible base for military operations. It became a successful and prosperous community where, despite some evidence for social integration, there was a strong Roman character with a predominance of Latin inscriptions and the eventual emergence in the third century AD of a famous Roman law school.[183]

On the other hand, in the opinion of Tacitus, far from bringing Romans and the provincials closer together, Roman colonies were sometimes detested as instruments of imperialism. Thus the representatives of the rebel leader Civilis tried to persuade the citizens of Colonia Agrippina (Cologne) to join the revolt by denouncing the city defences as 'the walls of their slavery'.[184] During the revolt of Boudicca in Britain it became clear that the local British hated the veteran colonists at Camulodunum (Colchester), who had apparently stolen land from the native population beyond their original allocations. The colony was overrun and sacked. Of course the Romans treated the British as providers of taxes and recruits, though it was recognized that fairness was an asset to efficient government. And during his governorship Agricola went out of his way to win over the upper classes to the Roman way of life, though it is not clear how much this percolated through to the ordinary British.[185] The contemptuous attitude of the Roman military establishment to the British was probably much more typical. A memorandum or intelligence report found at the fort at Vindolanda concerning British fighting techniques disdainfully dismissed them as 'little Brits' (*Brittunculi*).[186]

Romanization was a complicated process, very difficult to trace and with much depending on the often controversial interpretation of archaeological finds, artefacts, burial customs and architectural styles.[187] It is therefore problematical to what extent the military presence, and in particular veteran colonies or individual veterans, contributed either to economic development, or to the acculturation of non-Roman peoples, or even to the introduction of the Roman way of life. Ex-soldiers were probably pretty rough and uncultivated, their numbers were comparatively small, and although sometimes reasonably affluent they seem not to have formed an exclusive élite group dominating local life. Veterans were not at the top of the social scale, and were not the most influential people in society.[188] In Egypt at least, where there is useful evidence in inscriptions and papyri, there is little sign that veterans made a substantial impact on the development of local communities.[189] Many perhaps enjoyed an unadventurous life, living in small towns and villages, adapting to the ways of the local population, and playing their part in the community in a way that has not often been recorded for posterity. There is no sign that the government had any deliberate or consistent policy of using serving soldiers or veterans to further Romanization. If the soldiers made a contribution here, it will have been limited, indirect and largely accidental. Auxiliary veterans doubtless assimilated to the Roman way of life during life in the camps, but that would depend on individual receptiveness. They did receive Roman citizenship for their wives, and up to the 140s AD for existing children, thereafter for subsequent children. Those who returned to their native areas and did not settle among their ex-comrades may have brought with them some vague idea of Roman values. In general, veterans of the Roman army could provide local people with a model to imitate, and could perhaps encourage young men to join the army when they saw that it looked after its old soldiers, that they were at least men of respect in their communities, and that professional soldiering could be profitable whatever the fortunes of war.

Plate 4.1 Monument (reconstructed) of Lucius Poblicius
Source: By permission of the Rheinisches Bildarchiv

5

WAR AND POLITICS

Qualities in other directions could more easily be ignored, but good generalship should be the monopoly of the Emperor.[1]

Tacitus puts this thought into Domitian's mind in order to emphasize a dilemma confronting Roman emperors. They needed to employ competent commanders, but those commanders might be so militarily successful that they could challenge the emperor's control of the army and undermine his political domination. In all ages and societies the interrelation of war and political structures has provoked debate among historians and social commentators. On one level, mass participation in war by a citizen militia can lead to political changes through the sacrifice and suffering of the ordinary citizens serving as soldiers, who vote in the assembly to bring about permanent changes in the constitution or extort temporary concessions from the governing group if their military contribution is considered essential. Therefore the 'military participation rate' can be a significant indicator of social and political change, and in some circumstances is perhaps relevant to the ancient world. On another level, one group in society can sometimes exploit a special or superior contribution in war to impose its rule on the rest of the population, or an individual can exploit his military leadership to stage a coup or buttress his faltering political authority. When military commanders compete for control within a state, it sometimes happens that ordinary soldiers acquire a political influence normally denied to them. Once in power, a leader might use his personal association with the army, his prowess in war and the promise of frequent war-making to change the pattern of government by establishing a purely military autocracy. Finally, the emergence of a professional army with a low level of military participation among the population as a whole might lead to domination by the soldiery in one form or another.[2]

Leaders and soldiers

During their conquest of Italy and the Mediterranean, Roman citizen-soldiers seem not to have used their military muscle significantly to change the political structure of the Republic. Changes eventually came about for other reasons, largely through the political rivalry of upper-class factions,

106

though in the end the fall of the Republic was encompassed by soldiers in the pay of ambitious military leaders.[3] In this process the army effectively ceased to be the army of the Roman state as soldiers were absorbed into the forces of individual military dynasts, to whom they swore oaths of personal loyalty and obedience. In the 80s BC, and in the war between Caesar and Pompey, the influence of the troops had been largely passive, in that the situation developed according to their willingness to follow or abandon certain leaders. After the murder of Caesar they sometimes played a more active role, forcing the leaders to take action that they could not themselves have initiated. Thus Caesar's veterans were keen not only that Caesar should be avenged but also that their rights to land distributions be upheld, and therefore they wanted Antony and Octavian to stand together against Caesar's murderers. But they had no fine political principles or ideas on the future government of Rome; they were motivated by individual loyalties and the expectation of personal profit. Similarly, the soldiers who fought for Brutus and Cassius were not driven on by Republican principles. They were more influenced by greed for land and booty, and were swayed by powerful personalities in the leadership. After the battle of Philippi, the victorious armies hoped for peace, not for political reasons but so that they could enjoy the fruits of victory.[4] The soldiers did not prevail, and when, after more civil conflict, Augustus emerged in 31 BC as supreme leader, he was in the tradition of the great military dynasts of the previous twenty years, who won the loyalty of their soldiers by promises of enrichment, and then went on to organize the political world to suit them without consulting their army.

Augustus' victory nevertheless confirmed the political dimension of the Roman army. He was in control of the empire because of the support of his legions, and those legions did exercise political power in so far as he would fall if they deserted him. But in real terms the situation was not so clear-cut. In the late Republic the Roman army had not been a single entity, and became even less so after Augustus' victory. It was instead divided into several armies based in many different locations as far apart as Spain and Syria. The soldiers did not speak with one voice, since armies in different provinces, or even different legions, had their own views and there was often intense rivalry between units. Therefore activists would find it difficult to concert action for political objectives. There was no direct channel of communication from the army to the emperor that could change the mechanisms of government or fundamentally reshape the nature of the Roman state. There was no army council, or even an informal group of senior officers, and there were no *ex-officio* army representatives to badger the emperor. Furthermore, the army was a professional force with set pay and conditions, and not a casual levy; and, since the legions and auxiliaries were based outside Italy for twenty-five years, they were separated from the political life of Rome and any previous familial or political ties. Indeed, the soldiers were virtually the emperor's employees, and because recruits came increasingly from outside Italy he was unlikely to face hostile political opinion in the homeland because of public concern about casualties and military setbacks.

In fact Augustus had no intention of using the army to support him politically by voting for his proposals. Many soldiers recruited during the civil wars were not even Roman citizens, and Augustus brought many non-citizens into the formal structure of the army as auxiliaries. In any case, few soldiers would be in a position to vote in the people's assembly, and such votes would count for little in the new political set-up. Augustus based only the praetorians in Italy, and there were only three cohorts on duty in Rome. Upper-class senators commuting from their estates to Rome and attending meetings of the senate will not have noticed much difference around the streets and buildings of the city. It was not until the end of the second century AD that a legion was permanently stationed in Italy.

In terms of the political changes that Augustus introduced, when Dio describes the constitutional arrangements of 27 BC and later, he does not suggest that Augustus thought of consulting the army, much less that he took account of any views expressed by the soldiers. He decided what he wanted to do with the help of his chief henchmen and high-ranking advisers, although taking care to have proposals discussed and approved by the senate. Of the powers and attributes granted to Augustus, only procon-sular *imperium* implied military command. In the provinces within the sphere of his *imperium*, which contained most of the legionary troops, he appointed the governors personally; in the remainder the governor was technically appointed by the senate. Augustus was granted greater proconsular power (*proconsulare imperium maius*) in 23 BC, which enabled him formally to give orders to any governor in the empire. By the end of his reign there was only one province containing legionary troops (Africa, with legion III Augusta) to which the senate appointed the governor. When Gaius shifted command of this legion to his separate appointee, the emperor was in practice commander-in-chief of the whole army.

From the start of the imperial period the army's role in political life, though potentially important, was entirely extra-constitutional. This emerges most clearly in Dio's comments on the formation of the praetorian guard in 27 BC: 'His [Augustus'] first action was to have a decree passed granting to the members of his future bodyguard twice the rate of pay of the rest of the army, to ensure that he was strictly guarded. So it was perfectly clear that he intended to establish a monarchy.'[5] Dio sarcastically places this after his account of how Augustus allegedly offered to return the administration of affairs to the senate and people. In fact Augustus astutely organized all political matters as he wanted. He was polite to the senate, appeared to consult them, respected the traditional prerogatives of the Roman people, and kept the soldiers at arm's length. As the bringer of peace and order after the chaos of civil war, Augustus could not be seen to be at the mercy of his troops. Famously, he declined to call the troops 'comrades' after the civil wars were over, because the term was 'too flattering for the demands of military discipline, the peaceful nature of the times, and his own majesty and that of his house'.[6]

Augustus' apparent deference to traditional practices, and his careful and piecemeal acquisition of powers, contributed to the lack of a clear constitutional framework for the emperor's position. Eventually, according to the jurist Ulpian, the source of the emperor's power was formally defined as a law passed by the people.[7] The formal vote of the people would be taken on the recommendation of the senate, and it is true that a new emperor normally sought acceptance and recognition by the senate as soon as he could. Of course, the senate retained a considerable mystique, and it was probably always important for an emperor to make a show of approaching it, for the senate and the people, so it seemed, represented a significant body of opinion. Therefore, as he left to fight Vitellius, Otho invoked 'the majesty of Rome and the approval of people and senate'.[8] Now, although the senate had an important political role to play, it had no *right* to confer the imperial powers because it had no power to initiate such a move or to reject a man who had gained the backing of a sufficiently large number of soldiers.

Naturally the acclamation and obvious support of the soldiers was of great practical importance in persuading the upper classes and army commanders in the provinces, who might at the outset doubt the new emperor's capacity to rule and his ability to obtain the full backing of the troops. We see this in Tacitus' description of the accession of Nero: 'Nero was brought into the praetorian camp, and when he had said a few suitable words and offered a donative on the scale of his father's generosity, he was hailed as *imperator*. The decree of the senate followed the decision of the soldiers, and there was no hesitation in the provinces.'[9] The practical, extra-constitutional power of the army was sometimes embarrassingly obvious. Vespasian was acclaimed emperor by his troops in the east on 1 July AD 69, but his powers were not formally voted by the senate until six months later, in late December 69, and he took 1 July as his *dies imperii*, the formal inauguration of his reign.[10] In the third century AD, Dio was still concerned enough to complain that Macrinus had assumed the imperial titles before the senate had voted them, but his words reveal the true situation, since he says merely that it was 'fitting' for the senate to play this role. Macrinus' letter to the senate indicates the realities of power politics: 'I was well aware that you agreed with the soldiers, since I knew that I had benefited the state in many ways.'[11]

Augustus had prepared the way for a politicized army which his successors inherited. Yet, despite their importance as potential imperial power-brokers, the soldiers seem to have shown little sign of political awareness. It is certainly not true even in the third century AD that they set out to protect their own social class, namely the rural peasantry from whom most soldiers were recruited.[12] Apart from the fact that much of the injustice suffered by poor civilians was inflicted by soldiers, the troops' loyalty was to their own unit, just as loyalties in the ancient world were in the main local and parochial, and not based on large groups or classes. In fact soldiers with no firm political opinions of their own were ideal supporters of the emperor. They had little motivation to change a political system that secured regular pay and rewarded them when their military service was over. In any case the most they could achieve by revolt, even if their leaders were from the upper classes, was to bring about a change in emperor. The one common view among soldiers was probably that the emperor should be competent to maintain his rule and consequently their benefits, be strong enough to avoid civil war with other Roman legionaries, and possibly provide opportunities for plunder.[13] To this end they might be influenced by a prospective emperor's family connections (e.g. relationship to the family of the previous emperor), and his record and attributes, in so far as these could be made known.

But the soldiers' interest in an emperor's attributes did not extend to his moral qualities, his style of government, or the diligence and effectiveness of his administration. Nero ruled for fourteen years, as untroubled by military discontent as the respected Antoninus Pius. The praetorians were slow to desert and needed to be prompted by prominent men.[14] Despite widespread revulsion among the senatorial class at the excesses of Commodus, and his lack of interest in military affairs, he ruled for twelve years. It is true that Herodian claims that the emperor Macrinus (AD 217–18) offended the troops by his effeminate habits while on campaign in the east.[15] Doubtless soldiers would not want to see an emperor living luxuriously while they faced the hardships of life on campaign, but it is clear that they turned against Macrinus because he threatened to reduce their pay and benefits. And they were happy to support the usurper Elagabalus, who by all accounts dressed and behaved in a bizarre fashion.[16] When, in a rare concerted move, the praetorians forced Nerva to execute the murderers of Domitian, they were not making a disinterested intervention for justice and equity but were reaffirming their rights and privileges, perhaps threatened by the change of emperor.[17]

Roman soldiers had no particular affection for the traditions of the upper classes, or loyalty to the Roman state or to any imperial ideal. The entire basis of the army's position in the state was a personal relationship with the emperor. When in January AD 69 the legions in Upper Germany abandoned their allegiance to the emperor Galba and eventually swore loyalty to 'senate and people', this was not a recognition of higher political loyalties, but rather an attempt to cover their real intentions, namely support for Vitellius in his bid for power.[18] It was certainly true that in 193 the way in which Didius Julianus was proclaimed emperor made him an object of derision in Rome and provoked two senators in provincial commands to make their own bid for the purple,[19] but the soldiers who supported Septimius Severus hardly shared whatever concern he may have felt at the way in which Julianus had seized power or the way in which he was conducting his government, however much Severan propaganda may have alleged this. They were doubt-less won over by the promise of money and other rewards if Severus won.

When soldiers intervened directly with an emperor, they were usually trying to win concessions for themselves or increase their benefits. It is possible that they would have more leverage in time of war or political turmoil. Such isolated examples, arising from particular circumstances, are not necessarily politically significant. They are important, however, because they show that the emperor from his position as commander-in-chief could not entirely distance himself from the demands of the soldiery. The notorious mutinies of AD 14 brought military activity on the Rhine and Danube to a stop and seriously embarrassed the new emperor, Tiberius. The troops objected to low pay, poor conditions and over-long service. They were also worried about their future after the death of Augustus, so closely did they associate their military career with him. Under Claudius the soldiers stationed in Germany wrote secretly to the emperor in the name of all the armies protesting about the hard work they were subjected to by commanders who tried to win imperial approval by engaging in building or mining projects.[20] This is apparently a very rare example of concerted action, though it is not clear how the soldiers in various armies communicated with one another or conveyed their letters to Claudius. Similarly, we hear from Josephus that the soldiers of several auxiliary units in Judaea, who objected to being transferred, sent a deputation to Claudius and won their case.[21] Commodus politely received a large group of legionary soldiers who had travelled from Britain to Rome to complain about the conduct of his powerful praetorian prefect Perennis.[22] It was of course also possible for an individual soldier to use his right to petition the emperor directly (a right theoretically enjoyed by all citizens) to support his interests or those of his friends. Thus the petition of the peasants at Scaptopara who were aggrieved at the oppressive con-duct of soldiers and other officials was presented by a soldier in the praeto-rian guard who was a landowner there, and who presumably, owing to his position, had an excellent chance to deliver the petition.[23] In AD 193, just after Septimius Severus had occupied Rome and was about to set out against his rival for the purple, Pescennius Niger, his troops burst into the senate demanding a donative equal to that given by Octavian in 43 BC.[24] Severus managed to placate them by paying a token sum, but this episode raises the question of the enhanced role of the army in civil wars and disputed accessions.[25] The common factor in all the examples discussed above and in other minor mutinies and disturbances is a complaint about immediate problems or the conduct of individuals. They were not directed against the system of imperial government. This kind of military intervention cannot be seen as significant in social or political terms.

In an army that could hold the balance of political power but lacked real political awareness, it was important for emperors to build up an ideal relationship of loyalty and affection, so as to make it difficult for rebels to win the soldiers over to their side. Thus soldiers swore an oath of personal loyalty and obedience to their emperor, who would address his men as 'comrades' (*commilitones*), sometimes in terms of great affection, as when Trajan in official instructions to his governors referred to 'my excellent and most loyal comrades'.[26] On campaigns emperors at least made a show of behaving as true fellow-soldiers, wearing military uniform and sharing the privations of their men. In their nomenclature and titles they boasted of their military attributes, they received acts of veneration on numerous occasions scrupulously set out in the military calendar, and they maintained their personal responsibility for the soldiers' pay, decorations and other benefits. Whole legions were sometimes granted special honorific titles for conspicuous service and loyalty: for example, the two legions (VII and XI) that remained loyal to Claudius during the abortive revolt of the governor of Dalmatia in AD 42 were named 'Claudian Loyal True' (*Claudia Pia Fidelis*).[27]

Association with the troops encouraged emperors to take more interest in military affairs and to assume personal command of campaigns.[28] This translated easily into the use of warfare for political ends. Emperors could of course exploit the trappings of war and military leadership by clever manipulation and self-presentation, however limited their achievements were in practice.[29] But real war often offered a direct way to enhanced status, wealth, and even an increase in centralized imperial authority, since the administrative structure followed the emperor out of Rome. An emperor therefore could become a 'military entrepreneur' in that he might gamble that the political benefits of a successful war would outweigh any risks.[30] Thus he might be driven to provoke war and exploit the blood and effort of his soldiers in order to boost his own political standing in Rome. Since he controlled foreign policy he was answerable to no one if he decided to launch an offensive.[31] Indeed, Augustus had cynically exploited his large army by using it to conquer lands whose annexation he then celebrated by word and deed, helping to establish his legitimacy and standing as *princeps*. Claudius also realized that military conquest was a way of quickly placing himself beyond all competition and criticism. The annexation of Britain was skilfully exploited to emphasize his personal role.[32] Septimius Severus fought two bloody civil wars in 193 to 197, but the campaigns were mostly under the command of others, and he was present at only one of the battles that decided his fate. His skills in generalship were questionable, and he was certainly not one of the empire's great commanders. Once secure in power, he looked for a legitimate military target to distract attention from the thousands of Roman soldiers killed in the cause of his personal ambition, to enhance his own military credentials and to confirm political loyalty. Severus' successful war against the Parthians and the creation of the new province of Mesopotamia splendidly served this purpose.[33]

Civil war, militarism and praetorianism

Modern commentators and theorists, who are interested in the links between warfare and social and political change, have developed methodologies that might be useful in an analysis of the political role of armies. The so-called 'military participation ratio', that is, the proportion of the citizen body involved in military service, is particularly relevant.[34] Military participation affects social stratification; and, if participation becomes restricted and military service professionalized, this can lead to a more steeply stratified society. In his theoretical analysis Andreski referred to six 'ideal' types of military organization. The 'mortazic' type, which combines a low level of participation with high levels of cohesion and subordination, could be applied to the Roman imperial army. In his view this often led to praetorianism or the domination of the military in one form or another, exercised not along customary or legally recognized constitutional channels, but through mutinies and *coups d'état*. This is characteristic of professional troops who have no particular ideology. Soldiers are more likely to be the arbiters of politics if they are the main plank of the government's authority, and military might is liable to be decisive in politics in a society where there are no clear and universally accepted beliefs about the legitimacy of power.[35]

Some of these generalizations may be applied to the Roman empire. The army was professional and the troops had no strong political beliefs beyond the preservation of the source of their service and benefits. There was no dynastic succession or undisputed mechanism for selecting a successor. But the situation in Rome was far more complex than this. Although all emperors adopted the attributes of a Roman commander in dress and titles, they also displayed other civic attributes, and many did not take the field in person. They were not expected to be great warriors, still less to fight in battle. The military did not dominate political life in Rome. Even in the case of an emperor like Domitian, whom senators regarded as a tyrant, it was not military domination that Tacitus and others complained about, but his failure to find a working relationship with the senate. The army was not singled out as the main plank in the government's authority, which also depended on the senate and the people, and the rule of law. Augustus had expressed the hope that he had created the foundations of government that would last long after him.[36] Indeed, the system he established proved a workable and relatively stable means of preserving a government in which the emperor and the upper classes collaborated.

Nevertheless, the emperor was in total control of the army, and depended ultimately upon its armed support, however much he might try to conceal this. He kept a bodyguard, which from early in the first century AD was stationed permanently in Rome. Augustus had tried to keep the praetorians out of politics. He saw that they had potentially great political influence since they were the only substantial military force at the centre of power. Therefore at the start of his reign he based the bodyguard in several Italian communities, did not appoint an overall commander until 2 BC, and when he did so he appointed two commanders of equestrian rank (praetorian prefects). But the praetorians were drawn into the political intrigue that inevitably surrounded the emperor. The guard commander became closely associated with the emperor personally and became a major player in imperial politics. Since in practice on many occasions only one praetorian prefect held office, the scope for intrigue was greater. The career of a prefect like Aelius Sejanus under Tiberius revealed that the prefect could exercise an influence far beyond his formal legal powers.[37] Gradually the power and attributes of the prefect came to match his latent influence as guard commander; he was a confidant and imperial adviser, was often given special military responsibilities on campaign and gradually acquired legal jurisdiction. Indeed, the prefect became such an important officer of state that when Constantine abolished the praetorian guard in AD 312 the office of praetorian prefect remained.

Thus Augustus failed to isolate either the guard or its commanders from the politics of the imperial family. The praetorians' most significant intervention in politics came in AD 41, when in the confusion after the murder of Caligula they escorted Claudius to the praetorian barracks. From here he exploited the backing of the troops, who wanted another emperor of the Julio-Claudian line, and used intermediaries to negotiate with the reluctant senators. His proclamation by the soldiers, encouraged by a generous payment, was a public demonstration of his military support, and ensured that there could be no serious opposition. Coins minted in the early years of the reign showing Claudius shaking hands with a praetorian, and bearing unique legends, 'The Reception of the Emperor' and 'The Reception of the Praetorians', emphasize the debt he owed to the praetorians.[38] Nevertheless, we cannot say that after the initial phase Claudius was especially indulgent towards the army or that the general tenor of his government was disturbed by a pro-military bias.[39]

. When the succession was resolved by civil war the implications of the army's intervention were even more damaging. Tacitus analyses the events of AD 68 to 69, a time of battles, extreme violence, murder, destruction of property and the disruption of the normal process of administration. The army was of course at the centre of this, but it was what Tacitus calls the 'madness of the leading men', that is, the ambition of important men for power and profit, that sustained the conflict.[40] Of course, everyone would have agreed that autocratic government must continue; the fight was over who should be emperor. The troops who survived the fighting gained some benefits; they had opportunities for plunder, they received donatives, a relaxation of discipline, and in some cases the chance to serve in the praetorian guard or to choose their own officers; the victors had the prestige associated with winning. But nothing really changed as a result of the fighting in 68 to 69. The same system of government remained; Vespasian reimposed military discipline, and there was not even a pay rise for the troops, who had no more real or formal political standing than before. The unseen, long-term consequences are another matter. The overthrow of Nero and the subsequent civil wars demonstrated the success of appealing to the army to overthrow the existing government, and they also showed that a provincial governor in command of an army could march on Rome and seize power. It is probable that everyone in public life in Rome had known this, but the public confirmation of it set an example for the future. Tacitus summed up this political truth in a famous epigram: 'The secret of ruling was revealed. An emperor could be made outside Rome.'[41]

The stability of the Augustan system and the difficulty of winning over the soldiers from their loyalty to the emperor contributed to the fact that it was not until the late second century that a reigning emperor was again overthrown by a provincial governor marching on Rome. In AD 193 Pertinax was murdered by the praetorians because they thought that he was parsimonious and a strict disciplinarian. His death was followed by the notorious 'auction' of the empire, in which two senators, Didius Julianus and Sulpicianus, father-in-law of Pertinax, made rival offers to the praetorians for their support. Julianus, who was outside the camp, shouted out the sums he was offering, even counting out the amount on his fingers, and was eventually proclaimed emperor by the troops. When Julianus first appeared in the senate he was surrounded by praetorians in full armour carrying their standards. Contemporary sources thought that the whole episode was disgraceful and tended to blame the praetorians, forgetting that it was the two senators who exploited the troops, who simply went with the highest bidder and took no further interest in politics.[42] However, Julianus had little authority, and the mood in Rome was exploited by ambitious provincial governors, first Septimius Severus in Pannonia and Pescennius Niger in Syria, and then Clodius Albinus in Britain. The civil wars lasting from 193 to 197, in which Septimius Severus eventually secured power, were the worst that Rome had experienced since the late Republic, and involved unprecedented ferocity, loss of life, and damage to provincial communities, although Italy escaped the worst of the violence. What were the political consequences of these tumultuous events?

It is possibly in this period that theories of military participation rate and praetorianism have most relevance. Scholars have identified a sinister watershed during the reign of Septimius Severus, the development of militaristic tendencies, the undermining of the senate and traditional practices of government, and the upsetting of the balance established by Augustus. Perhaps Severus' open reliance on the support of his army helped to bring about a fundamental change in the way the state was run and in the ways of winning military support, even if Severus himself did not intend this or recognize what was happening. He was perhaps eager to inspire a committed loyalty that did not ask too many questions, which we see in the inscription set up in Poetovio in Pannonia by a tribune of the praetorians 'setting out to suppress the Gallic faction' (that is, the emperor's rival, Clodius Albinus).[43] Indeed, Severus had disbanded the praetorians in 193, replacing them with legionaries. There were good reasons for this in that they had murdered Pertinax, sold their support to Didius Julianus and then abandoned him. They could not be trusted, and Severus also needed to reward the soldiers of his own legions who had first supported him. However, symbolically this highlights the political relationship between emperor and praetorian guard that Dio had pointed out in respect of Augustus' creation of the guard in 27 BC.[44] On his deathbed Severus allegedly said to his sons, 'Stick together, enrich the soldiers, and despise the rest', which suggests that he was well aware of the political reality of the army's power.[45]

Did the army now have a more dominant political role to play and, if so, how was this manifested? Is there any real evidence that Septimius Severus brought about an increase in militarism? We must look first at the criticisms of Cassius Dio, a contemporary senator, which are echoed by another contemporary writer, Herodian. Dio was angered at the cost of the army (Severus granted a pay rise) and frequent military campaigns, and the burdensome presence of so many troops in Rome.[46] These criticisms seem to relate to the immediate situation, but perhaps more significant is his analysis of the emperor's relationship with his troops. Severus placed his hopes of secure government on the strength of the army rather than on the goodwill of those around him, by which he means those members of the upper classes who could assist his rule.[47] This might indeed suggest a changed balance of power with more open reliance on the army, or even some kind of military participation in government, but Dio may be reflecting on the early part of the reign immediately after the coup of 193 when the emperor's intentions were still unclear. Dio's general verdict on the reign is rather more favourable.[48]

However, it is possible that a greater reliance on the army, greater specialization in military affairs and the frequent military campaigns of this era promoted social mobility. Perhaps the emperor, spending more time in the company of soldiers, turned to them or their junior officers for advice and guidance, accepted their militaristic outlook and tried to use them in various levels of government. But, so far as we can tell, Septimius Severus seems to have employed henchmen and advisers drawn from the usual quarters, that is, senators and *equites*. He was supported by his fellow governors of the Danube provinces, notably C. Valerius Pudens, governor of Lower Pannonia, later destined for high honours, and Severus' brother, P. Septimius Geta, governor of Lower Moesia. In charge of the food supply for the march to Rome was M. Rossius Vitulus, a former equestrian officer, while the commander of the advance guard was Julius Laetus, possibly a legionary legate or governor of Raetia or Noricum. In the campaign against Niger several senators who were old friends of Severus played a leading role, especially Fabius Cilo, Tiberius Claudius Candidus and Cornelius Anullinus. Claudius Claudianus, a man of equestrian rank, was brought into the senate, made praetor and soon sent as legionary legate in Dacia.[49]

Men like Claudianus were doubtless absorbed into the senatorial ethos, but it is possible that, as the regime settled down, the greater military experience or aptitude of equestrians persuaded Severus to ignore the usual social conventions and promote *equites* to jobs of major responsibility, and encourage them to edge out senators. The emperor then would have devoted henchmen from outside the top social class who had talent, a more professional attitude to military service and a hard edge of military thinking. In time this could change the character of government. Most striking is the appointment of an equestrian to the governorship of the new province of Mesopotamia, the only person of this status to be permanently in command of legionary troops apart from the prefect of Egypt. But this was probably not part of any *policy* to promote equestrians. Severus was always concerned with security, and he may have wished to break up the pattern of five armed provinces in the area, all governed by senators.[50] Or he may have found it difficult to find a suitable senator willing to serve in a newly conquered province that might prove fractious. The legionary commanders in Mesopotamia were necessarily of equestrian rank because it would have been unthinkable even at this date to ask a senator to be subordinate to an equestrian. In this Severus was protecting the interests of senators. The newly recruited legion (II Parthica) stationed in Italy at Albanum was also under an equestrian prefect, but it was traditional for troops in Italy to be commanded by equestrians, and in any case it may have been under the ultimate authority of the praetorian prefects.

We must ask if Severus pursued a more subtle approach by trying to infiltrate equestrians quietly into posts normally held by senators, so that gradually the position of senators in the administration was undermined. Inscriptions recording the careers of individual office-holders provide the only evidence and there are not enough to give a clear answer. From the reign of Severus we have about seven cases where a man of equestrian rank was appointed to a post of governor that would normally have been held by a senator. This is only a small number of examples, and the title usually held by these men ('acting in place of the governor') suggests that they were intended to be temporary appointments. In one instance there was clearly an emergency, since the governor had died suddenly in office. The men appointed to these temporary positions rarely commanded troops, and there is little to suggest a sinister motive. Severus was not the first emperor to think of using *equites* as temporary replacements for senators, a practice attested at least as early as the reign of Domitian. In a way typical of Roman administration, the emperor was making an *ad hoc* response to immediate circumstances. In general, it made sense to exploit fully the talents of equestrians and promote them as required, as Augustus had done.

Thus, when it suited him, Severus was prepared to encourage this avenue of social mobility provided by service in the army, which in turn added a further dimension to the political culture in Rome.[51]

It would be particularly interesting if promoted soldiers were significantly better off in terms of career prospects in the reign of Septimius Severus. This would show how far social mobility had improved under the new regime. Many equestrian office-holders such as procurators had begun their career with military service of some kind, often holding one or more of the military posts traditionally held by men of their rank, such as military tribune or commander of an auxiliary cohort or *ala*. There was a gradual increase in the proportion of men who rose from the position of centurion to equestrian rank and were then promoted to hold further posts in the civil administration. Such men might be thought to represent a tougher, genuinely military influence. Perhaps indeed Severus aimed deliberately to change the basis of Roman government by appointing men with a tough military background to junior positions, and then ensuring that gradually they could be promoted to form a new group of administrators. However, on the available evidence, in the Severan period just over 30 per cent of equestrian procurators who had held some military post in their previous career were promoted centurions, while over 57 per cent had held traditional equestrian military posts.[52] Furthermore, it is clear that the practice of employing ex-centurions went back at least to Hadrian and was well established before Severus. This is not likely to be a deliberate or long-term policy, or a sign of militarism. Rather, emperors were sensibly using more intelligent or well-educated soldiers to fill gaps in the administration.

To sum up, under Septimius Severus it seemed like business as usual for *equites*, although there was some increase in their status and responsibilities. The emperor certainly had many henchmen and confidants from the equestrian class. But so had Augustus, for example, Maecenas, and Cornelius Gallus, who was appointed as first prefect of Egypt in charge of legionary troops in defiance of precedent. In fact it does not appear that Severus had any preference for equestrians or trusted them more. When the Severan dynasty finally came to an end in AD 235, senators still held most of the major governorships and army commands. As for the army, when Severus died in AD 211 ordinary soldiers were of course financially better off, had been enriched by the plunder and donatives from civil and foreign wars, and could legally marry. Furthermore, the army did contribute to social mobility and offered a route to higher posts, but for a comparatively small number of soldiers, as before. The troops had no more legal privileges than previously. They did not dictate military policy, since the major foreign military expeditions were undertaken at the emperor's personal decision. In fact soldiers had virtually no direct political influence under Severus, and had no impact on the succession he had arranged, or subsequently when Caracalla murdered his brother Geta.

It is striking that the high-ranking lawyer Ulpian, a contemporary of Severus, confirmed that a law still formally defined the emperor's position: 'Whatever the emperor has decided has the force of law; inasmuch as through the law which was carried concerning his power, the people confers all its power and authority on him and in him.'[53] Indeed, in the Severan period the character and order of society are similar to that under the respected Antonine emperors, and Dio's description of Severus' daily routine and conduct of government business also suggests an emperor not untypical of previous years.[54] There was always a balance to be found between the emperor's civilian attributes and his military responsibilities, since he needed to preserve the loyalty and goodwill of the senatorial class, from which most of the governors and army commanders came. Indeed, Tiberius famously described the emperor's task of dealing with a possibly seditious nobility, the senate, and the demands of the soldiers as 'holding a wolf by the ears'.[55]

It is therefore impossible to sustain sweeping generalizations about militarism and praetorianism in the Roman world. There was no real military hierarchy or caste of generals, and it certainly cannot be said that the 'Roman imperial guard stands as a classic example of the rule of soldiers'.[56] Nevertheless, we can see that the balance of power was beginning to change and that important trends were slowly developing. Septimius Severus did not deliberately set out to increase the role of the army, and he would not have been at pains to define 'militarism'. But the inevitable consequence of the first capture of Rome with an army for 124 years was a closer relationship between emperor and army, which made it more difficult to conceal the reality of an autocracy backed by military force. After Severus four emperors in succession were violently overthrown, three by military insurrection, though the mutinies were instigated by plotters among the imperial family or senior officials. Dio reflects on the increasing influence of the soldiery: 'For whenever people, and especially the soldiers, have become accustomed to be contemptuous of their rulers, they feel that there is no limit to their power to do whatever they want; indeed they use their weapons against the man who gave them that power.'[57] The army was now more important in politics and potentially less controllable, and the emperor's position as a military leader and commander in war was more significant. The new relationship between emperor and soldiers was announced by Caracalla in a characteristically excitable way: 'I am one of you and it is because of you alone that I want to live so that I can do all kinds of good things for you. For all the treasuries belong to you.' An emperor must be willing to fall in battle, for 'there a man should die, or nowhere'.[58]

The later empire

By the later third century an emperor generally needed to be successful in war to survive. It is true to say that emperors were compelled to think more and more about their personal security against revolt, preparation for warfare and the waging of war. Maximinus, who overthrew the last member of the Severan dynasty, Severus Alexander, emphasized in his propaganda campaign that Alexander was a mummy's boy, militarily incompetent and parsimonious – in contrast to Maximinus, who was a real soldier's man.[59] The fact that Alexander was involved in long wars made these jibes more effective. However, as emperors became more associated with military life it became more difficult to distance them from military failure, and setbacks were directly laid at their door. We may remember by contrast how Augustus had skilfully isolated himself from the destruction of three legions in Germany, which was blamed on the incompetence of the luckless commander, Varus.[60] Indeed, an emperor's military ability became more important as foreign wars became more frequent and dangerous, and the empire faced serious foreign invasions. If men felt that they needed someone of imperial rank on hand to command the troops, repel incursions and keep the empire together, then that would lead to frequent usurpations as ambitious contenders promised to rescue the empire by their military prowess and tried to persuade senior officers and the soldiers. This in turn could lead to an increased role for the army in politics, as soldiers supported various candidates for the purple, and also to fragmentation of the imperial structure as strong leaders emerged who based their rule on their ability to protect a single territorial area, like Postumus and his Gallic empire, and later Odenathus in Palmyra.[61] Diocletian recognized these developments when he reorganized the empire in the late third century by creating a structure in which two emperors (*Augusti*) ruled jointly, supported by two junior partners (Caesars). In practice, this system, known as the Tetrarchy, meant that each of the four rulers took responsibility for a part of the empire, increasing military efficiency and personal security through the speed of reaction to invasion or revolts. This was perhaps the only way in which central control could be re-established. Eventually, in the fourth century as the government became desperate for good soldiers, warlords in command of private armies offered their services and supported Rome's interests as suited their personal inclinations.

It is doubtful, however, if soldiers had any more say in political life than before. They were essentially the pawns of groups of officers or other important men who bribed or cajoled them to support certain candidates. In constitutional terms the senate, and through it the people, were still the legitimating bodies, however much in reality the leading generals dictated the choice of emperor. In the dissemination of information and the promotion of their image, emperors still maintained the traditional slogans about imperial qualities and the government of the Roman state. Policy was not formulated in the interests of soldiers or any specifically military ideology.

Andreski thought that praetorianism became particularly acute in Rome 'when promotion from the ranks to the highest posts became common'.[62]

From the mid-third century there was certainly greater social mobility, in that men of equestrian rank were now being appointed to more senior posts previously held by senators, such as the command of a legion. These men usually had more military training and experience than senators, and it will have made less sense to appoint a senator with limited military experience as governor of a province where he was in command of several legions and *auxilia*. Gradually equestrians began to be appointed to more senior posts, often with the title *dux*, in command of substantial bodies of troops. Senators were phased out of provincial governorships involving the command of legionary troops, and AD 260 saw the last known example of a senator in command of a military campaign. Equestrians employed in this way tended to be schooled in military affairs and were often promoted from highly experienced centurions and senior centurions. Thus the way was opened for people from different regions and social backgrounds to assume a greater role in Roman society and government, as the empire moved further away from its Italian homeland and the army became steadily less Roman in character. Many of these tough military officers came from the Danubian provinces, and the marriage of military ability and imperial responsibilities eventually brought emperors of Illyrian stock like Diocletian and Constantine. Yet Augustus would still have recognized the political and military framework, and when Constantine died in 337 he had secured the unity and prestige of the empire while remaining the master of his army and preparing for an orderly, hereditary succession.

6

WAR AND PUBLIC OPINION

Augustus and military glory

> Next to the immortal gods he [Augustus] honoured the memory
> of the leaders who had raised the power of the Roman people
> from obscurity to greatness.[1]

When Augustus built his new forum as the centre-piece of his construction
projects in Rome, the adjoining hemicycles and colonnades provided room
for statues of distinguished men, many in military dress, which had their
original inscriptions and also an explanatory notice of their deeds. One
such statue was that of Marcus Valerius Corvus, who had allegedly killed
a Gallic leader in single combat with the assistance of a raven, which pecked
at his eyes. The statue had a raven on its head.[2] Augustus also decided that
all commanders who won triumphal honours should have a bronze statue
in this forum,[3] which in addition contained the *columna rostrata*, a column
decorated with the beaks and anchors of captured warships, and surmounted
by a gilded statue of Octavian. This had been erected in 36 BC to celebrate
his victory over Sextus Pompey.[4] The niches in the upper tiers of the
colonnades may have been decorated with additional war trophies of various
types (see Figure 6.1).[5] The hemicycle to the right of the temple of Mars
included a statue of Romulus, and that to the left a statue of Aeneas and
members of the Julian family. This demonstrated the unique historical
importance of Augustus' own family and linked it with the tradition of
the foundation of Rome. The building of the forum was financed by
Augustus' military conquests, as he himself explains in the *Res Gestae* – 'I
built the temple of Mars the Avenger and the Forum Augustum on private
ground from the spoils of war' – and was constructed on land he had
purchased.[6] Although this new forum was apparently designed to accommodate the increasing number of lawsuits, it also propagated Augustus'
name and associated him with a resounding declaration of Roman military
prowess, past and present. On the occasion of the dedication of the forum
in 2 BC he declared by edict his view that 'the Roman people should

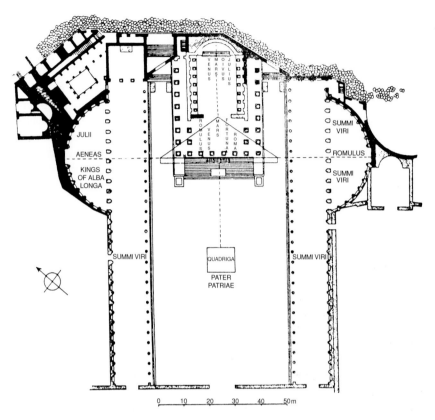

Figure 6.1 Forum of Augustus
Source: Adapted from Southern (1998, 178)

judge him, while he was alive, and future leaders, by the standards of these men'. The senate responded by erecting a statue of a four-horse chariot with an inscription listing all Augustus' victories.[7]

The temple of Mars the Avenger (Mars Ultor) stood in a dominant position, filling one end of the open square of the forum. Octavian had vowed a temple of Mars the Avenger immediately before the battle of Philippi in 42 BC, and it was eventually dedicated on 12 May 2 BC.[8] The temple symbolized vengeance upon the murderers of his father Julius Caesar, but also chastisement of all those who had dared to challenge Roman arms. Thus the military standards recovered from the Parthians in 20 BC were eventually lodged there, and it was intended that all standards recaptured from the enemy in future were to join them.[9] But, more than this, the temple was intended to play an integral part in Roman life. There was an annual festival conducted beside the steps; young Roman boys came here to assume the toga of manhood, and governors formally set out to their

123

provinces from the same spot. The senate met in this temple to debate questions of war and the granting of triumphs, and those who celebrated triumphs dedicated their sceptre and crown to Mars, the presiding deity.[10] For foreign ambassadors and visitors to the city or those who had travelled from Italian rural communities and towns, the forum will have been a great show-piece of the power and stability of Augustus' regime, its control of foreign affairs, and also of the military glory and durability of Rome. We may be sure that the chieftains of foreign tribes who were compelled by Augustus to swear in the temple of Mars the Avenger to keep the peace were suitably impressed by their surroundings.[11] The military ambience of this area was increased in AD 19 by Tiberius, who built two arches on either side of the temple at the back to celebrate the victories of Germanicus and Drusus in Germany.[12]

In the old Forum Romanum, the traditional centre of Roman life, stood the temple of Augustus' father, the Divine Julius, whose reputation as an outstanding commander far outlasted the political embarrassment of his dictatorship and murder. In the third century AD, according to the Roman military calendar, his birthday was still being celebrated.[13] Between the temple of Divus Julius and the temple of Castor stood an arch with three gateways, which should probably be identified with the arch erected in 29 BC to celebrate Augustus' victories in Dalmatia, in Egypt, and at Actium. This arch may have been modified in 19 BC in celebration of the return the previous year of the captured Roman standards and prisoners from Parthia. In its final form it was apparently surmounted by a four-horse chariot, and showed barbarians offering standards to a triumphing general.[14]

Augustus everywhere displayed the visual images of victory. He had transported from Heliopolis in Egypt as a symbol of his conquest an enormous obelisk of Aswan granite (23.7m high), and in 10 BC (the twentieth anniversary of the conquest of Egypt) he placed it in public view on the *euripus* or *spina* (the central divide) at the eastern end of the circus. In the same year he set up another obelisk (21.79m high) surmounted by a tall pedestal and a spiked bronze globe, suitably inscribed in commemoration of his victory: 'Egypt having been brought under the power of the Roman people.' This acted as the pointer in the huge sundial that was dedicated close to the Altar of Augustan Peace.[15] In Roman ideology victory was worshipped in the form of a winged female figure (*Victoria*). A statue of *Victoria* surmounting a globe stood proudly on the top of the pediment of the new senate house finished in 29 BC, while inside Augustus set up another statue and altar in her honour.[16] *Victoria* was the guardian of the empire and symbolized Roman military power, but also Augustus' courageous leadership. Even when he was not present in person his statues reminded people of what he had achieved on the battlefield, since many showed the emperor in the uniform of a Roman commander. The famous statue found at Prima Porta in the villa of his wife Livia portrays a noble and heroic Augustus, soldier and protector of his people. The decoration on his breastplate shows a humbled Parthian returning the lost military standards to a figure in military dress, perhaps representing the legions or Mars Ultor himself. Other symbols of Roman victory and domination of subject peoples accompany the tableau.[17] The image of the kneeling, humbled Parthian had such an impact on the public imagination that individuals wore rings engraved with it.[18]

The military victories won by Augustus enabled him to close the doors of the temple of Janus on three occasions, symbolizing peace (*pax*) throughout the empire. Peace accompanying military supremacy was an honourable concept, and perhaps had its most famous expression in Augustan Rome in the Altar of Peace (*Ara Pacis*), which the senate voted on 4 July 13 BC on Augustus' return from Spain and Gaul. It was constructed in the Campus Martius on the Via Flaminia, the route by which Augustus had entered the city, and was dedicated in the presence of the emperor on 30 January 9 BC.[19] The enclosure wall facing the Via Flaminia depicted the goddess Roma seated on a pile of arms, accompanied by personified figures of Military Valour (*Virtus*) and the Respect due to it (*Honor*), highlighting again Augustus' military achievements. On the panel on the other side there is an allegorical figure, variously identified as Mother Earth, Italy, Venus Genetrix or *Pax*, but which perhaps combines elements from all of these, emphasizing the benefits Augustus had brought to a now peaceful and prosperous Italy. The upper part of the sides depicts a public parade, containing figures at about three-quarters life-size, apparently including Augustus, Agrippa, and other members of the imperial family, priests and senators engaged in some kind of religious thanksgiving, presumably in honour of *Pax*.[20] Peace was often personified as a female figure and specifically associated with Augustus himself in the form *Pax Augusta*. As such *Pax* also represented the achievement of Augustus in putting an end to civil wars. His life and good health were therefore important to the senate and the Roman people. Their need for Augustus, often expressed in physical terms as they clamoured for his return, was demonstrated visually by the Altar of 'Fortune Who Brings You Home' (*Ara Fortunae Reducis*), erected by the senate in 19 BC on the Via Appia outside the Capena gate to celebrate Augustus' return from the east.

Augustus claimed to have found Rome built of brick and to have left it built of marble.[21] He was referring probably to his political reconstruction, but his buildings and restorations, and those of his associates, especially Agrippa and Maecenas, left an impressive mark. Augustus also had a substantial impact in the provinces.[22] He founded two cities called Nicopolis (City of Victory), on the site of Actium and near Alexandria in Egypt.[23] In the west the foundation of new communities and new building initiatives displayed the grandeur of Rome and promoted the idea of assimilation into a larger world with common values that enjoyed the protection promised by Roman government. On the other hand, numerous arches and trophies suggested the invincibility of Roman arms and 'promoted the idea of peace achieved through the agency of military might'.[24] But this was also a warning. Those who rejected the image of Romanness or who persisted in resisting Roman consolidation could expect to meet the fate of the cowed captives so graphically carved on the trophies. For example, the famous monument at La Turbie in the Alps dedicated in 6 BC celebrates how under the auspices and leadership of Augustus all the Alpine tribes from the Adriatic to the Mediterranean had been brought under the control of the Roman people. Forty-five tribes are listed.[25]

No remains of the ancient world are found in greater numbers than coins.[26] The government had complete control of their issue and design, and also a captive audience, since people must look at a coin to confirm its value and authenticity. There was potentially a large area of circulation, and the coins could convey a message in words and pictures. However, it is not clear if the numerous different coin types were minted with the intention of influencing public opinion, or if we can use the word 'propaganda' since this can imply deliberate falsehood. It is also reasonable to question the effectiveness of pictures on coins as a way of persuading people of anything, especially since some coins stayed in circulation for such a long time that messages became outdated or even contradictory. Then, again, many people in the Roman empire will have been illiterate and incapable of understanding even simple slogans.[27] It is possible therefore that coin types were not intended in the first instance to supply information to the public that they could not get from other sources, and were perhaps less noticed than other types of publicity.[28] On the other hand, it does seem likely that both the obverse and the reverse of the coin by their joint message underlined the importance of the emperor, and that the imperial coinage tends to engross 'the whole potential of the coin for making value-laden statements for the benefit of the emperor'.[29] Thus the portrait of the emperor's head, which both validates the coin and identifies the ruler and his titles, is backed up by symbols of his honours, his achievements, and even his supporting deities. Coins identified imperial concerns, produced valuable publicity for the emperor, and highlighted his activities in a way to which people could relate. Therefore both upper classes and ordinary people could see him as a kind of charismatic leader with outstanding qualities that marked him out from the rest of mankind.[30]

The context of these developments lies in the last years of the Republic, when public display of various kinds had become more common in keeping with the intense political rivalry. Traditional coin types became more variable and specific, sometimes evoking contemporary events and powerful people.[31] Military images were an important factor, and coins minted during Sulla's lifetime depict his two trophies for the battle of Chaeronea and cite his double acclamation as general (*imperator*); another shows Sulla as a triumphing general in a four-horse chariot.[32] In 44 BC, Julius Caesar became the first living person in Rome to have his head depicted on the coinage. This idea was taken up by his murderers and by the triumvirs. Indeed, Brutus deliberately used a particular coin type and slogan (the cap of liberty and two daggers, with the caption 'freedom') to demonstrate that he and his followers had liberated the Republic from Caesar.[33] Gradually, after 31 BC all official Roman coin issues in gold, silver and bronze came to portray the head of Octavian-Augustus and this perhaps had the most important role to play in attracting attention.[34] In the case of non-Roman coin issues between 31 BC and AD 14 more than 200 cities struck coins with the imperial portrait, representing a revolutionary change in the symbolic character of coinage.[35]

The emperor's military prowess was an important though not predominant theme on the coinage. It picked up ideas also expressed through the medium of public buildings and statues, such as the emperor's personal qualities and his bringing of peace through victory. Coins also provided publicity for specific victories won under Augustus, and it is fair to say that the moneyers, like good public relations executives, presented the best possible interpretation of the emperor's policy, which is indeed a form of propaganda. For example, a coin bearing a picture of a crocodile with the legend 'The Capture of Egypt' tastefully celebrated the overthrow of Cleopatra's realm and the end of the civil war (see Plate 6.1).[36] A coin showing an archer's quiver with the message 'The Capture of Armenia' suggested another Roman conquest, conveniently ignoring the fact that Armenia had not been annexed, as Augustus admits in the *Res Gestae*.[37] A famous issue shows a humbled Parthian kneeling and handing back a captured Roman military standard reinforced by the legend 'The Return of the Standards'. Augustus made much of this diplomatic achievement, giving the misleading impression that the Parthians had been forced into surrender by Roman military action.[38] Coins were also used to portray buildings erected to celebrate military achievements, and in this way served to reinforce information provided more dramatically elsewhere, for example, by the triumphal arch of 29 BC.[39] The coin issues, however, have nothing to say about individual legions or the personal relationship between emperor and army, which of course had political overtones. Imperial coinage was presumably still in an experimental stage as the emperor and his advisers discussed what themes and issues should be publicized and in what way.

Buildings and coins were the tangible expression of the glory of Rome under Augustus. The emperor's personal presence gave added meaning to this, either through travels in the provinces, or more importantly in Rome itself, which Tiberius had described as the 'head of things'. It was important that Augustus appeared in person at games and shows and other great public ceremonies.[40] Early in his reign he spectacularly promoted the spirit of military success by celebrating three triumphs on 13–15 August 29 BC.

Plate 6.1 Denarius of 28 BC: 'The Capture of Egypt'
Source: *Roman Imperial Coinage* (2nd edn), no. 288, by permission of Spink, St James's, London

He will have driven in the ceremonial chariot along the traditional route from the Circus Flaminius through the triumphal gate in the old city walls and then on to the Capitoline hill. There, in the tradition of a victorious commander, he dedicated in the temple of Capitoline Jupiter the bay-leaves with which he had wreathed his *fasces*. Augustus proudly tells us that nine kings or children of kings were led before his chariot.[41]

Forty-three years later his public funeral celebrated the death of a great commander, but also of a man who had displayed a whole range of qualities to achieve prosperity, reconciliation and stable government in Rome. Augustus had left written instructions for the ceremony. His body was enclosed in a coffin, but wax images of him were carried in procession, one in triumphal dress, while another was pulled on a triumphal chariot. Behind were carried images of his ancestors and other distinguished Romans, and representations of all the peoples he had added to the empire.[42] After the eulogies, his funeral couch was carried through the triumphal gateway in a procession accompanied by senate, equestrians, praetorians and huge crowds of the Roman plebs. His body was placed on a pyre in the Field of Mars, and praetorian guardsmen ran around it and threw on to it all the military decorations they had received from Augustus. Finally centurions set light to the pyre.[43]

As a permanent monument for his life Augustus left a short catalogue of his achievements (*Res Gestae*), which were to be inscribed on bronze tablets and set up in front of his mausoleum.[44] Our text for this document comes from the province of Galatia where it was inscribed (in Latin with a Greek paraphrase) at Ancyra (Ankara) on the walls of the temple of Rome and Augustus. Parts of two other copies have been discovered at Apollonia and Antioch in Pisidia. The *Res Gestae* may be seen as an extension of the idea of the eulogy delivered by a relative at the funeral of a great man, or the inscriptions set up to celebrate distinguished careers, proportionately longer because Augustus' achievements were extraordinary. In this selective account of his actions, celebrating his restoration of peace and political stability, his generosity to the Roman people and the honours granted to him, Augustus' role as military leader features prominently. By carefully listing all his triumphs and other military honours and titles (4), he makes a statement of unmatchable glory and success. He fought genuine wars which, while just and necessary, brought spectacular additions to Roman territory in every direction, and brought back from Parthia Roman standards lost by previous commanders (26–7, 29–30). Unbroken military success allowed the Romans to intervene at will, pick and choose which lands to occupy, and graciously receive kings, hostages and ambassadors from far-off places (31–3). No Roman had ever had achievements like this to his name: 'Embassies from kings in India were frequently sent to me; never before had they been seen with any Roman commander' (31.1). The vigilance, leadership and inspiration of Augustus brought peace through military victory (13; cf. 26.2, 34.1), even if many of the battles were fought by others. The language used throughout, which was presumably intended to appeal to ideology shared by the reader, suggests the value in contemporary society of a reputation as a great conqueror, and presupposes an interest in celebrations of imperial power and glory, not only in Rome and Italy, but also in the provinces.[45] Indeed, the person who composed the preamble for the inscription of the *Res Gestae* in Ancyra responded to the triumphalist mood: 'The achievements of the Divine Augustus, by which he brought the world under the empire of the Roman people.'

We can perhaps find a further indication of the thinking of those at the heart of Augustus' government in the writings of Strabo and especially Velleius Paterculus. Strabo, from a prominent family in Pontus, enjoyed the patronage of Aelius Gallus, who while prefect of Egypt led an abortive invasion of Arabia in 25 BC. Strabo's *Geographia* helps to set Augustus' rule in the context of the Mediterranean world, with which it was closely linked and which it had consolidated. He professed that the study of geography was useful to political leaders and army commanders, 'who bring together cities and peoples into a single empire and political management'.[46] He also claimed that the Roman empire now included all that was worth conquering, having omitted infertile regions and the territories of nomads.[47] Little profit could be expected from peripheral areas like Britain.[48] Strabo may be articulating the government's explanation of some of its foreign policy decisions. If so, he thought that there were no moral and few strategic military considerations involved. The only limit on the Romans' acquisition of territory was their judgement of the likely profit.

Velleius Paterculus from the Italian municipal aristocracy enthusiastically supported Augustus, and also Tiberius, under whom he served from AD 4 to 12 as a cavalry commander. He became a senator and was marked down for election as the 'emperor's candidate' to the post of praetor.[49] In his history of Rome he gave the version of those at the centre of power and their supporters. Among Augustus' achievements he placed his military record to the fore: 'The civil wars were brought to an end after twenty years, foreign wars were suppressed, peace was restored, and the frenzy of fighting was lulled to rest everywhere.'[50] The emperor succeeded in bringing total peace to Spain, which had defied Roman armies for 250 years, other areas were pacified, and the Parthians returned captured military standards.[51] He defends war against the Pannonians on the grounds of their proximity to Italy, and the rebellion of the Pannonian peoples in AD 6 was a real threat to Italy itself; indeed, Velleius uses the emotive word 'slavery'. It is in this context that we are meant to understand the massive assembly of Roman forces to deal with the rebels.[52] On the other hand, it was enough to say that in Germany there were warlike tribes, a military challenge and the pride of reaching the River Elbe, which a Roman army had never attempted before.[53] After the defeat of Varus in AD 9, he explains Tiberius' vigorous counter-attack across the Rhine by the fear of a possible German invasion of Italy.[54] Then, again, Velleius describes how the planned attack on King Maroboduus of Bohemia in AD 6 was justified because he was talented and had a large army partly trained on the Roman model. In addition, the edge of his territory was only 200 miles from the Alps, which marked the boundary of Italy itself.[55] These are the views of a serving officer who was probably privy to military councils at the highest level, and who had great respect for Tiberius as a military commander. Velleius believes that in military situations Rome should be on the offensive, and expresses the self-evident dynamic of Roman power, authority, territorial expansion and military glory. Augustus also sought to isolate and destroy by whatever means available those who could be a threat, either as charismatic leaders or through geographical proximity to Roman interests. We can deduce perhaps that this is how the senior members of the imperial entourage discussed matters of warfare and diplomacy.

It is more difficult to discover how far these ideas had spread among the upper classes generally. Were they receptive to the aggressive Augustan view of empire or did they need to be persuaded? There is a good range of contemporary poetry and prose, which provides a useful commentary on some of the principal events of Augustus' reign, including the emperor's dealings with foreign peoples, diplomatic contacts, and, of course, warfare. These authors recount enthusiastically, often with poetic embellishment, the idea of Roman military conquest – for example, describing the fighting methods of the Parthians and the skill of their archers and cavalry. The disgrace of the defeat of Crassus in 53 BC and the loss of military standards are to be expunged under the leadership of Augustus by the annexation of Parthia. Rome's advance will inexorably swallow up the Chinese, Indians and British. But there is a clear change in tone in respect of eastern affairs after 20 BC, after Augustus' diplomatic accommodation with the Parthians. Now we hear that Roman objectives have been achieved and that the subservient Parthians have accepted Augustus' jurisdiction and power. His reputation was enough to bring them to heel without fighting.[56]

These writers, who moved in upper-class circles and whose works were presumably read by some of the eminent men of the day, were not mere puppets. But they did live in an autocracy, were naturally susceptible to influence and patronage, and would hardly go out of their way to express sentiments known to be at odds with Augustus' views. It is entirely possible, though there is little evidence, that Augustus or members of his entourage gave a lead on government policy by dropping hints, which might then be understood in different ways. Perhaps, indeed, Augustus faced an uphill task in persuading the upper classes and the Roman people to take an interest in warfare and campaigns against foreign peoples. For much of the Republic war had been a regular feature of life – indeed, at times almost commonplace. Interest in armies and warfare was high; thousands of Italians served in the legions and fought in numerous wars of conquest, which were therefore a source of attention and concern throughout Italy. Senators served in the army as military tribunes and higher officers and commanders, and the senate was intimately involved in decisions of war and peace. By the end of the Republic more than 200,000 Italians were under arms, though compulsion or the allure of booty had much to do with this.

However, by 31 BC the Roman people had every reason to be war-weary, and part of Augustus' appeal was that he 'seduced everyone by the enjoyable gift of peace'.[57] Gradually war came to be remote from ordinary people as fewer Italians served overseas in the legions.[58] Augustus took into his own hands important decisions on war and peace, and tended to restrict army commands largely to members of his family or trusted henchmen. Thus during his rule opportunities among senators for military glory, prestige and aggrandizement were restricted. It follows that they had less experience of war, little knowledge of frontier provinces, and perhaps little reason to find out. Life in the military camp could become an alien and hostile world in which soldiers were feared and despised and senators gradually lost their taste for military command.[59] But it is easy to exaggerate the disillusionment of the upper classes with military affairs. In all ages there is often a wide divergence in opinion about warfare and military leadership, and what is best for the state and the ruling classes. There is also frequently a difference between private views and opinions required by public duty. Even those who feared the army might still support an active policy of warfare, since that would keep the army occupied, disciplined and out of mischief elsewhere.

Augustus' attempts to influence public opinion by all kinds of publicity have to be understood in the social and political context in which he made decisions on foreign policy and decided how to propagate a suitable military image. In my view he was dealing with an audience that traditionally had taken a great interest in foreign affairs and with which he could interact, rather than imposing his views on a reluctant or indifferent citizenry. It is likely of course that he gave a strong lead to the viewpoint of the upper classes, whose skill and expertise he needed to exploit. But he did not have to contend with deeply held views against conquest or military action, or the annexation of land or the killing of large numbers of people.

War and public opinion after Augustus

Emperors after Augustus, many of whom lacked his accumulated prestige, perhaps had to work harder to maintain public interest in foreign affairs. Yet conquest continued, though admittedly at a slower rate, and a fairly wide cross-section of senators continued to participate at some level of military command and to hold most of the senior governorships until well into the third century AD. It seems that many influential Romans remained interested in warfare, military life and martial glory, and at least affected to admire these qualities and activities.[60] Opinion about foreign peoples, warfare, diplomacy, the welfare of Rome, and the security and self-interest of the upper classes does not seem to have changed much over the years. Emperors and their advisers in government will have interacted with this by turning towards the same kind of publicity and opinion management used by Augustus. Appian, a Greek and a Roman citizen who received the status of procurator from Antoninus Pius, wrote about the peoples whom the Romans had encountered and subdued on their way to imperial power. His views on the rationale of Roman imperialism are very much like those of Strabo:

> Possessing the best parts of the land and sea, in the main they intelligently choose to consolidate their rule rather than extend it endlessly over destitute and unproductive barbarian peoples. I have seen some of them in Rome negotiating and offering themselves as subjects, but the emperor would not accept men who were going to be of no use to him.[61]

Similarly, Pausanias, a Greek writer who lived c. AD 150 and who produced a guide to the most important historical sites in Greece, describes in pragmatic terms Roman penetration into Thrace and the land of the Celts:

> All Thrace is in the hands of the Romans. But they have deliberately ignored that part of the Celtic country that they think useless because of its extreme cold and the poverty of the soil; but whatever they [the Celts] have that is worth getting, the Romans own.[62]

On the other hand, Florus, celebrating the military accomplishments of the Roman people, stated that it was just as splendid and honourable to acquire provinces which brought great titles to imperial greatness, though they served no useful purpose, as it was to acquire rich and powerful provinces (1.47.4–5).[63] Even those left outside the empire nevertheless appreciated the greatness of Rome and revered the Roman people as conquerors of the world (2.34.61). Florus contemptuously dismisses many peoples subdued by Augustus as savages who could not recognize the value of peace (that is, Roman domination); they were mere raiders and bandits of a ferocious and brute courage. He makes no attempt to distinguish differing policy objectives; those who resisted are simply to be annihilated (2.21–34). He also believed that further military action was eminently desirable. After Augustus, so he claims, for almost 200 years, emperors were militarily inactive, and the Roman people, as if growing old, lost its strength; but under Trajan, against all expectation, youthful vigour was restored (1, Preface 8).

Florus illustrates the limited and unanalytical response of some reasonably intelligent and literate Romans to government policy on conquest and warfare, and has an unthinking pride in Roman imperial achievement. He also agrees with writers like Appian and Pausanias in his contempt for peoples outside Graeco-Roman culture. Naturally Romans and their Greek apologists would have agreed that all their wars were justified. Augustus had summed up the violent and bloodstained clearing of the Alpine tribes with this boast: 'I secured the pacification of the Alps . . . yet without waging an unjust war on any people.'[64]

But what about historians of Rome who came from the government class, especially those who had held high office, notably Tacitus and Cassius Dio? Did the ruling classes in the first and second centuries AD have an idea of the ideology of war, the rights and wrongs of fighting and diplomacy, and any understanding of other peoples and how they should be treated? How did they react to imperial publicity, and what qualities in an emperor were particularly valued? Neither Tacitus nor Cassius Dio makes any attempt to explain Roman conquests or military activity. They merely relate what happened with occasional comments. Vital war decisions may be satisfactorily explained on the grounds that the emperor wanted to acquire military glory or to protect the Roman concept of military honour or to expiate the disgrace of a mutiny or to keep family harmony.[65] There is no discussion of the moral dynamics of empire or the treatment of foreign peoples beyond occasional comments on Roman misgovernment. Dio, who had been governor of Upper Pannonia, sneers at the Pannonian people, who had 'the most miserable existence of all mankind'; they suffered poor soil and climate, produced no olives or decent wine, and 'possessed nothing that makes an honourable life worthwhile'.[66] But he does not question Roman occupation of their territory. In Tacitus' opinion the British were barbarians and the climate appalling, though Britain had enough precious metals to make it worth conquering. He believed that it was only imperial jealousy that prevented his father-in-law Agricola from conquering the entire island. In Agricola's opinion Ireland, too, could have been added to the empire with a single legion, and no further considerations were necessary.[67] Tacitus also wrote an ethnography of the German tribes seen through Roman eyes, in which he recognized that they had good qualities. Indeed, some of their practices could be favourably compared to the dubious moral climate of Rome, but one consequence of this was that they were potentially a threat and therefore further conquest was desirable. As he reviewed Roman wars with the Germans, Tacitus wistfully commented: 'How long it is taking to conquer Germany.'[68]

When it suited Tacitus he was belligerent and set no limit to the advance of Roman arms. He berates Domitian for Rome's military setbacks that placed the very maintenance of the empire in jeopardy.[69] In the *Annals* he laments 'his narrow and inglorious task' in recounting the history of the early principate, with the empire sunk in torpor and the emperor Tiberius uninterested in territorial expansion; foreign potentates could mock him as old and unwarlike.[70] Yet Tacitus appreciated that in certain circumstances diplomacy was valuable and also a careful calculation of Rome's self-interest.[71]

Dio, although he never questioned the wisdom of the empire, also saw the value of a peaceful solution in some cases, and in general tends to be critical of major wars and annexation of new territory.[72] Thus Trajan's campaigns in Parthia are branded as being simply an expression of the emperor's 'desire for glory', and the invasion of Britain launched by Claudius is clearly seen as a show-piece demonstrating the emperor's military valour.[73] Dio's comments on the annexation of Mesopotamia by Septimius Severus offer a rare analysis of both sides of a debate about the wisdom of territorial aggrandizement.[74] Dio has sensible objections – the annexation was provocative, expensive, and ultimately destructive because it led to more wars – but it is unlikely that he felt strongly enough to pursue the matter. Indeed, most upper-class Romans were probably happy to accept the empire and to agree that war should be made on its behalf. They had little concern with what happened to other peoples. Dio of Prusa, a well-connected Greek philosopher and rhetorician, was a lone voice, as far as we know, in criticizing (in a speech before Trajan) war waged merely for the sake of glory.[75] On another occasion he visited the Danube frontier and witnessed the preparations for a campaign in Dacia. He said that he saw one side fighting for empire and power, and the other for freedom and their native land, though he makes no moral judgement on their motivation, and indeed has little to say on the morality of contemporary warfare.[76]

The question of publicity, propaganda and the winning of support for imperial policy is bound up with public opinion, and in particular the views of senators and equestrians on the qualities an ideal emperor should possess. How much did they admire and yearn for a great conqueror? Here the case of Trajan and Hadrian is instructive. Trajan was popular with senators, and the ritual acclamation of the senate was: 'May you be luckier than Augustus and better than Trajan.'[77] However, as we have seen, Cassius Dio is critical of the latter's military exploits, which he believes were motivated by a personal greed for glory. The emperor's great campaigns in the east against the Parthians ultimately failed, and his conquests, which had cost so much loss of life, could not be maintained.[78] Hadrian by contrast was not so respected by the upper classes, and the opening of his reign was clouded by the execution of four senators of consular rank. But Dio praises his tough discipline and training of the army. Foreign peoples kept the peace because of their respect for him, and he provoked no wars.[79] Yet not everyone agreed. Cornelius Fronto said that Hadrian preferred to surrender rather than defend by force the provinces won by Trajan, and produced the outrageous false-hood that the emperor had abandoned the province of Dacia.[80] These opinions perhaps indicate something of the debate that attended these events among eminent men in Rome. Were Trajan's conquests justified and worth-while? Did Hadrian's policy sensibly consolidate and preserve the strength of the empire, or was it an excuse for indolence? We may have Hadrian's defence of his actions in the clever epigram attributed to him: 'I have achieved more by peace than others by war.'[81] In fact it seems that both Trajan and Hadrian needed to explain and justify their actions, and that warfare, conquest and the direction of campaigns remained serious and relevant topics of dis-cussion. Even if this was at the simplistic level suggested by the comments in Tacitus and Dio outlined above, it helped to establish the context in which Roman emperors after Augustus set out to influence or interact with public opinion, and to create an image of an effective military leader. The means they used owed much to Augustus, and involved a series of integrated visual and verbal images that embraced buildings, monuments, coins, public displays and ceremonies, and the constant repetition of honorific names and titles. Publicity was therefore part of the environment of day-to-day life and com-mercial transactions. On the other hand, we must beware of thinking that the dissemination of publicity was top of the government agenda. There were many factors involved including the artistic freedom and input of the archi-tects, artists and designers, and the amount of direct influence the emperor had remains obscure, though it is unlikely that significant initiatives were undertaken without his approval.

Buildings, monuments and statues

The most strikingly innovative construction was Trajan's column. This was simultaneously a landmark (it stood about 128 Roman feet (38m) high surmounted by a 3m statue of the emperor in military dress), a building (it had a room in the base, a spiral staircase lit by forty slit windows, and a platform for the statue; there was a metal fence, and visitors who climbed to the top would have had a panoramic view of Rome), and a monument (there is a frieze 200m long carved in low relief on the outside of the column's shaft, with 155 scenes in continuous sequence and 2600 figures, carved in about two-thirds life-size, depicting the course of the Dacian wars in AD 102 to 103 and 105 to 106) (see Plates 2.1, 2.2, 3.1 and 6.2).[82]

Plate 6.2 Trajan's Column
Source: Ancient Art and Architecture Collection

It is frustrating that we are so badly informed about ancient opinion on this building. Dio says that it was intended to serve as the emperor's burial monument, and indeed his ashes were deposited there. But the height of the column was also designed to show how much land had been excavated in order to construct Trajan's forum, and this is confirmed by the dedicatory inscription on the column: 'The senate and people of Rome to . . . Trajan, to show the height of the hill excavated and the extent of the work in the place'.[83] Nevertheless, the column must have made a dramatic impact in Rome, looming over Trajan's forum and Basilica, with its enormous statue of the emperor in full military dress. In the colonnades adjoining the forum, gilded statues of horses and military trophies were set up 'from the spoils of war'; there were also statues of great generals, figures of Dacian captives, and in the centre of the square a magnificent statue of Trajan on horseback. Much of this recalls the forum of Augustus.[84]

The column base portrays piles of captured Dacian weapons, and the circular plinth on which the cylinder itself sits takes the form of the laurel wreath of a victorious general. The sculptures depict the unfolding story of the military campaigns, and in an exciting narrative the overwhelming military grandeur of the emperor shines out through his frequent appearances. He seems to dominate the war, by offering inspirational leadership and by personally directing the military operations, sometimes on horseback and always close to the centre of the action. He makes speeches of encouragement to the soldiers, he meets embassies, interrogates prisoners and sees the horrors of war. Clearly the success of the campaign depends on him. The result is a great Roman victory and the annexation of a new province. The Dacians are portrayed as wild and uncivilized with little to offer except torture and violence. They evoke little sympathy, and in the end face death or humiliation and captivity. The severed head of King Decebalus is presented on a platter in the emperor's camp, while the remains of his people abandon their ancestral lands.[85]

But what is the point of this intricate artistic work, which reminds us of a roll of film or a book of folding pictures? It was surely not to give an account of the workings of the Roman army, though it is mainly studied for this reason by modern scholars, nor was it a factually accurate account of the Dacian Wars. A structure as different and unprecedented as this must surely celebrate the emperor's personal glory. It would not matter that spectators could not follow the whole story with the naked eye. The point is its overall impact and its relationship with other buildings, especially the forum and the Basilica, both provided at Trajan's expense. These physical memorials erected by the emperor spectacularly demonstrated that the civil and military life of the empire were in safe hands.[86] We cannot know how much artistic leeway was allowed to the sculptors, though it would be very odd if the emperor and his advisers did not set out some general themes that they wanted to get across. But the intention was perhaps not to seek an individual response, but to invoke more general feelings shared by the mass of the people and the upper classes relating to the profits of war, imperial responsibility, opportunities for army command and military glory.[87]

The column of Marcus Aurelius, probably erected by Commodus in honour of his father and his mother Faustina in celebration of Marcus' victories in the wars against the Marcomanni and Sarmatians in AD 172 to 175, deliberately evokes the design of Trajan's column. It was 100 Roman feet high, and was nicknamed *centenaria* ('hundred-footer'), with an internal spiral staircase and a platform on which stood a statue of the emperor.[88] A sculptured frieze is carved in high relief on the outer casing and tells the story of the military campaigns. Once again, the emperor is present throughout the campaigns, and his inspirational guidance of the troops seems crucial in the successful outcome of the war. The fighting brings the reward of victory for Roman arms, though it seems that the artistic style gives a more violent and passionate and less mannered representation. Battle, Roman superiority and the ruthless destruction of the enemy are the central themes, and there is less extraneous detail.[89] This funeral monument celebrated the glory of the imperial family, and Commodus could enjoy the military achievements of his father, even though he did not himself conduct any campaigns. Its importance in later years was apparently undiminished. In AD 193 the freedman procurator responsible for looking after Marcus' column was given permission to build a shelter nearby.[90]

The same tradition of monumental architecture and intricate carving of individual scenes appears also in the great triumphal arches, which were dotted throughout Rome and other cities in Italy and the provinces. The arch was originally associated with an entrance or passageway and served as a triumphal memorial, since a general celebrating a triumph entered Rome through the triumphal gate (*porta triumphalis*) and formally crossed the city boundary. However, especially in the early empire they were being built everywhere. More than a hundred are known from Rome and Italy, and examples have been identified in every province, with more than a hundred discovered in Africa alone.[91] In the simplest design, a single archway flanked by columns supported an entablature and attic, which formed a base for statuary, usually including a four-horsed chariot. Triple arches appeared as early as the second century BC, and the carving on the columns and entablature became more elaborate.

The predominant image in Rome was military triumphalism, a celebration of victory and the propagation of the empire. The honour belonged exclusively to the emperor since a grateful senate and people usually set up arches to him.[92] Thus, for example, in AD 51/52 the senate voted a triumphal arch in honour of Claudius' conquest of Britain: 'He was the first to bring the barbarian peoples across the ocean into the control of the Roman people.'[93] Statues of other members of the imperial family and scenes of military combat adorned the arch. The arch erected on the *Via*

Sacra after the death of Titus celebrated both his capture of Jerusalem (Titus is seen in a triumphal procession with the spoils of the Jewish campaign) and his apotheosis.[94] Another arch in the Circus Maximus was erected in AD 80 to 81 in honour of Titus 'because under the direction, advice, and auspices of his father [Vespasian], he subdued the Jewish race and destroyed the city of Jerusalem, which had been either besieged fruitlessly or left completely untouched by all commanders, kings, and peoples before him'.[95] In AD 203 the senate dedicated a triumphal arch in the Roman forum to Septimius Severus and his sons Caracalla and Geta, 'because they restored the state and extended the rule of the Roman people through their out-standing qualities at home and abroad'.[96] This refers in part to Severus' defeat of the Parthians and the creation of the new province of Mesopotamia. Carvings on the arch show Roman troops leading captured enemy soldiers, a triumphal procession and victory motifs. Four large panels provide an extensive panorama of the campaigns.[97] A six-horse chariot, in which rode the emperor and his sons, flanked by foot soldiers, surmounted the arch; there was a cavalryman at each of the outer corners.[98] The tradition of the commemorative arch remained important in the fourth century, and in AD 315 a triple arch was erected spanning the triumphal way in honour of Constantine's victory over his rival Maxentius and in celebration of ten years of his rule. It is notable that this arch celebrates victory over a fellow Roman and also borrowed sculptures from previous monuments. Scenes from the life of Constantine appear; there are also legionary soldiers, captives, and battles between Romans and Dacians.[99]

These great triumphal arches were integrated into city life, and, as people walked past them or through them, served as a vivid reminder of victory, imperial success, and of course the personal role of the emperor. These ideas were also expressed in the deliberate construction of buildings from the spoils of war, so that it was clear to all that their physical enjoyment was sustained by the profits of their army's success in battle. For example, the massive building projects of both Augustus and Trajan that saw the construction of the imperial *fora* were financed 'from his general's share of the booty' (*ex manubiis*). Furthermore, the recently reconstructed inscription from the Colosseum, which once formed part of one of the original dedicatory inscriptions in the building, proclaims: 'The emperor Vespasian ordered this new amphitheatre to be constructed from his general's share of the booty.'[100] The amphitheatre was in fact another triumphal monument, paid for out of the treasure captured after the sack of Jerusalem, which was celebrated in the triumph of 71.[101]

Although many buildings in Rome had military associations, the Circus Maximus was particularly significant. The central spine (*euripus* or *spina*) had the enormous obelisk that Augustus had brought from Egypt,[102] and indeed the Circus apparently incorporated within its structure the triumphal arch celebrating Vespasian's conquest of the Jews.[103] In the case of religious buildings, apart from the temple of Mars Ultor there were two other temples of Mars in Rome, one between the first and second milestones outside the Porta Capena, the other in the Circus Flaminius. The temple of Jupiter Feretrius also had strong military connections since a commander who had killed an enemy leader in single combat dedicated there his armour and other spoils (*spolia opima*). Augustus had restored this temple.[104] The theme of military success was also emphasized by the temple of Victory on the Palatine hill. Other parts of the city were closely associated with the rituals that were traditionally part of Roman warfare. The Armilustrium was a square on the Aventine hill, decorated with pillars containing representations of weapons. Here the festival of purification of weapons took place on 19 October. At the *Columna Bellica* in front of the temple of Bellona, who personified warlike frenzy, was a plot of land that the Romans took to represent foreign territory. According to the ancient rites of the Fetial priesthood, a priest threw a spear over the column into enemy territory to begin formal hostilities. A form of this rite was still being carried on in the time of Marcus Aurelius.[105]

Although statues were commonplace in the ancient world as a mark of honour, the emperor's statue also had the weightier political message that he was in unchallenged control. Therefore the design of these imperial images was important, and statues of the emperor as a soldier followed a particular style, exploiting the traditional armour and military dress of a Roman commander, since he had to show that he was competent in warfare and that victory was assured under his leadership. The famous statue of Augustus from Prima Porta had shown the way.[106] Emperors who had fought great campaigns sometimes preferred an equestrian statue, like that set up by Trajan in his forum. The most striking example shows Marcus Aurelius on horseback wearing military tunic, cloak and military boots. The statue was gilded and twice life-size, and underneath the horse's right hoof was originally the kneeling figure of a barbarian.[107] In official thinking, a statue took the place of the emperor himself. Therefore in the frequent diplomatic negotiations with the Parthians, when the emperor was not present in person, acts of reverence were performed to his statue.[108] During the civil wars of AD 68/69, to throw stones at an imperial portrait or to knock over a statue was tantamount to an act of rebellion.[109]

Coins

Buildings and statues made an impression only on those who saw them, mainly in Rome and important provincial cities, but coins minted and distributed in large quantities could reach a much wider audience. They were also one way in which imperial imagery could pass into the private context.[110] To the educated classes and probably to many others as well, Roman imperial coins demonstrated the wealth and standing of the empire, the supremacy of Rome, economic prosperity and political stability. Augustus had disseminated the message that this happy state of affairs was based upon the victorious progress of Roman arms, and that the security and permanence of the empire were closely linked to the emperor's well-being. He gave the lead in the exploitation of phrases and images that were to become well established: 'Roman imperial coin types and their inscriptions drew their concerns and forms of expression from a highly developed visual and verbal language of imperial ideology.'[111] Well-known words in Roman diplomatic and political vocabulary appear on the coinage of Augustus' successors: *pax*, *victoria*, *virtus*, *providentia*, *concordia*, *fides*, *disciplina*. All these words could assume a military connotation when required. A coin of Trajan shows *Pax* dramatically setting fire to a pile of Dacian arms.[112] Some of the concepts were personally identified with the emperor (e.g. *victoria Augusta*), and in Roman eyes 'victory' and 'peace' continued to be closely associated as personified female figures, and the symbolism was often completed by the addition of a globe, showing Rome's domination of the world.[113]

The emperor loomed over this background of traditional words and activities, having his image and titles on the obverse of each coin, which of course often had military implications.[114] Furthermore, he often appears on the reverse in a martial context, usually in the military dress of a Roman general, marked out by his dominant position in the scenes, and sometimes by a sweeping gesture.[115] His actions are those of an authoritative leader who commanded personally, addressing the troops, leading them on horseback or on foot, setting out on campaign, and receiving the surrender and obeisance of foreign rulers.[116] A consistent picture emerges of an active, concerned and effective leader who looked after the empire's interests. But how was this related to specific events? How did it prepare the population for foreign policy decisions, the emperor's personal role as military leader, great achievements or possibly embarrassing setbacks? What incidents were chosen and why? How were they presented? What was left out?

Naturally the inhabitants of the empire got to hear about only what the imperial government decided was acceptable, and sometimes the truth suffered. Coins issued under Domitian after the defeat of the Chatti optimistically celebrate 'The Capture of Germany'.[117] 'Germany' probably sounded more romantic and comprehensible than a tribe's name. Emperors are generally keen to glorify the wars they fought, exalt success and ignore failure. The defeat of other peoples is graphically depicted by a trophy, or by a trophy with bound captives, or by a personification of the defeated nation, who sits in mourning. The emperor is linked to this by his portrait on the obverse, but sometimes he is more directly associated with the victory. Vespasian eulogized his triumph over the Jewish rebels with coins showing him in military dress armed with a spear and towering over the mourning province.[118] Trajan, too, is depicted in this way, as well as standing with his foot on the head of a Dacian, or riding down a Dacian soldier.[119]

The slogans on these coins boast of the destruction of the enemies of Rome: 'The Total Defeat of Judaea.' In the diplomatic contacts that followed war with foreign peoples, the emperor takes on a dominant role. Trajan appears in military dress sitting on a high platform surrounded by his officers and looming over a figure who crouches humbly to receive his crown by the emperor's grace. The slogan 'The Bestowal of a King on the Parthians' once again proved premature, as Trajan's arrangements in the east collapsed after his death (see Plate 6.3).[120]

Military victory, it might be argued, involved the whole state, united in the furtherance of Roman power. Thus it was politically expedient for Vespasian's coins to show *Victoria* inscribing *SPQR* (The Senate and People of Rome) on the shield of victory after the Jewish revolt. Some coins of Trajan are artistically even more direct in showing the emperor presenting a Dacian prisoner to the senate, or supporting the globe of the world with a togate senator.[121] In another interesting representation we find Marcus Aurelius in military dress, holding a spear and extending his hand to raise the kneeling personification of Italy. The slogan 'The Restorer of Italy' reminds us of his military campaigns against the enemies of Rome on the Rhine and the Danube.[122] Military victories were of course proof of the emperor's unique and exceptional character; but, rather than celebrate in detail individual success, the Romans often found it more effective to demonstrate in general terms the link between victory in war, political stability and public contentment.

Imperial coinage throughout the period spoke firmly of the Roman heartland. Hadrian moved outside the established pattern with his unique series of coins celebrating the armies in their provincial stations (e.g. 'The Army of Germany').[123] Perhaps he was trying to emphasize the empire's military readiness in the context of criticism of his withdrawal from Trajan's conquests in the east.[124] He also celebrated the provinces, which were depicted by appropriate symbols and personification, and this also marked a contrast with the normal Roman practice of depicting non-Roman people on coins in attitudes of subjection to the Roman conqueror.[125]

There were many provincial mints, which continued to produce coins in the imperial period. The central government did not necessarily have close control over these mints; indeed, they seem to have operated with a degree of independence, though with imperial permission.[126] However, the mints were doubtless controlled by the local élites, who identified with Rome, which sustained their privileged position, and accepted the government ideology, which in turn was taken up by the provincial civic coinages. The coin reverses were dominated by local themes, with few references to topical events apart from the relationship between the emperor and individual cities. In the third century there was something of a change, as the emperor appears more often in a military role, perhaps reflecting concerns about the developing threat of the Persians in the east from the reign of Severus

Plate 6.3 Sestertius of AD 114 to 117: 'The Bestowal of a King on the Parthians'
Source: *Roman Imperial Coinage*, no. 667, by permission of Spink, St James's, London

Alexander. In general, local provincial communities looked for dynastic stability and political continuity, and for an emperor who would be victorious against external enemies and also a font of patronage.

Public display

The citizens of Rome had the opportunity of watching the physical enactment of military ceremonial and the national celebration of military victories. The triumph was the most spectacular and important of all Roman military ceremonies, with a tradition going back to the early Republic. The victorious general put on ceremonial dress consisting of a purple cloak and star-spangled toga, and rode in a chariot at the head of his army, behind which trudged prisoners of war, along the processional route to the Capitoline hill and the temple of Jupiter Best and Greatest. This had once been the climax of the career of aristocrats in the Republic, but after 19 BC no one in private station was allowed to hold a triumph. The emperor alone enjoyed this honour, or, by his permission, a member of his family. The triumph continued to be respected because it took place relatively rarely, and was usually a celebration of genuine military success, in which the emperor had himself taken part.[127] Thus Claudius argued that only the conquest of Britain could bring a proper triumph, for triumphs were earned only in victories over unconquered peoples and kingdoms.[128] Between 31 BC and AD 235 there were only thirteen triumphs celebrated by nine emperors, with five holding more than one triumph. It was perhaps a mark of Vespasian's need to build up prestige quickly for his dynasty that he and his son Titus triumphed for the suppression of the Jewish rebellion of AD 66, rather than a war of conquest.

The ceremony of the triumph was heavily militaristic, with a special breakfast for the soldiers, a speech by the emperor, a full military parade and the acclamation of the emperor as general. There followed the parade of the spoils of war, with a pictorial account of the campaign carried on tableaux, and then the public execution of the enemy leader. The triumph brought emperor and soldiers together in their most honourable function of waging war for the good of Rome, and presented the emperor as a great military leader, the directing force of the campaign. However, the ceremonies also involved the senate and *equites*, and the whole people had a chance to view the spectacle.[129] The high point of the day was undoubtedly the personal appearance of the emperor. Tertullian, writing in the third century AD, thought that 'in that most exalted chariot' he was at the very height of his glory, and the golden triumphal chariot also impressed the Greek sophist Philostratus.[130] The coming together of the emperor and the whole Roman people in celebration is brought out by Josephus in his vivid account of the triumph of Vespasian and Titus over his own people: 'All that day the city of Rome celebrated the victory in the campaign against its enemies, the end of civil war, and the beginning of hopes for a happy future.'[131] Here we see how the military presentation of a Roman victory blended in with political ideology.

Emperors astutely managed and exploited the popular acclaim and publicity associated with military ceremonies by staging gladiatorial and other shows and making a great public holiday. After the Dacian Wars, Trajan arranged spectacles lasting for 123 days in which approximately 11,000 animals were killed and 10,000 gladiators fought.[132] Septimius Severus celebrated his victory against the Parthians with distributions of money to the people, and seven days of elaborate games and spectacles.[133] Gradually, more military ceremonies were revived or invented, where the emperor could be in public view. Whereas Augustus had preferred to enter and leave the city discreetly, by the late second century the arrival (*adventio*) or departure (*profectio*) of the emperor was a formal military procession, celebrated on coins and sculpture.[134] Already in the Julio-Claudian era special events were staged to emphasize the emperor's military success and the power of Rome. Claudius displayed two kings captured in war: Mithridates of the Bosphorus and the British king Caratacus.[135] According to Tacitus, Caratacus inspired real public interest. The people were summoned 'as if to a remarkable spectacle', the praetorians paraded in full armour, Claudius presided in military dress on a high platform; and, when Caratacus and his family were brought in, the emperor formally tried and eventually pardoned him. In AD 66 a similar spectacle was staged at which Nero crowned Tiridates king of Armenia. There was a parade of soldiers in full armour with their military standards, and then Nero in triumphal dress welcomed Tiridates in the presence of the senators and the people drawn up in ranks, and was acclaimed general with a great roar. He then made a speech and an interpreter translated Tiridates' reply. Although the Romans had won no substantial victories in the east, the imperial imagery was again of Roman power and the emperor's military splendour. Even writers normally hostile to Nero spoke of a magnificent event.[136]

These celebrations and spectacles of course took place in Rome but, like coins, imperial names and titles, served to export far and wide around the provinces news of the emperor as a successful war leader. Important men in Roman society traditionally recorded their life and achievements on relatively simple stone inscriptions set up in life and also after death. These monuments usually identified their name, family and tribe, and then set out posts, magistracies and commands held in public life, and often benefactions made to local communities. Emperors, too, belonged to the upper classes, and inscribed stones became another expression of imperial ideology, over which they had a significant degree of control. Inscriptions were easy to reproduce, and could carry an emperor's titles, attributes and record of achievement, which were attached to his name whenever it was read out or carved in Rome, Italy, the provinces, and of course in military camps. The inscribing of the full imperial titulature combined a visual and verbal language to express concepts of authority, grandeur and unsurpassed achievement.

Augustus had daringly adopted the battlefield acclamation of *imperator* (general) as his forename, styling himself Imperator Caesar Augustus, which marked out his unparalleled military achievements.[137] From Nero's time all emperors consistently used this name, which became virtually a designation of power. Augustus also continued to receive acclamations as *imperator*, in many cases for successes gained by his generals, which were added to his titles and amounted to twenty-one by the end of his reign. Augustus thought highly of these honours: 'I celebrated two ovations and three curule triumphs, and I was twenty-one times saluted as *imperator*.'[138] Eventually senators found the way to this honour blocked, as Augustus granted it to only a few close friends. The last acclamation as *imperator* made to a senator was in AD 22.[139] Emperors, however, accumulated *imperator* acclamations throughout the first two centuries. The Flavian dynasty, which came to power disreputably through civil war, amassed fifty-nine between them.[140] Pliny in his speech in praise of Trajan (*Panegyric*) stated the ideal by comparing Trajan to leaders of old 'on whom battlefields covered with the slain and seas filled with victory conferred the name *imperator*'.[141] In practice, the title was now simply a mark of imperial military honour that was often exploited and abused. Claudius had twenty-seven acclamations, but several of these were for the British campaign, although traditionally a commander was acclaimed only once for the same war.[142] But when the emperor was present on campaign the acclamation could still be staged with all the Roman flair for spectacle. A scene from Trajan's column depicts the victorious emperor, accompanied by his officers, addressing his troops at the end of the First Dacian War. The soldiers are drawn up with their standards, and raise their right arms aloft to acclaim Trajan.[143]

The 'surname from courage' (*cognomen ex virtute*) given to a victorious commander was usually derived from the name of the people he had defeated. Emperors adopted this practice and added the names of defeated peoples to their nomenclature.[144] Traditionally, an emperor accepted such a *cognomen* only if he had taken personal leadership of the military campaign and won a genuine victory. Thus Dio notes that when Trajan captured the Parthian capital Ctesiphon in AD 116 'he established his right to the title *Parthicus*' (Conqueror of the Parthians).[145] The formal process for the granting of the honour can be seen from an inscription referring to the same event:

> On 20 (or 21) February a despatch decked with laurel was sent to the senate by Imperator Trajan Augustus. For this reason he was named conqueror of the Parthians, and for his safe deliverance a decree of the senate was passed, offerings were made at all the shrines, and games were carried on.[146]

Senatorial commanders were soon excluded from such honours, which became the personal preserve of the emperor.[147] By the second century AD emperors usually took personal charge of all significant military campaigns,[148] and these 'surnames from courage' became more common. Trajan, for example, held three (*Germanicus*, *Dacicus* and *Parthicus*) and Marcus Aurelius five (*Armeniacus*, *Medicus*, *Parthicus Maximus*, *Germanicus*, *Sarmaticus*). The cheapening of the honour meant that emperors had to find something better, and by the late second century the adjective *Maximus* had appeared as an indication of surpassing achievement. Therefore *Parthicus Maximus* means 'Greatest Conqueror of all time of the Parthians'. The cumulative effect of these names was impressive, and physically they will have taken up a lot of space on inscriptions, coming after the emperor's other names and attributes and before family connections, magistracies, priesthoods, and the all-embracing 'Father of the Fatherland' (*Pater Patriae*). They were traditional, but also sounded romantic with their evocation of far-off peoples, and brought the usual message of overwhelming Roman power and the personal military leadership of the emperor.

Imperial communication and response

Roman emperors had no information office or press secretaries to ensure favourable publicity by putting the best interpretation on imperial policy. They did, however, have substantial control over the dissemination of information to the senate, Italy and the provinces through speeches, despatches, edicts, letters, and formal responses to enquiries and embassies. In the Republic a military commander usually sent despatches to the senate. Emperors carefully preserved this tradition, even using the old opening formula: 'If you are in good health, it is well, I and my army are in good health.'[149] The despatch, like a *communiqué*, provided an opportunity to give a favourable slant to events; the emperor could describe the defeat and conquest of dangerous foreign peoples, military policy, diplomacy, and of course, his personal role.[150] Caligula, who had a good idea of the dramatic, ordered that the messenger carrying his dispatches from Germany should ride in a carriage at full speed through the forum and present them to the consuls in person before the meeting of the senate in the temple of Mars Ultor.[151]

Claudius missed few opportunities of reminding everyone about his conquest of Britain, and when he addressed the senate on the matter of the admission of citizens from Gaul to senatorial status, with due diffidence he mentioned it again: 'I am afraid that I may seem somewhat arrogant and to have looked for an excuse for boasting of my own extension of the boundaries of the empire beyond the ocean.'[152] Septimius Severus used letters to convey much the same message to provincial communities, such as Nicopolis on Ister. He wrote commending the people on their enthusiastic celebration of his message that peace had been attained throughout the world 'because of the defeat of those savages who are causing disturbance to the empire'.[153] Similarly, in a letter to the city of Aphrodisias, Severus apparently commended the citizens because they rejoiced at his success over 'the barbarians and [conducted] a festival to celebrate them'.[154] Here the presentation of imperial success and the response to it locally were part of a quasi-diplomatic process in which the city ensured that its existing rights were preserved. Sometimes the official version was elaborated by local enthusiasm. So a dedication from Cyrenaica in honour of Trajan claims that he had captured the Dacian king Decabalus, who in fact had committed suicide.[155] But Trajan will not have objected to this exaggeration. It was important that the emperor be seen as the guiding force behind the military success of the empire. The perfect response to this message is found in an inscription from the Dacian town of Sarmizegethusa, which celebrated its rescue by Marcus Aurelius – 'saved by a display of courage from two threatening dangers'.[156]

Emperors in the main belonged to an articulate and literate aristocratic society, in which composition in Greek and Latin was common. Nero dabbled in poetry, Hadrian wrote Greek verses, and Marcus Aurelius composed in Greek a record of his inner thoughts and reflections on life as he campaigned on the Danube. Autobiography could explain or defend a man's actions, and of course propagate military achievements. The *Res Gestae* of Augustus, as we have seen, had a strong military content. Vespasian and Titus wrote about their campaign against the Jews, and Trajan wrote an account of the Dacian Wars, of which just one sentence survives. Septimius Severus' autobiography certainly covered the civil war which he fought against Albinus.[157]

By means like these emperors set out to reinforce the official version, and that is what in the main has come down to us. Therefore, in the language of war, *bellum* was used to denote an officially sanctioned and divinely approved war against the declared enemies (*hostes*) of Rome, and the war was often identified by the name of the vanquished people or their territory.[158] However, *bellum* could be used to refer to a war that really did not deserve the title, and sometimes concealed a sordid civil war, as in the *bellum Germanicum*, describing the suppression of the rebellion against Domitian in AD 89 of Saturninus legate of Upper Germany.[159] The agency of the government perhaps appears most clearly in the explanation of defeats. One of the most damaging in terms of psychological, material and human loss was the death of P. Quinctilius Varus in Germany in AD 9, along with his three legions. But, although Varus had been Tiberius' brother-in-law and had already been governor of Syria, the official version ruthlessly put the blame on him. According to the pro-government Velleius, he had been careless, failed to appreciate the imminent danger, and did not use proper military procedures. In a way he had betrayed his soldiers and, by implication, the trust his emperor had put in him.[160] As the blame was transferred, so the dishonourable word *clades* (disaster) was attached to the defeat, with the commander's names in adjectival form: *clades Variana*.[161] Similar publicity surrounded the incident in which Sedatius Severianus, governor of Cappadocia, was defeated and killed by the Parthians, apparently with the loss of at least one legion. Again the official version blamed it on the incompetence of the governor, who was described as 'the foolish Celt'.[162]

By the same token, wars in which the emperor did not participate personally could well have been kept out of the limelight. In the reign of Augustus, there was clearly a deliberate attempt to play down the campaigns fought by Marcus Crassus, proconsul of Macedonia, against Thracian tribes in 27 BC. Not only was he in line for an acclamation as general and a triumph, but he had even killed an enemy leader in single combat and claimed the *spolia opima*. This was not good news for Augustus, who of course wanted to be the supreme, unchallenged military leader. Thus legalistic objections were raised, and Crassus was deprived of his due reward on the grounds that he was not acting under his own auspices. Rather inconsistently he was permitted to celebrate a triumph, but not until several years later, when most people would have forgotten him.[163] This is a rare case where we can see the manipulation of publicity and public opinion by the imperial government. Naturally, when an emperor was present in person on campaign, it was much more difficult to distance himself from failure. But increasingly from the end of the first century AD emperors believed it important to take control of military operations in person, and to run the risk of moving away from Augustus' practice of taking the credit for victories but rarely visiting the front.

When they met, gossiped or wrote, the reaction of the upper classes to government publicity was very important. It would be especially helpful if there were talented people prepared to write up an emperor's exploits.

Augustus and his friends had carried on the tradition of the Republican nobility in offering encouragement, patronage and even financial support to writers. None of these writers was expected to pen slavish panegyrics, but occasional references to Augustus were appreciated. The general picture that emerged in the literature of the Augustan age of a secure but expanding empire in the safe hands of the courageous *princeps* must surely have pleased Augustus and his advisers. Ovid, in exile at Tomi and seeking to regain Augustus' goodwill, is particularly keen to praise the dutiful leader who has brought peace based on Roman domination through his military superiority over all peoples.[164] Similarly, in the reign of Domitian, the poems of Statius and Martial are generously adorned with praise of Domitian's wars against the Germans and the Dacians, the emperor's personal leadership and his total victory.[165] After Trajan's Dacian Wars, Pliny was approached by a budding poet from his home town of Comum asking for advice on a poem about the emperor. Pliny enthusiastically suggested themes – the achievements of Roman military engineering, the building of new bridges and camps, the defeat and death of a foreign king, and Trajan's personal leadership.[166] The distinguished lawyer Cornelius Fronto, who was a family friend of Marcus Aurelius and Lucius Verus, wrote a history of the Parthian War of AD 162 to 166, in which Verus was praised for successful leadership, the restoration of discipline and control of strategy.[167] More critical views of Verus' conduct of the war were current, and it is not surprising that he was very keen for a particular version to be propagated. For this reason he wrote to Fronto suggesting that his policy and actions should be explained, and that his achievements should be made clear by emphasizing the lack of success before he arrived. So concerned was he that he arranged for the senatorial officers in the war to send their campaign notes to Fronto.[168]

But emperors did not have things all their own way, and sometimes did not obtain the reaction they wanted, because in the end Rome was not a totalitarian society. Seneca's satirical commentary on the deification of Claudius ('The Pumpkinification of Claudius') mocks the emperor, who turns up at his own funeral and is delighted to hear his funeral lament, which praises his military success, the subjugation of the very ocean and the conquest of Britain.[169] Juvenal also directed his satirical attacks at individuals who were already dead, but his writings could nevertheless ridicule imperial ideology, as in his fourth satire about Domitian's council meeting. He also refers to the military disaster that saw the death of Domitian's praetorian prefect, Cornelius Fuscus, and the destruction of his army. The incomplete sixteenth satire starts by poking fun at the military and their privileges.[170] Lucian of Samosata (born *c.* AD 120), who wrote witty commentaries on contemporary life and literature, has a particularly devastating account of some of the panegyrical writing that passed for history of the campaigns of Lucius Verus in Parthia. This reminds us of Fronto's embarrassing efforts to write a history that pleased Verus. According to Lucian, writers greatly exaggerated the emperor's military achievements (one compared Verus to Achilles and the Parthian king to Thersites, the loud-mouthed, ugly upstart in Homer), and wrote up what he did in enormous detail, in one case spending hundreds of lines describing his shield.[171] Thus, although an emperor could present his activities in the best light and sometimes alter the truth, it would not do to indulge in shameless exaggeration or complete fabrication. Everyone would remember the scathing though probably unjustified comments of Tacitus and Pliny on the military triumphs of Domitian, who allegedly bought Germans on the market and dressed them up to look like prisoners of war for his sham triumph. Tacitus may well have expressed contemporary criticism when he said: 'In recent times the Germans have been more triumphed over than defeated.'[172] Similarly, during his speech in the senate in praise of Trajan, Pliny effectively contrasted Trajan's genuine military record to the posturing of Domitian.[173]

At all times the main advantage the government had in propagating its views on warfare and foreign policy was that Romans and most of the privileged élite in the provinces agreed on what they wanted: not to surrender the revenues and other benefits of empire, and to maintain the imperial grandeur of Rome. There was no strong public opinion against warfare, no clear moral stance on the ethics of warfare, no anti-imperial sentiment or pressure for disengagement from occupied lands, although some people might discuss the value of individual annexations of territory.[174] For many people throughout the empire it was self-evident that the gods had indeed granted the Romans 'power without limit'.[175]

7

EPILOGUE

The Roman army seems curiously modern with its professionalism, structured bureaucracy and detailed military organization. Indeed, John Keegan has called it the 'mother-house' of modern armies. It is not surprising that this army, which had such an impressive record of success, has often played a part in modern analysis of the nature of war and the impact of military practices and warfare on society. However, the Roman army does not fit easily into any pattern or theory derived from analysis of the armed services of communities in different eras, and its diversity and close links with a unique society and culture make generalizations very difficult. Furthermore, we should remember that the army of the imperial period had been initially moulded to suit the wishes and needs of one man, Augustus. He determined its size, structure, disposition and command, and in this he had at least one eye on the straightforward matter of his own survival. Augustus engaged in frequent warfare and kept personal control of his army, which he stationed permanently in the provinces, especially Germany, the Danube lands and the east. In this he influenced the direction of Rome's military and strategic interests for generations to come, and indirectly the future course of European history. Yet he managed to combine his proclaimed role as a great conqueror with a system of government largely free from the trappings of military autocracy.

From this complex legacy emerged significant features that were to have enduring importance: above all, the idea of professional, specialist soldiers paid by the state, who earned rewards by their service and an entitlement to a kind of pension on discharge. Increasingly legionaries were recruited from outside Italy, and large numbers of non-Romans were also accepted to play an integral part in the military as auxiliaries. On completion of their service these men received citizenship for themselves and their children, and there was a significant degree of assimilation and integration into the Roman way of life. There was also an avenue of social mobility through promotion in the army to the rank of centurion and above. It was a conspicuous achievement to recruit this army largely from subject peoples and to preserve its loyalty and commitment for over four centuries in the west.

151

The Romans developed a framework of military organization and a pattern of thorough training throughout the army, and commanders exploited this by using battlefield tactics that involved the simultaneous operation of infantry and cavalry and the deployment of reserves. With its highly developed unit loyalty, excellent ordnance, technical support, medical service and effective siege artillery, the army had an ability unparalleled in the ancient world to fight long campaigns and wear down an enemy. In response to changing conditions, tactical thinking could be flexible and adaptable, and the army's skill on campaign exemplified Maurice's maxim in his *Strategicon*: 'Warfare is like hunting. Wild animals are taken by scouting, by nets, by lying in wait, by stalking, by circling round, and by other such stratagems rather than by sheer force' (Book 7). Not that the Romans avoided the use of force, and it was the reputation of their tough and seemingly invincible army that sustained the diplomacy they chose to employ on occasion. As Vegetius pointed out, 'those who seek peace must prepare for war' (*Epitome of Military Science*, 3, Preface).

This professional army was the largest state-sponsored organization in the ancient world and was a perpetual burden on provincial communities whether in war or in peace. They sustained its immense cost through the payment of direct taxes and other irregular exactions, and the presence of soldiers often brought misery to civilians, especially those living along main roads or near military camps that became permanent structures. Not for the last time in history a government proved unable to restrain its own agents. However, the army's presence was two-edged since it could also provide a stimulus to the local economy and create fresh activity in its wake. As soldiers formed unions with local women and produced children they became more integrated into the local society of the settlements that developed round the military camps in parts of the empire. In some cases these settlements survived to become important cities and capitals in the modern world. Furthermore, veteran soldiers often chose to settle close to where they had spent their military service. Not only were they Roman citizens, but they also had experience and connections that could potentially enhance the community where they lived.

From the time of Augustus the Roman emperor was effectively commander-in-chief of the army, had complete control of the military resources of the state, made all decisions on war and peace, and commanded in person on major campaigns. Yet, although he was often depicted in the dress of a Roman general, he was not part of a warrior élite, and even in the later third century society in Rome was not really militaristic. In fact the emperor was symbolically a military leader who ruled in a largely civilian context and made sure that his military commanders formed no military hierarchy. Indeed, army commanders were rarely specialist military men, and many senators and equestrians were not involved in military affairs at all. The professional army protected a civilian political structure in which the soldiers and their commanders had no direct say by virtue of their military role. Only in times of rebellion and civil war could the army make a direct impact on politics, though of course successful warfare against foreign peoples could enhance an emperor's political standing. It was not until the later third century that a clique of tough military officers appeared whose support was needed to fight Rome's wars and give government the necessary credibility to survive. By this time an emperor's capacity to rule was virtually tantamount to ability in military command, partly because from the late first century emperors had assumed a more active role in military command by taking charge of major campaigns, and therefore found it impossible to distance themselves from military failure.

Throughout the first three centuries of the imperial period the Romans engaged in exceptionally vigorous and aggressive warfare; campaigns were conducted with a ruthless determination, and the army was capable of inflicting enormous casualties even with the rather primitive weapons of destruction in the ancient world. New territory was added regularly either by conquest or by more peaceful assimilation and annexation. The Romans recognized no boundaries, crossing the ocean to invade Britain, the Danube to attack Dacia, and the Euphrates to annex Mesopotamia. The destruction and loss of life caused by the Roman army in the pursuit of imperialist goals are beyond calculation. Entire populations were killed or sold into slavery or deported and brutalized; cities that resisted sieges were subjected to systematic pillaging and destruction. In the early Republic, warfare was an ingrained part of Roman culture; campaigning was seasonal for the citizen-soldiers, battle was an integral part of life, and excellence in war was a great attribute. Under the emperors warlike instincts were less prevalent, and many more senators than in the Republic had little if any military experience. Nevertheless, there was still a general interest in warfare and army command, and many *equites* now had more extensive army careers. In particular, there was no doubt among eminent Romans about the imperial mission and they were not concerned to justify the morality of conquest; they believed that it was right to protect and expand imperial territory and they did not think about the cost. They simply expected the army through successful warfare to impose the physical infrastructure of imperial government and stable rule, whose benefits were self-evident to them. The propertied élite in the provinces accepted the army and the imperial system on which they relied for support, since they had no other credible means of preserving order or protecting themselves, and cooperated in assisting Roman local administration.

Emperors smoothed over the more questionable aspects of the army's role in the Roman world by skilfully using the means at their disposal to disseminate favourable information and shape public opinion. They systematically presented to the Roman people and provincial communities their role as leaders in war, and the army's record of military success, which involved both the defence and extension of imperial territory. The Romans seemingly understood that propaganda has to be comprehensible at various levels, through the cumulative impact of the repetition of relatively simple messages. Their methods and themes were remarkably coherent and consistent, and developed organically from what had already been done. Some of the methods, especially the use of patriotic slogans and formal military displays and ceremonies, became a significant part of the propaganda employed by states right up to the present day. Indeed, what we may call the emotional impact of the Roman army is still important, and Hollywood screenwriters and film-makers have appreciated and exploited not only the army's military prowess, but also its glittering appearance as a disciplined and well-accoutred force splendidly suited for pomp and spectacle.

In the Roman empire an effective army represented control, power and the ability to govern consistently. This army was relatively unobtrusive in political terms but placed enormous demands on the state to organize its pay and support. From the mid-third century the army lost some of its effectiveness in the face of numerous foreign invasions and internal rebellions. As political instability increased, the army became more obviously the determining factor in politics. Diocletian re-established strong government and successfully reorganized the army, which was able once again to reassert Roman territorial integrity. But the continuation of the empire-wide recruiting of a professional army and a probable increase in the number of soldiers confirmed the importance of revenues organized by the central government. The quest for secure sources of funding became paramount as the role of the army and its demands assumed ever greater importance in the life of the empire. It is significant that Diocletian tried to improve tax collecting through changes in the provincial system and to develop a system of paying the army in kind. In the east, new ways were found to fund the army, and this was a crucial factor in the survival of the eastern empire with its capital at Constantinople. In the west, the people of Italy had long since lost the tradition of bearing arms, and when the expensive army could no longer be maintained warlords with private armies appeared who suited their own interests. As the soldiers who had sustained the burden of defending and patrolling the empire melted away, much of the infrastructure collapsed with them. Many years of violence, dislocation and decline were to pass before anything remotely comparable could be put in its place.

BRIEF CHRONOLOGICAL
TABLE

31 BC	Battle of Actium
AD 6–9	Revolt of Pannonians
AD 9	Defeat of P. Quinctilius Varus in Germany
42	Revolt of L. Arruntius Cammilus Scribomanus
43	Invasion of Britain
66	Jewish revolt
69	Two civil war battles at Bedriacum, first the defeat of Otho by Vitellius, then the defeat of the Vitellians by the Flavian forces
70	Capture of Jerusalem by Titus
73 or 74	Fall of Masada
77–84	Agricola governor of Britain
85	Oppius Sabinus, governor of Moesia, defeated and killed by the Dacians
85–92	Wars against the Dacians and Pannonians
89	Rebellion of L. Antonius Saturninus, governor of Upper Germany
101–2	First Dacian War
105–6	Second Dacian War; creation of province of Dacia
106	Annexation of kingdom of Nabataeans and creation of province of Arabia
113	Trajan launches campaign against Parthia
116–17	Uprising of Jews of the Diaspora
121–5	Hadrian's first provincial tour
122	Start of building of Hadrian's Wall in Britain
128–32	Hadrian's second provincial tour
130	Aelia Capitolina founded on site of Jerusalem
132–5	Bar Kochba revolt in Judaea
131–7	Arrian governor of Cappadocia
161	M. Sedatius Severianus, governor of Cappadocia, defeated and killed in Armenia
162–6	Parthian War of L. Verus
167–75	Northern Wars, especially against the Marcomanni and Quadi

175	Revolt of C. Avidius Cassius, governor of Syria
178–80	Northern Wars
194	Final defeat of Pescennius Niger by Septimius Severus
195	Annexation of Osrhoene
197	Defeat of Clodius Albinus at Lugdunum
197–8	Parthian War
198	Creation of province of Mesopotamia
208–10	Campaigns in northern Scotland
213	War against the Alamanni in Germany
214–17	War against Parthia
231–3	War against the Persians
234–5	War against the Alamanni
238	Legion III Augusta cashiered in disgrace
251	Decius defeated and killed by Goths at battle of Abrittus
260	Valerian defeated and captured by Persian king, Shapur
272	Defeat of Zenobia by Aurelian and surrender of Palmyra
274	Defeat of Tetricus and the Gallic Empire
277–8	Probus defeats the Alamanni and Franks and restores the German frontier

NOTES

1 THE ORIGINS OF WAR

1　Ferguson, in Raaflaub and Rosenstein (1999, 427, n. 3). I take 'material' to include winning prestige and renown and maintaining status.

2　Momigliano (1966), esp. 120–4, traced this problem back to Greek writers and their view that war was inevitable, whereas constitutions, which could be changed, were a suitable area of study for philosophers and political historians. Furthermore, ancient writers did not pursue the social, moral and economic aspects of warfare.

3　Note particularly Andreski (1968), Marwick (1974, esp. 3–6), Keegan (1976, 1987, 1993), Holmes (1985), Paret (1992). Ferguson, in Raaflaub and Rosenstein (1999), esp. 389–94, 402–14, 423–7, provides a good survey of the causes of war from an anthropological perspective. Modern parallels are used carefully to good effect for the later Roman Republic by Patterson, in Rich and Shipley (1993). See also Garlan (1975, 180–8).

4　Livy (9.17.3), referring to the Republic. For Romans as the sons of Mars, see below, n. 72.

5　*Pro Murena*, 75.

6　For the history and development of the army of the early Republic, see Keppie (1984).

7　See Polybius, 6.14.10–11.

8　The mentality of ordinary soldiers is discussed by Harris (1979, 41–53). There was possibly a change of feeling in the 150s BC with garrison duty in Macedonia and longer, less profitable wars.

9　Fergus Millar (1984, 1986, 1998) has argued against the conventional view, emphasizing the sovereignty of the Roman people, often expressed through public meetings.

10　See Harris (1979, 9–41).

11　ibid.; see also 1984.

12　For discussion, see Sherwin-White (1980), North (1981), Rich, in Rich and Shipley (1993), who dispute some of Harris's conclusions. It is doubtless right to avoid schematic solutions. Wars came about for a variety of complex reasons, any one of which could be uppermost on any one occasion.

13　Plutarch, *Crassus*, 2.

14　Sallust believed that Caesar wanted a new war in which his *virtus* could shine out (*Catiline*, 54.4); see Brunt, *Roman Imperial Themes* (1990, 309–14).

15　Cornell, in Rich and Shipley (1993, 154–60), argued that major imperialistic ventures became increasingly rare in the last century of the Republic. But, as he admits, there were still some spectacular campaigns, and the putting down

of revolts and internal conflict was part of imperialist aggression in the determined building of a territorial empire. Furthermore, civil war or the threat of
civil war after the time of Sulla may have inhibited or distracted from plans
for imperial expansion. Cf. Appian (*Illyrica* 15) describing how war with Pompey
interfered with Caesar's plans for Illyricum.

16 See Botermann (1968) for the relationship between soldiers and commanders
    in the late Republic.
17 For Augustus' organization of the army, see Raaflaub (1980); Keppie (1984,
    145–71); *CAH²*, vol. 10, 376–87.
18 17.3.25 (840). Strabo was writing in Augustus' lifetime. Dio (53.17.6), though
    speaking generally, is referring to events in 27 BC.
19 For senatorial commanders, see Chapter 2, pp. 40–2.
20 2.30 for Florus, see also below, p. 12.
21 Dio, 53.22.5.
22 *Res Gestae*, 26.5.
23 See Campbell (2001, 10–11). An Indian embassy, which had spent four years
    on the road, had to be sent on to Samos where Augustus was staying; only
    three members survived the journey (Strabo, 15.1.73 (719); Dio, 54.9.8–10).
24 Dio, 55.33.5.
25 For problems of logistics and information see below, pp. 17–18.
26 Josephus, *The Jewish War*, 2.25, 81; *Jewish Antiquities*, 17.301.
27 2.30.22.
28 54.9.1, quoting Augustus' comments to the senate after the settlement with
    the Parthians in 20 BC.
29 Brunt (1963, 172).
30 Suetonius, *Augustus*, 21.2. See Brunt, 'Roman imperial illusions' (1990, 465);
    Suetonius saw Augustus as a model emperor and, writing under Hadrian, who
    did not fight wars of conquest, could not present Augustus as governed by
    ambitions that Hadrian had rejected.
31 *Res Gestae*, 26–33.
32 Suetonius, *Augustus*, 8.2, 10.4, 13.1, 16.2.
33 Appian, *Illyrica*, 20, 27.
34 Suetonius, *Augustus*, 25.4.
35 See Chapter 6, pp. 145–6.
36 Suetonius, *Augustus*, 18. Pompey and Caesar had also been admirers of Alexander.
37 Suetonius, *Divus Julius*, 44.3.
38 There have been many conflicting interpretations; see most importantly Brunt
    (1963, 'Roman imperial illusions' 1990), Wells (1972), who undermine the idea
    of a defensive policy and incline to the view that Augustus may have thought
    of world conquest; Gruen, in Raaflaub and Toher (1990, 409–16), sees Augustus
    as a pragmatist, following diverse and flexible policies; Cornell, in Rich and
    Shipley (1993, 141–2, 161), believes that Augustus followed a programme of
    imperialist expansion but had to stir up a war-weary people; note also the
    cautious comments of Syme (1978, 51–2.)
39 For public opinion and warfare in Augustus' time, see Chapter 6, pp. 129–32.
40 Interestingly, Dio makes Livia, Augustus' wife, say, 'We have many soldiers to
    protect us, both those arrayed against outside enemies and those who guard
    us, and a large retinue so that through them we can live safely both at home
    and abroad' (55.15.3); note the comments of Goodman (1997, 81–4).
41 The close connection between the military and political control is illustrated
    by Dio's comment on Augustus' setting up of the praetorian guard in 27 BC:
    'By doing this he clearly aimed to establish a monarchy' (53.11.5).

42 Velleius claims that Octavian's campaigns in Illyria were partly intended to prevent military discipline from being corrupted by inactivity (2.78); see also Goodman (1997, 82–3).

43 *Illyrica*, 15.

44 16.4.22 (780).

45 Dio, 56.23; Suetonius, *Aug.* 23; Velleius, 2.119–20. It seems likely that the site of the battle was in the Teutoburgiensis Saltus at Kalkriese, about 100km north-east of Haltern. Archaeological finds here have included coins of Augustan date, pieces of military equipment and carefully buried human remains. Tacitus tells us that Germanicus found the site of the battle and buried the lost legions in AD 15 (*Annals* 1.62). See Schlüter (1993); Schlüter and Wiegels (1999, espc. 61–89); Berger (1996, 11–46, 58–9) discusses the significant finds of Augustan coinage with fourteen examples countermarked with VAR (P. Quinctilius Varus).

46 See Dio, 49.38.2, 53.22.5, 25.2; Horace confidently predicted the conquest of Britain (*Odes*, 3.5.3–4); Strabo voiced the official view that the Britons were not a threat, and that invasion and occupation would cost more than could be raised by taxation (2.5.8 (115)); for Parthia, see Campbell, in Rich and Shipley (1993, 220–8).

47 Pompeius Trogus, *apud Justin*, 42.5.10.

48 This is summed up by Florus, 2.34: 'When all the peoples of the west and south had been subdued, and also the peoples of the north, at least those between the Rhine and the Danube, and of the east between the Cyrus (?) and Euphrates, the remaining peoples too, who were not under the control of the empire, nevertheless felt the greatness of Rome and revered the Roman people as conqueror of the world'; cf. Dio, 53.7.

49 Tacitus, *Annals*, 1.11. This is misleadingly translated by M. Grant in the Penguin Classics as 'the empire should not be extended beyond its present *frontiers*' (40); cf. also Dio, 56.33.5. Ober (1982) argued that this last advice of Augustus was inspired by Tiberius.

50 *Res Gestae*, 13.

51 *Annals*, 4.72–4.

52 See below, pp. 14–15.

53 Smallwood (1966, no. 23, lines 8–13).

54 Dio, 68.9, 10.3.

55 *ILS*, 451.

56 *Satire*, 4.

57 Tacitus, *Annals*, 15.25.

58 Dio, 72.1–2; Herodian, 1.6.

59 For the emperor's role in the civil administration of the empire, see Millar (1977).

60 Tacitus, *Annals*, 11.20; *Agricola*, 39; Pliny, *Panegyric*, 18, cf. 14.5. Of course hostility to 'bad' emperors could colour senatorial judgement, and in any case many senators were not interested in the responsibilities of military commands and provincial governorships.

61 As, for example, responsibility for the German defeat of AD 9 was placed entirely on the shoulders of Quinctilius Varus; see above, n. 45.

62 See Isaac (1992, 388–9); Whittaker (1994, 86); Cornell, in Rich and Shipley (1993, 160–8), discusses reasons why war might not be desirable. Note also Dio's comments on the cost of unexpected campaigns (52.28.5). For public opinion, see Chapter 6.

63 Tacitus, *Annals*, 1.47.

64 See Campbell, in Rich and Shipley (1993); (2001); for diplomatic contact with peoples on the Rhine and Danube, see Pitts (1989).

65 See further, Chapter 5.

66 Marwick (1974, 4), referring to Germany before the First World War.

67 See Campbell (1987).

68 *Roman History*, Preface, 6.

69 1.1 introd.

70 For the views of Tacitus and Dio, see Chapter 2, p. 33. I cannot agree with Tim Cornell's view (Rich and Shipley, 1993, 164–8) that there was a declining interest in war among the literate upper classes and that those interested in military affairs were confined to a few. If true, this might have influenced emperors towards a cautious approach, but the careers of senators and indeed *equites* often show a mixture of civilian and military posts. Specialization in a military 'career' is comparatively rare, though it might of course appear in periods of prolonged war. Military culture and ideology were still important in Roman society, and it is not possible to say that Roman writers show a lack of interest in war. It must be remembered that we have only part of what they wrote. For much of the work of our main narrative historian, Cassius Dio, we rely on an excerpted text, and it may be that those who edited his text omitted much military narrative. Furthermore, writers may have found it difficult to get information on Wars in distant provinces. It is true that Pliny apparently had no interest in the Dacian Wars except as a literary venture, but he was not slow to praise and emphasize Trajan's military prowess in the *Panegyric*. Furthermore, it is relevant that, apart from three major campaigns of conquest from the mid-first to late second century, Trajan also aimed to include Armenia and Mesopotamia in the empire (see Lightfoot, 1990, 121–4), while Marcus Aurelius aimed to exterminate the Sarmatians and create a new province of Sarmatia (A. Birley, 1987, 183, 253–4). Military setbacks and revolts stopped them. This does not sound like a society uninterested in war.

71 See Brunt, 'Roman imperial illusions' (1990, 475–80); see also below, Chapter 6.

72 Livy, Preface, 7. Cf. 3: 'I shall take pleasure in having done my best to commemorate the achievements of the foremost people in the world.'

73 Livy, 1.16.7.

74 Tacitus, *Annals*, 3.73.

75 Ammianus Marcellinus, 30.5–6.

76 See Chapter 2 for the recruitment of soldiers. That the loss of the lives of citizen-soldiers *could* be a concern may be deduced from Tacitus' comments on the battle of Mons Graupius in Scotland (*Agricola*, 35) that victory would be much more glorious without the shedding of Roman blood, because the *auxilia* bore the brunt of the struggle.

77 Isaac (1992, 383) suggested that soldiers might seek war for their own profit. However, the only example he cites does not support this (Herodian, 6.7.9–10). In this case what annoyed the soldiers was Severus Alexander's lazy lifestyle and the fact that German arrogance had not been punished. In fact this looks suspiciously like a typical upper-class view put into the mouth of the soldiers by Herodian.

78 Note the deputation of soldiers that came from Britain apparently to complain to Commodus about his praetorian prefect Perennis; see Brunt (1973).

79 53.19.

80 68.17.1. Other explanations have been rather unconvincingly based on economic considerations or frontier rectification; see the discussion in Lepper (1948); Lightfoot (1990).

81 Dio, 68.8.2.

82 Dio, 68.6.

83 See below, Chapter 6, pp. 135–8

84 Note the view of Isaac (1992, 417) that control over peoples and towns was the essence of sovereignty. 'Territory was important only as a source of income.' Whittaker (1994, 98–131) examines the spread of Roman control into usable areas on the frontiers.

85 Suetonius, *Claudius*, 17; Dio, 60.19–22; see also Chapter 5, p. 112; Chapter 6, pp. 138, 145, 147.

86 For Domitian's military activity, see Jones (1992, chs 6 and 7).

87 Dio, 76.11; Herodian, 3.14.1–2; see in general A. Birley (1988, 170–87).

88 Suetonius (*Tiberius*, 41) unjustly criticizes Tiberius' foreign policy. Tacitus also disliked Tiberius and subtly casts doubt on his conduct of foreign affairs (e.g. *Annals*, 4.32, 6.31); he is similarly sarcastic about Domitian (*Agricola*, 39–41).

89 Nero – Suetonius (*Nero*, 18); Hadrian – Fronto (ed. Haines (Loeb), 2, 206).

90 More than 13 per cent of Rome's military strength; see Kennedy (1996, 85).

91 Isaac (1992, 393–4) plays down the importance of this motive.

92 2.105.3, cf. 2.103.

93 *Stratagems*, 1.1.8.

94 *ILS*, 986.

95 *ILS*, 8938.

96 *Roman History*, Preface, 7. The role of the army is apparently to protect the inner core of provinces, and also to discipline neighbouring peoples; see further discussion in Whittaker (1996, 36–7).

97 *Annals*, 1.9.

98 A. Birley (1987, 183).

99 See above, p. 1.

100 Luttwak (1976), esp. ch. 2.

101 Ibid., ch. 3. Note the distinction between power and force in Luttwak's theory. Power was the ability to enforce obedience because people were overawed by Rome's superior military strength. Power is not consumed by its use, whereas force is.

102 See below, pp. 18–20.

103 Luttwak's views have been criticized notably by Mann (1979); Isaac (1992, 372–418); Whittaker (1994, 1996). Whittaker (1996) analyses recent scholarly debate, especially Ferrill (1991), who argued in support of Luttwak. See also Mattern (1999) for a good discussion of the factors and principles that underlay Roman foreign policy. For Roman attitudes to war and peace and the motivation for military activity, see also Woolf, in Rich and Shipley (1993, 179–84); Cornell, in op. cit., 166–8.

104 See Nicolet (1988, 82–95); Talbert (1990).

105 See above, p. 9.

106 See e.g. Isaac (1992), referring to the eastern provinces.

107 Cf. Mann (1974); Johnston (1989).

108 It is difficult to decide why the Romans continued to fight in some areas and not in others, beyond the usual motives of profit, opportunistic imperialism, the protection of Roman interests at the time, and simple loss of enthusiasm for further conquest; there may also have been more complex reasons such as economic factors within entire frontier zones; see discussion in Mann (1979); Whittaker (1994).

109 Nicolet (1988, ch. 3) discusses the intellectual tendency in Rome to identify the frontiers of their empire with those of the inhabited world.

110 Goodman (1987, 1997, 254–7).

111 For the creation of new provinces, see above, pp. 14–15 (Dacia, Mesopotamia, Britain, also Arabia); territories more stealthily annexed included Cappadocia, Commagene, Amanus, Thrace, Mauretania, Lycia.

112 See in general Kennedy (1996, 85) for legionary dispositions.
113 *Concerning his Return*, 134–7 (the translation is that of H. Isbell, *The Last Poets of Imperial Rome*, Penguin, 1971).

2 SOLDIERS AND WAR

1 See e.g. Keegan (1976, 114–16, 187–94, 274–84); Holmes (1985, 270–315).
2 For the history of the army in the Republic, see Harmand (1967); Keppie (1984).
3 See chapter 1, p. 2.
4 See discussion in Hopkins (1978, 30–7); Harris (1979, 44–5); see also Brunt (1971, 391–415).
5 Battle narrative – *Amphitruo*, 188–262; see in general Harris (1979, 43).
6 10.15.4–6. It is possible of course that Polybius exaggerates from a few cases; soldiers do sometimes get out of hand and feel resentment against the enemy after a campaign.
7 Livy, 31.34.4.
8 Harris (1979, 51).
9 Brunt (1971, 393–4).
10 Appian, *Iberica*, 84.
11 Polybius, 35.4.2–6.
12 Brunt (1971, 403–5) (in 214 BC and before 129). Harris (1979, 44–50) thinks that up to the mid-second century BC Roman citizens were fairly willing to serve in the army.
13 Brunt (op. cit., 405–12; Keppie (1984, 61–3)). Conscription continued to be employed.
14 See Brunt (op. cit., 413–15, and 509–12).
15 See Mann (1983, 3); *Diz. epig.* s.v. *legio*, 552.
16 Suetonius, *Caes.*, 68, cf. also 69–70.
17 Appian, *Civil Wars*, 5.17.
18 *Diz. epig.* s.v. *legio*, 555; perhaps around 250,000 men. See also Keppie (1984, 132–44).
19 *Digest* 49.16.4.10; Brunt, *SCI* (1974, 90–3).
20 See Mann (1983, 49).
21 See Forni (1953, 29–30); Brunt (1974).
22 See below, p. 29.
23 *Auxilia* – Cheesman (1914); Saddington (1975); Holder (1980). Fleet – see Chapter 3, pp. 49–50 and n. 20.
24 See Gabba (1976, 16–19) for the social background of soldiers from Marius onwards; see also below, pp. 32–4.
25 See Mann (1983, 50–1).
26 The evidence is scattered and uneven but has been brilliantly analysed by Forni (1953, 1974, 1992).
27 See below, n. 51.
28 For the view that units were often under strength see below, n. 38.
29 See below, Chapter 4, pp. 97–8.
30 I cannot agree with Alston (1995, 43) that the description *castris* could refer to a soldier's origin in any camp and not the one in the environs of which he served. It seems to me that without qualification the phrase *castris* should refer to men born in the camp locally.
31 Mann (1983, 36–7); Mócsy (1974, 117, 154–5). Wilkes, in Goldsworthy and Haynes (1999, 98–100), has shown on the basis of a monument from Viminacium

in Upper Moesia that in the late second century two-thirds of the recruits to the legion VII Claudia came from the province, mainly from its two long-standing veteran colonies, Scupi and Ratiaria.

32 Le Roux (1982, 254–64); Mann (1983, 22).

33 The importance of regional variations is emphasized by Mann, op. cit. Saller and Shaw (1984, 139–45, 152–5) argued that the lack of local recruiting in provinces like Britain and Lower and Upper Germany explained the fact that soldiers in these areas appear to develop fewer family relationships. Cherry (1989), however, held that this has more to do with the strict enforcement of the ban on military marriages in provinces where there was great military danger. It should be remembered that the evidence for the origins of recruits is uneven and certainly rather limited in the case of Britain (Mann 1985).

34 Mann (op. cit., 12–16); Shaw (1983, 143–8).

35 Mann (op. cit., 42).

36 Forni (1953, 77, 167); Alston (1995, 41–5).

37 See above, n. 30. For the unusual case of recruits to legion II Traiana in AD 132/3, see below, p. 29 at n. 50.

38 Alston (op. cit., 44–8). He argued that some of the larger intakes could be tied to a crisis, for example, the large number of recruits who joined the III Augusta in 173, when war may have broken out in Africa. See also Gilliam (1986, 227–51).

39 Alston also cited an inscription relating to legion II Traiana in Egypt in 194 which in his view suggests that there was a delay in replacing centurions and that the whole unit therefore was not up to strength. But there are many possible reasons why this unit had at this moment an apparently reduced complement of centurions. Corrupt governor – Pedius Blaesus in Crete and Cyrene was expelled from the senate for his role in the recruiting in Cyrenaica – 'for accepting bribes and solicitations to falsify the recruiting rolls' (Tacitus, *Annals.*, 14.18).

40 Holder (1980, 5–13); Goldsworthy (1996, 23–4).

41 See Mann (1983, 52–5).

42 Tacitus, *Annals*, 13.7.

43 Ibid., 35.

44 Tacitus, *Histories*, 2.57.

45 Ibid., 21; see also Keppie (1997, 95).

46 Tacitus, *Histories*, 2.82.

47 Ibid., 3.50.

48 Mann (1983, 53).

49 Ibid.

50 *AE*, 1969–70, 633, with 1955, 238; Mann (1983, 46–7); Alston (1995, 44) argues that the inscription indicates normal recruiting policy. However, this idea seems to be contradicted by the other evidence for recruitment in Egypt.

51 Cf. Mann (1963), arguing that all new legions were raised in Italy; Brunt, *SCI* (1974, 97–9). Note the evidence for the levying of troops in Italy under Marcus Aurelius between 163 and 166 (*ILS*, 1098), and under Septimius Severus (*CIL*, X 1127), both possibly connected with the recruitment of new legions; see Mann (1983, 63) for recruitment of I and II Italica by Marcus Aurelius, and I, II and III Parthica by Septimius Severus; Pavan (1991, 459–63) argues that the legion II Parthica stationed at Albanum in Italy had a mixture of recruits with strong representation from Italy and Pannonia. A levy conducted under Hadrian in the Transpadana region of northern Italy was probably connected with losses sustained in the Jewish revolt (*ILS*, 1068). See also Keppie (1997, 99).

52 Dio, 55.31, 56.23; Velleius, 2.111; Tacitus, *Annals*, 1.31.

53 *Annals*, 1.16.

54 Brunt, *ZPE* (1974), implying also the recruiting of freedmen; see also Pliny, *Natural History*, 7.149; Suetonius, *Augustus*, 25.

55 75.2.5.

56 See Le Roux (1982, 93–6).

57 See Cheesman (1914, 57–85); Kraft (1951); Saddington (1975); Holder (1980).

58 Roymans (1996, 20–4).

59 Tacitus, *Histories* 4.12–15. The legionary fortress at Vetra (Xanten) came under prolonged assault as the Batavi had learned Roman siege methods (4.21–3). The remaining troops eventually surrendered to Civilis, and the camp was destroyed (4.60).

60 Roymans (op. cit., 40–1). Note that Roymans argues that in the pre-Flavian first century AD the Roman army was closely interwoven with Batavian society and that Batavian soldiers continued to 'function in the organisational structures of their own community'.

61 See also Chapter 4.

62 Kraft (1951, 43–68).

63 Kraft (ibid., 50–1) argues that *auxilia* recruiting came to have a more strictly local basis.

64 *Agricola*, 32, in the speech he gives to the British chief, Calgacus.

65 Cheesman (1914, 83–4).

66 Tacitus, *Annals*, 4.4.

67 *Annals*, 1.17.

68 Brunt *SCI* (1974, 111–14).

69 When the troops of Vitellius burst into Rome in AD 69, they were amazed at the city and crowds of people, who in turn thought that the soldiers had an extraordinary appearance (Tacitus, *Histories*, 2.88).

70 *ILS*, 2671.

71 See further below, pp. 35–6. Gilliam (1986, 282) estimates that in the east between Augustus and Caracalla about 600,000 men received Roman citizenship as a result of military service.

72 Note Tiberius' low opinion of Italian volunteers (above, n. 66).

73 Pliny, *Letters*, 10.30.

74 Some letters are translated in Campbell (1994, 13–14, 30–1, 33, 89); Alston (1995, ch. 7); for the military bureaucracy, see Daris (1964); Fink (1971).

75 Adams (1994).

76 Adams (1999), on two centurion poets at Bu Njem.

77 See below, Chapter 5.

78 52.25.6.

79 52.27.4, cf. n. 66.

80 49.16.2.1, 49.16.4.1–9.

81 See above, n. 55.

82 75.2.6.

83 Campbell (1984, 365–71).

84 68.7.5, 54.25.6.

85 Velleius' praise of the Roman soldier (2.112.5) is based on his fighting qualities in a crisis.

86 See Cornell, in Rich and Shipley (1993, 164–8). But Alston (1995, 100–1) argues for the deep involvement of the soldiers in civilian society and a substantial level of integration, at least in Egypt. For discussion of what has been described as 'the military participation rate', see Chapter 5, pp. 106, 115.

87 For discussion of modern armies, see above, n. 1. For the Roman army, see esp. MacMullen, *Historia* (1984); Lee, in Lloyd (1996); Goldsworthy (1996, 248–82).

88 Note that Aristotle (*Nicomachean Ethics*, 1116b) discussed whether courage might be equated with experience of what was likely to happen in battle. Thus professional soldiers 'faced dangers on the assumption that they were stronger'.

89 For booty see Goldsworthy (1996, 259–61).

90 See M.A. Speidel (1992); Alston (1994). A legionary under Augustus received 900 sesterces annually, rising to 1200 under Domitian, and about 1800 under Septimius Severus.

91 Discussion in Alston (1995, 106–7); for soldiers' wealth see Campbell (1984, 176–81). Auxiliary cavalrymen could be quite well off. Longinus Biarta, a Thracian cavalryman in the Ala Sulpicia, had an expensive tomb monument at Colonia Agrippina (Cologne) in Upper Germany (*CIL*, 13.8312; see cover illustration).

92 For colonies of veterans, see Chapter 4, pp. 101–4.

93 Campbell (1984, 311–14).

94 See Webster (1969, 195–7, 248–54); Davies (1970, 1972, 1989).

95 Campbell (1984, 210–36).

96 Campbell (1978, 1984, 439–45).

97 See further below, pp. 45–6.

98 See Swoboda (1958); Mócsy (1974, 126–9, 139–40, 218–19); below, Chapter 4, p. 97.

99 See Curchin (1991, 74–7); Richardson (1996, 181–9). Note that legion VI Victrix was in Spain from 30 BC to AD 69.

100 *CIL*, 2.5084 = *AE*, 1974.390.

101 See Chapter 4, p. 97.

102 It is unlikely, however, that it was deliberate government policy to foster fighting spirit in the army. See also above, p. 27, on the limitations of local loyalties.

103 Tacitus, *Histories*, 2.80 (translation by K. Wellesley (Penguin, 1964, p. 129)). Tacitus also points out that they had formed liaisons or 'marriages' with local women.

104 Herodian, 6.7.3. There was a similar incident in the Late Empire when Julian (AD 361–3) enlisted locals on the promise that they would not have to serve beyond the Alps; they rebelled at the prospect of being sent to the eastern frontier and leaving their families unprotected (Ammianus, 20.4.4, 10).

105 See in general Jones (1964); Williams (1985); Southern and Dixon (1996).

106 This is part of the speech that Livy attributes to Aemilius Paulus before the battle of Pydna in 168 BC (44.39.5).

107 Goldsworthy (1996, 264–71) discusses to what extent individual acts of bravery by Roman soldiers were inspired by a wish to impress or emulate their comrades; see also below, n. 111. There is no evidence that the Romans relied on the stimulation of alcohol in battle.

108 *AE*, 1928.27.

109 Campbell (1984, 32–9); below, pp. 41–2.

110 Richmond (1962, 146–8).

111 For the importance of unit cohesion, see Goldsworthy (1996, 252–7). For parallels in modern armies, see Holmes (1985, 290–315). Note also MacMullen, *Historia* (1984), 448.

112 Scholars are not in agreement about this; but, given the tactical importance of the cohort, it is difficult to believe that it did not have its own standard; cf. Parker (1958, 36–42); Webster (1969, 134–41); Connolly (1981, 218–19). Tacitus (*Annals*, 1.18) refers to 'standards of the cohorts'.

113 For unit rivalry see Goldsworthy, in Goldsworthy and Haynes (1999, 202).

114 II Augusta, III Augusta, III Cyrenaica, III Gallica, IV Scythica, V Macedonica, VI Ferrata, VI Victrix, VII (subsequently called Claudia), VIII Augusta, IX Hispana (destroyed in second century), X Fretensis, X Gemina, XI (subsequently called Claudia), XII Fulminata, XIII Gemina, XIV Gemina, XV Apollinaris, XX Valeria Victrix, XXII Deiotariana (destroyed in the second century).

115 The religious aura of the eagles appears in the story of how the rebellion against Claudius by Scribonianus, governor of Dalmatia, petered out when the soldiers could not adorn them or move the standards (Suetonius, *Claudius*, 13.2); see also below, n. 45.

116 *Res Gestae*, 29.2.

117 The *vexillum* also served as a cavalry standard and had a role in the legion; see Webster (1969, 139–40). In the later empire the *draco* standard was adopted, which had a hollow, open-mouthed dragon's head to which was attached a long tube of material that hissed in the wind (Ammianus, 16.10.7).

118 Tacitus, *Annals*, 1.18.

119 There were also *cohortes equitatae* containing infantry and cavalry, probably in the proportion of 4:1; see Keppie (1984, 182–3).

120 Vegetius, *Epitome of Military Science*, 2.5. This oath probably dates from the late empire; see Milner (1993, 35); Campbell (1984, 23–32).

121 Much of this is described by Vegetius (Milner (1993, 10–18)), who, although writing in the fourth century AD, was probably using a medley of information gleaned from earlier periods. For the importance of drill in building morale in all armies, see Holmes (1985, 36–49, esp. 43): 'Not only does it [close-order drill] make men look like soldiers, but, far more important, it makes them feel like soldiers.'

122 Tacitus, *Histories*, 1.38.

123 *AE*, 1979.643 = Campbell (1994, no. 181; also nos 180, 182–4).

124 Campbell (1994, 136–9).

125 *RIB*, 200. Note also the memorial of Longinus Biarta (above, n. 91).

126 Campbell (1984, 303–10). For desertion, see also Goldsworthy (1996, 251).

127 Suetonius, *Augustus*, 24. Other generals made their reputation by strict enforcement of discipline, e.g. Domitius Corbulo (Tacitus, *Annals*, 13.35–6), Ulpius Marcellus (Dio, 72.8.2–5), Pontius Laelianus (Fronto, ed. Haines (Loeb), 2, 148).

128 Note, however, the measures for the return of deserters after Marcus Aurelius' northern wars (Dio, 71.11.2, 13.2, 72.2).

129 *Jewish War*, 3.72–6. Tacitus believed that it was *Romana disciplina* that distinguished the Roman army from its German opponents (*Germania*, 30). Like all generalizations, these should be treated with some caution, but can be taken as what had impressed these writers about aspects of Roman military practice.

130 See Maxfield (1981); for some examples, see Campbell (1994, 104–7). Polybius (6.39) describes the importance attached to military rewards in the Republic, emphasizing the public honour and the encouragement for soldiers to emulate the exploits of others.

131 Pontiroli (1971).

132 Josephus, *Jewish War*, 7.13–16. See in general Goldworthy (1996, 276–9).

133 Ibid. and cf. *ILS*, 7178 = Campbell (1994, no. 92).

134 *CIL*, 16.160 = Campbell (1994, no. 326); see in general Maxfield (1981, 218–35).

135 Their duties were: 'to keep the soldiers in camp, to lead them out for exercises, to keep the keys of the gates, to inspect the guards regularly, to look after the soldiers' rations, to check the corn, to prevent fraud by the measurers, to punish offences in accordance with the level of their authority, to be present frequently at the headquarters building, to hear the complaints of the soldiers, to inspect the hospitals' (*Digest*, 49.16.12.2).

136 *Agricola*, 5.

137 *ILS*, 1098. He was governor of Dacia, killed *c.* AD 170.

138 That of course suited the emperor because it made it more difficult for commanders to become popular enough to foment revolts among their men; see Chapter 5.

139 See above, p. 36.

140 For the career and role of centurions, see Dobson, in Breeze and Dobson (1993, 201–17). Some centurions, however, were appointed straight from civilian life, sometimes by exercise of patronage (Goldsworthy 1996, 31–2). For the appointment of auxiliary centurions, see Gilliam (1986, 191–205).

141 As such they often bore the brunt of the soldiers' rage when discipline broke down, as in AD 14 and 68 to 69; see Campbell (1984, 101–9). The symbol of the centurion's rank was the vine stick (*vitis*), which can be seen on the tombstone of M. Favonius Facilis from Colchester (above, n. 125).

142 56.13. Note also that Titus observed the siege of the Temple at Jerusalem from the captured fortress of Antonia 'so that none of the courageous might go unnoticed and without reward' (Josephus, *Jewish War*, 6.133–4).

143 Herodian, 2.11.2

144 M.P. Speidel, *Roman Army Studies* (1992, 306).

145 For this theme see Campbell (1984, 32–59).

146 Campbell (1984, 76–88); Lepper and Frere (1988), scene x, plate XI; Goldsworthy (1996, 145–8). Note also that the theme of the imperial speech before battle is a common feature of the sculptures on Trajan's column (see below, Chapter 6). Hansen (1993) maintains that the details of such speeches in ancient historiography were usually fictitious.

147 According to Josephus, *Jewish War*, 6.33, 7.5–6.

148 Herodian, 7.2.6–7. Campbell (1984, 59–69).

149 For a survey of religion in the Roman army, see Watson (1969, 127–33); *Diz. epig.* s.v. *legio*, 616–18; Helgeland (1978); E. Birley (1978); Campbell (1994, 127–39).

150 *ILS*, 4795. He may have been on the Parthian campaign of Lucius Verus in AD 162–6.

151 See Lepper and Frere (1988, scene viii, plates IX–X.).

152 *RIB*, 2139.

153 *ILS*, 451.

154 See Beard *et al.* (1998, vol. 1, 324–8); translation in Campbell (1994, 127–30).

155 For the importance of standards in the army, see above, p. 38.

156 *ILS*, 2355 = Campbell (1994, no. 218).

157 Edmonds (1988, 34).

158 *AE*, 1985.735.

3 THE NATURE OF WAR

1 *ILS*, 939, set up on Mt Eryx in Sicily.

2 Keegan (1993, 267).

3 See Campbell (1987).

4 See further below, pp. 61–5.

5 Goldsworthy (1996, 39–68) discusses the nature of the Germans, Gauls and Parthians, who fought against the Romans in this period, but the information he uses is largely derived from Roman sources.

6 Keegan (1976, 61–8). In my view Keegan's criticism of Caesar's *Gallic War* (2.25) is misconceived. (The same passage of Caesar is cited by Keegan (1993, 269) as 'a graphic depiction of the reality of legionary warfare'.) This is an

exceptional case of personal intervention by Caesar in a serious crisis, and he attempts to explain what happened when many centurions had been killed, a battle line began to give way, and more and more soldiers started to slip away from the action. He does not in fact suggest that legionaries were automatons, but enough remained in position to hold the line. The comparison with Thucydides' battle description is unhelpful since this was a different (hoplite) battle, the experience and character of the troops were different, and the role of the commander was different.

7   Woodman (1979) argued that Tacitus, for example, in his description of the discovery of the site of Varus' defeat (*Annals*, 1.61–2), effectively invented the details, which he derived from a passage of the *Histories* about the scene after the battle of Cremona. I am entirely unconvinced that tangential literary similarities in passages with related themes amount to 'substantive imitation'.

8   See Goldsworthy (1996), for the theme of the Roman army's experience in battle; he places particular emphasis on individual soldiers and how they react to the stress of conflict; also Lee, in Lloyd (1996); Sabin (2000).

9   There were twenty-five legions in AD 14, and thirty-three in the second century. For *auxilia* see Holder (1980).

10   See Chapter 2, p. 25. *Cohortes equitatae* (Chapter 2, n. 119) apparently did not fight as a composite tactical group.

11   Dio, 68.32.

12   Evidence in Cheesman (1914, Appendix 1); Holder (1980, 7–13); Saddington (1975).

13   Vegetius, 2.25.

14   Dio, 71.16.2.

15   Jones (1964, 619–23); de Ste Croix (1981, 509–18).

16   In general see Braund (1984).

17   *Alexandrine War*, 34.4

18   Strabo, 16.4.23 (780).

19   *Ectaxis*, 7; translation in Campbell (1994, no. 153). It is not clear what use the Romans made of local militias, which were of very uncertain quality and reliability; see E. Birley (1988, 387–94).

20   See in general Starr (1960; 1989, 67–81); Reddé (1986).

21   Josephus, *Jewish War*, 2.507–8.

22   Tacitus, *Annals*, 1.60, 63, 2.5–6, 23–5.

23   For example, Trajan's campaign in AD 116 (Dio, 68.26).

24   Tacitus, *Histories*, 3.25.

25   See in general Isaac (1992, 77–89; ch. III); see also Alston (1995, 74–9).

26   See Campbell (1987); also Goldsworthy (1996, 141–5).

27   See above, Chapter 2, p. 36.

28   Figures cited by Goldsworthy (1996, 138). See further below, p. 57, for the space required by a legionary. In this formation two centuries (eighty men in each) could line up side by side, with the remaining four centuries in the two ranks behind. M.P. Speidel (1992, 20–2) suggested that each century formed a line four deep and was deployed one behind the other, producing a width of twenty files and a depth of twenty-four ranks in the unit. But in open battle this depth would be excessive and would unreasonably limit the number of soldiers who could get to grips with the enemy.

29   Goldsworthy (op. cit., 140) calculates that the frontage of a legion with three cohorts of 480 and one of 800 in the front line would be about 1125 m (allowing for gaps between the cohorts).

30   See discussion in Goldsworthy (op. cit., 137–9, 176–83).

31   See the convenient summary in ibid., 22.

32 *Ectaxis*, 1, 3; translation in Campbell (1994, 92).
33 See Goldsworthy (op. cit., 133–7).
34 Tacitus, *Annals*, 14.34; Dio (62.8.2–3) thought that the enemy's overwhelming numerical superiority forced Paulinus to ensure that the three parts of his army could fight independently.
35 Tacitus, *Annals*, 2.16–17; see also Campbell (1987, 28–9).
36 Dio, 75.7.
37 At the battle of Mons Graupius, Agricola sent away his horse and stood in front of the standards, just behind the main battle line of auxiliaries (Tacitus, *Agricola*, 35.4). For the question of morale, see Chapter 2, pp. 34–46.
38 Goldsworthy (op. cit., 150–63).
39 Onasander, *Art of the General*, 25.2. Onasander was writing in the first century AD.
40 Arrian, *Ectaxis*, 14–24; translation in Campbell (1994, 97–8); see also Goldsworthy (op. cit., 131–3, 140–1).
41 See further below, p. 56.
42 They are represented on Trajan's column; see Richmond (1982, 17, and plate 3); Lepper and Frere (1988), scene XL, plate XXXI.
43 *Histories*, 3.23 (translated by K. Wellesley (Penguin, 1964), p. 159).
44 Tacitus, *Annals*, 3.74.
45 Coulston, in Freeman and Kennedy (1986); Campbell (1987, 24–7).
46 See Keegan (1976, 185–6), referring to the battle of Waterloo.
47 See Chapter 2, pp. 36–46.
48 Frontinus, *Stratagems*, 2.4.1, 3.
49 For the role of the commander in battle, see Goldsworthy (1996, ch. 4).
50 See e.g. Frontinus, *Stratagems*, 1.11, 12, 2.4, 7, 8, 3.15; Onasander, *Art of the General*, 1.13–14, 33.6. For an analysis of this work, emphasizing the importance of character and moral rectitude in the general, see Smith, in Austin *et al.* (1998). For speeches by generals to their army, see Chapter 2, p. 42. In the Republic it seems that military defeat was not necessarily damaging to a commander's career if he had led courageously and displayed personal *virtus*: Rosenstein (1990).
51 Onasander, *Art of the General*, 13.2.
52 Plutarch, *Marius*, 16.
53 *Germania*, 43.5.
54 *Gallic War*, 1.39.
55 Plutarch, *Crassus*, 23.
56 For soldiers' morale see Goldsworthy (op. cit., ch. 6).
57 Bishop and Coulston (1993, 48–50). Modern experiments suggest that the *pilum* when thrown from a range of 5m (16ft) can pierce 30mm (1in.) of pinewood or 20mm (3/4in.) of plywood (Junkelmann 1986, 188–9).
58 Note also Goldsworthy (op. cit., 217–18); pictorial evidence shows Roman soldiers using various different cuts and thrusts. Sabin (2000, 10–17) argues that close-range sword-fighting could not be carried on for long. Contact was likely to be sporadic as battle lines separated, and fresh fighters could come in from the next line. See further below, p. 60 (n. 81).
59 Vegetius, 3.15, with discussion in Goldsworthy (op. cit., 179–80).
60 Bishop and Coulston (1993, 92–3).
61 Ibid., 85–7.
62 Ibid., 81–4; see also Goldsworthy (op. cit., 209–12); for changes in equipment in the late second to third centuries, see Coulston, in Austin *et al.* (1998, 177–8).
63 See Bishop and Coulston (op. cit., 206–9). They argue that auxiliaries did not usually wear *lorica segmentata*. See Goldsworthy (op. cit., 19–20) for the fighting methods of auxiliaries.

64 For the range of the composite bow see Goldsworthy (op. cit., 184); slingers: ibid., 186; Celsus, *On Medicine*, 7.55.

65 In a speech put into his mouth by Tacitus, *Annals*, 2.14.

66 Hyland (1993); Dixon and Southern (1992, 113–34). The *Strategicon* or *Handbook* on military strategy usually attributed to the reign of the Byzantine emperor Maurice in the sixth century AD contains several brief Latin commands for cavalry (3.5), which might go back to Roman times: charge at gallop; follow in order; give way; turn, threaten; to the left, change front; to the right, change front; about face; change place (translation in Dennis (1984, 39)).

67 *Ars Tactica*, 37.

68 Ibid., 43. Roman cavalry were seemingly usually armed with lance and sword (see Roger Tomlin, in Goldsworthy and Haynes (1999, 136)).

69 *ILS*, 2487; translation in Campbell (1994, 19). He also advised cavalry from another unit to be careful while riding out from cover to engage in pursuit.

70 Discussion in Goldsworthy (1996, 182–3), who reckons that a cavalryman would need a space of 1m wide by about 4m deep; see also Hyland (1993, 78–88); Dixon and Southern (1992, 137–47). Cavalrymen in the ancient world did not have stirrups, but recent research has demonstrated that Roman saddles were cleverly designed to give the rider maximum support (Dixon and Southern, op. cit., 70–4).

71 Bishop and Coulston (1993, 93–5, 145–8); Goldsworthy (op. cit., 237–44).

72 Josephus, *Jewish War*, 3.16–18.

73 Eadie (1967); M.P. Speidel, *Epigraphica Anatolica* (1984).

74 See above, p. 56.

75 Tacitus, *Germania*, 3.

76 *Ectaxis*, 25. See in general Goldsworthy (op. cit., 195–7).

77 Dio, 62.12.1–2.

78 See *War in Africa*, 82. Tacitus, *Annals*, 1.68. Caesar, *Civil Wars* (3.92), noted that good commanders should encourage and not restrain their men's ardour for fighting, and commended the old custom of blowing trumpets and shouting out as battle was joined because this terrified the enemy and encouraged your own side.

79 *Spanish War*, 31.6.

80 Dio, 60.20. Caesar mentions a battle against Alpine tribes lasting for six hours continuously (*Gallic War*, 3.5).

81 See Goldsworthy (op. cit., 224); see also Sabin (2000, 11–17) on the duration of battles.

82 Dio, 65.12–13.

83 Ibid., 75.7.6.

84 Tacitus, *Histories*, 3.23.

85 Tacitus, *Annals*, 1.64.

86 Tacitus, *Agricola*, 37.

87 See above, p. 47.

88 Josephus, *Jewish War*, 2.542–55; translation from Campbell (1994, 95–7); see also Gichon (1981); Goldsworthy (op. cit., 84–90) gives possible reasons for Cestius Gallus' retreat: he had only a hastily raised force, he expected a quick success, and he did not have enough troops for a long siege when his first attack failed. Cestius had already suffered a set-back on the way to Jerusalem when a sudden Jewish attack broke through the Roman lines and the legion XII Fulminata lost its eagle (Josephus, *Jewish War*, 2.517–19; Suetonius, *Vespasian*, 4.5).

89 For the career of Josephus during the rebellion, see Rajak (1983, 144–73).

90 Tacitus, *Agricola*, 35–7. The exact site of the battle is unknown.

91 The translation of this sentence depends on the text and interpretation of Ogilvie and Richmond (1967, 276–7).

92   For the pursuit, see above, p. 61.
93   *Agricola*, 38.
94   Livy, 31.34.4.
95   Wheeler (1943, 118–20, 351–6); Marsden (1971).
96   *On Medicine*, 7.5. Another doctor was Galen, court physician under Marcus
     Aurelius, who was summoned to provide skilled medical treatment at the front
     (14.649–50); he also warned medical assistants in the German wars of Marcus
     Aurelius not to dissect the bodies of dead German soldiers in order to improve
     their knowledge of anatomy (13.604).
97   6.87. Paul of Aegina was a physician living in the seventh century AD who
     wrote several works on medical procedures, in which he seemingly borrowed
     extensively from earlier writers. He also discussed fractures and dislocations,
     probably caused in battle.
98   Scarborough (1969, Pl. 18).
99   Discussion in Scarborough (op. cit., 66–75); Davies (1970, 1972).
100 See Scarborough (op. cit., Pl. 19; also this volume, Pl. 3.1). The Byzantine army
     had medical corpsmen whose job it was to pick up and give assistance to men
     wounded in action (*Strategicon*, 2.9; see Dennis (1984, 29–30)).
101 Dio, 68.8.2.
102 Tacitus, *Annals*, 1.65.
103 Dio, 68.14.2. There is doubtless a measure of exaggeration in this story.
104 For Roman military hospitals, see Webster (1969, 195–7, 216–17).
105 For the danger of infection from penetrative wounds, see Keegan (1976, 112–14).
106 6.87. See also Celsus, *On Medicine*, 5.26C.
107 Strabo, 16.4.24 (782).
108 *Civil Wars*, 2.44.
109 Josephus, *Jewish War*, 3.19, 25.
110 *Jewish War*, 2.555; see above, p. 63.
111 *Agricola*, 37. There were 8000 auxiliary infantry, and about 5000 cavalry engaged
     in the battle; the legions present were not used.
112 Tacitus, *Annals*, 14.37. Tacitus merely cites the battle casualties as 'according to
     one report'. During the course of Boudicca's rebellion Tacitus says that there
     were about 70,000 civilian deaths. Note that during the minor rebellion of
     the Frisii tribe in AD 29 more than 900 Roman soldiers were killed, and 400
     who were trapped committed suicide (*Annals*, 4.73).
113 75.8.
114 Herodian notes that in their civil war accounts 'contemporary historians vary
     the total number of prisoners and casualties on either side to suit their own
     purposes' (3.7.6).
115 Scotland – 76.13.2. Cremona – 64.10.3. Elsewhere he says that 50,000 died
     in the sack of Cremona and the second battle (65.15.2). Another suspiciously
     round figure is 50,000 deaths during the Flavian assault on Rome (65.19.3).
116 See Chapter 1, n. 45.
117 *OCD*³, s.v. legion.
118 Tacitus, *Annals*, 1.62. Tacitus' emotive writing shows the significance of this
     event for his audience.
119 *ILS*, 9107; Richmond (1982) believes the altar to date from Domitian's reign;
     the third monument is a trophy (*Tropaeum*): see Lepper and Frere (1988, 295–304).
120 Dio, 68.8. Some have identified this with the *Tropaeum* at Adamklissi; see Lepper
     and Frere, op. cit.
121 See Appian, *Civil Wars*, 1.43.
122 Tacitus, *Histories*, 2.45, 70; Suetonius, *Vitellius*, 10.3; Dio, 65.1.3 (on the dead
     left unburied after the battle of Cremona). Tacitus, *Annals*, 4.73 – the Roman
     commander fails to bury the Roman dead after a battle against the Frisii.

123   *Agricola*, 35.
124   Velleius, 2.104.4. For examples in the Republic, see Goldsworthy (1996, 167).
125   69.14.
126   See Jones, in Mattingly (1997, 185).
127   See Goldsworthy (op. cit., 246–7).
128   *Germania*, 4, 20, 30.
129   See above, Chapter 2, p. 41.
130   Tacitus, *Annals*, 3.20–1; see also Chapter 2, n. 127.
131   See Chapter 2, p. 39.
132   For the problems of the Germans and others in fighting the Romans, see Goldsworthy (op. cit., 73–4).
133   For scouting see Austin and Rankov (1995); camps – Keppie (1984, 36–8); Goldsworthy (op. cit., 111–13); marching column – Josephus gives an excellent description of how Vespasian marched into Galilee (*Jewish War*, 3.115–26). First came auxiliary light-armed troops and archers to scout and deal with sudden attacks, then units of heavily-armed legionary infantry and a force of cavalry, then ten men from each century to survey and mark out the camp, then soldiers equipped to clear the route, then the baggage of Vespasian and his staff, escorted by cavalry, then Vespasian and his personal guards, then the cavalry of the legions, then the siege train, then the legates, prefects and tribunes escorted by picked troops, then the eagles and other standards followed by trumpeters, then each legion marching six abreast, accompanied by one(?) centurion to superintend the ranks, then the servants and baggage animals, then auxiliaries, then a rearguard of light and heavy infantry and auxiliary cavalry. See also Connolly (1981, 238). Note also Titus' marching column on the way to Jerusalem (Josephus, *Jewish War*, 5.47–50); Arrian's arrangement for marching out against the Alani (*Ectaxis*, 1–11; translation in Campbell (1994, 92–3)); Goldsworthy (op. cit., 105–11).
134   2.112.6. Of course, military tradition and legend probably outdistanced reality. The Romans liked to think that their troops would always fight to the end, and indeed sometimes they did (Tacitus, *Annals*, 4.73; Josephus, *Jewish War*, 6.185–8). But they did surrender and sometimes ran away ignominiously (e.g. Tacitus, *Annals*, 15.16; *Histories*, 4.60).
135   Diplomatic contact was possible (e.g. the First Dacian War ended on terms, with a formal treaty). See in general Campbell (2001).
136   Dio, 51.23–4.
137   Dio, 55.29–30; Velleius, 2.115. Note also that the Cantabri and Astures in Spain were subdued with enormous casualties (Dio, 54.5, 11).
138   Tacitus, *Annals*, 1.51.
139   Ibid., 1.56.
140   Ibid., 2.17–18. Note the extermination of the British after the defeat of Boudicca: 'The Romans did not spare even the women. Baggage animals also, pierced with weapons, added to the piles of dead' (ibid., 14.37).
141   Dio, 67.4.6.
142   Ibid., 54.22.4–5.
143   Ibid., 54.31.
144   Smallwood (1967, no. 228); translation in Braund (1985, no. 401).
145   1.39.7.
146   Josephus, *Jewish War*, 7.153–5.
147   10.15.4–6.
148   For Roman siege warfare, see Marsden (1969); Webster (1969, 230–45); Connolly (1981, 292–300); see also above, n. 95.
149   Jerusalem – *Jewish War*, 5.54–6.409; Masada – *Jewish War*, 7.252–3, 275–406.

150 Josephus, *Jewish War*, 3.141–339, esp. 271–8.
151 Ibid., 336–8.
152 *Stratagems*, 2.9.2–3, 5.
153 Tacitus, *Annals*, 12.17.
154 Ibid.
155 *Jewish War*, 2.362. For Josephus' attitude towards the war, see Rajak (1983, 78–103); Goodman (1987, 5–25).
156 See Levick (1999, 101).
157 *Annals*, 11.9, 12.50.
158 See now Roth (1999).
159 Chevallier (1989, ch. 3).
160 See above, pp. 49–50.
161 Velleius, 2.114.
162 See above, pp. 66–8.
163 *Annals*, 15.16.
164 Campbell (1984, 311–14).
165 *ILS*, 2244.

4 WAR AND THE COMMUNITY

1 1.28–9.
2 *Oration*, 26 (*To Rome*), 67, 72, 87. Cf. also Velleius, 2.126.3; Epictetus, 3.13.9.
3 Dobson, in Breeze and Dobson (1993, 113–28), distinguishes between a wartime and a peacetime army on the basis that a wartime army is mobilized for specific hostilities; therefore the army of the empire is a peacetime army in which warfare did not change the essential nature of army organization.
4 For the question of recruiting see Chapter 2.
5 See Chapter 1, pp. 15–16.
6 For example, the community of the Treveri in Germany set up an inscription in honour of Septimius Severus and his son Caracalla, in which they celebrated the legion XXII Primigenia 'for its glorious valour because it had defended them during a siege' (*ILS*, 419).
7 *Tiberius*, 41.
8 See Chapter 1, n. 45.
9 Dio, 56.23 (henceforth in Chapter 4 references to Dio mean Cassius Dio); Suetonius, *Augustus*, 23.2; *Tiberius*, 17.2.
10 Dio, 67.6–7; Suetonius, *Domitian*, 6; Jones (1992, 126–59).
11 *Agricola*, 41.2.
12 71.36.3.
13 Ammianus Marcellinus, 29.6.1.
14 A. Birley (1987, 163–9); Pausanias, 10.34.5; Richardson (1996, 231–5). There was also trouble in the east in the 160s, when the governor of Cappadocia, Sedatius Severianus, became embroiled with the Parthians and was defeated with the loss of a legion.
15 Mócsy (1974, 194).
16 Alföldy (1974, 152–4, cf. 180), suggesting a diminution in the circulation of coinage after the Marcomannic Wars. Disturbances in Dalmatia – Wilkes (1969, 85–6, 117–19).
17 *Digest*, 50.10.6.
18 *ILS*, 2287; I and II cohorts of Dalmatians also took part (*ILS*, 2616–17).
19 *CIL*, 3.7409.
20 Millar (1967, 217 and pl. 21).
21 See Chapter 3, pp. 53–5.

22 72.8.2; *Augustan History, Life of Commodus*, 13.5.

23 Herodian, 6.7.2–3 (by *Illyricum* Herodian probably means Noricum and Raetia); and see Chapter 2, p. 35 (soldiers' families).

24 For a general account, see Parker (1958, 141–220); Jones (1964, 21–36); Williams (1985, 15–23); Cameron (1993, 1–12).

25 Roman writers believed that he had been murdered by his praetorian prefect, Philip. However, the Persian tradition was that he was wounded in battle.

26 For a summary of the evidence, see Whittaker, in Finley (1976, 151–63); he warns that we should not exaggerate the extent of the devastation and dislocation of the empire in this period. See also Mócsy (1974, 263–5); Alföldy (1974, 169–71); by contrast, Dalmatia does not seem to have suffered extensively (Wilkes, 1969, 416). Spain – Richardson (1996, 249–56); Gaul – Drinkwater (1983, 212–27), also suggesting that the economic and social dislocation in Gaul may have been exaggerated, at least until the 270s. Mauretania – see below, n. 43.

27 See Campbell (1984, 365–71). Ash (1999) offers an analysis of the leaders and armies in AD 68 to 69 through the narratives of ancient writers, especially Tacitus. She argues that the soldiers mistrusted their immediate officers and that the self-destructive forces were generated by a combination of 'flawed emperors and frustrated armies' (169).

28 Tacitus, *Histories*, 1.51. For the sack of Cremona, see *Histories*, 3.33–4.

29 *Histories*, 1.63.

30 Ibid., 2.12–13; *Agricola*, 7.

31 *Histories*, 2.56, 87–8.

32 Ibid., 3.71–2, 83–4; for the effect of warfare on the food supply in Rome, see Garnsey (1988, 228–9).

33 Dio, 75.10–14.

34 See Drinkwater (1983, 81–2).

35 See in general Dyson (1971, 1975).

36 Tacitus, *Annals*, 4.72–4.

37 See Chapter 3, p. 53. Note also the rebellion of Florus and Sacrovir in Gaul (*Annals*, 3.40–6).

38 See Chapter 3, p. 69. For evidence of destruction in Britain (burnt glass, pottery and coins) see Ogilvie and Richmond (1967, 199–200).

39 Dio, 71.4.

40 See in general Smallwood (1976); Schürer (1973–87, 1. 529–34); disturbances in Egypt – Alston (1995, 75–7). The revolt in Hadrian's reign saw more than half a million war casualties alone on the Jewish side; see Chapter 3, p. 70; A. Birley (1997, 268–76).

41 *Digest*, 49.15.24.

42 See MacMullen (1966, 192–241, 255–68) Shaw (1984); Hopwood, in Wallace-Hadrill (1989); Isaac (1992, 77–89); piracy – Braund, in Rich and Shipley (1993); De Souza (1999, 179–224).

43 *ILS*, 2479 – military action in Numidia. Cornelius Fronto, preparing for his governorship of Asia, summoned from Mauretania one Julius Senex, who was expert in hunting down and suppressing bandits (Haines (Loeb), Vol. 1, p. 236).

44 Dio, 76.10. One of his famous sayings was: 'Feed your slaves so that they do not turn into brigands.'

45 Herodian, 1.10; *Augustan History, Life of Commodus*, 16.2.

46 See Shaw (1984, 41).

47 Isaac (1992, 77–89). There is, however, some dispute over the reliability of Rabbinic sources (see Mor, in Freeman and Kennedy (1986, 586–7)).

48 Shaw (1984, 16). For the provincial militia in the east, see Isaac (1992, 325–7).

49 See MacMullen (1966, esp. 256–61); Shaw, op. cit., 12.
50 *ILS*, 395.
51 *AE*, 1934.209. For a collection of such evidence, see Shaw, op. cit., 10, n. 25.
52 52.27–8.
53 Tacitus, *Annals*, 1.11.
54 54.25.5–6.
55 77.9.
56 77.10.4.
57 78.36.3.
58 Dio, 80.18.4.
59 4.4.7.
60 Herodian, 6.8.4–8.
61 Tacitus, *Annals*, 1.17. Certainly the government apparently made sure that it paid up on time, even though the mechanism for this is obscure. It was presumably a major preoccupation of imperial procurators to get sufficient cash to the military camps. According to Suetonius (*Nero*, 32) Nero allowed the army's pay to fall into arrears, but this may be a generalization from a single incident. It is hard to believe that Nero could have survived for fourteen years and retained the support of the army if this had been a common occurrence.
62 Dio, 67.3.5.
63 Attempts to calculate the cost of the army – Hopkins (1980, 124–5); MacMullen, *Latomus* (1984), Campbell (1984, 161–76). More recent discussions have reassessed the details of military pay – M.A.Speidel (1992); Alston (1994), who has argued convincingly that the pay of the auxiliary infantry and cavalry was on a par with the legionaries and legionary cavalry respectively.
64 In the following calculations (and at n. 66) a legion has been taken as 5240 men:

- **Legions** – 25 × 5240 = 131,000, paid 900 sesterces (with allowance for legionary cavalry, paid 1050 sesterces) – 118.35 million sesterces.
- **Legionary centurions** – 1350 × 13,500 sesterces, 125 *primi ordines* × 27,000 sesterces, and 25 chief centurions × 54,000 sesterces – *c.* 22.95 million sesterces (see M.A.Speidel (1992) for centurions' salaries).
- **Praetorians** – 9000 × 3000 sesterces = 27 million HS (taking no account of officers' salaries).
- **Urban cohorts** – 3000 × 1500 sesterces = 4.5 million sesterces (taking no account of officers' salaries).
- **Vigiles** – 7000 × 900 HS = 6.3 million sesterces (taking no account of officers' salaries).
- **Auxilia** – (if we accept Alston's argument (1994) that auxiliary infantry pay was comparable to that of legions and Tacitus' view that the *auxilia* were as numerous as legionaries) – 131,000 × 900 = 117.9 million sesterces (this takes no account of cavalrymen paid at higher rates or of officers' salaries (see M.A.Speidel (1992, 106)) and is therefore an underestimate).
- **Fleet** – minimum number of about 15,000 (see Starr, 1960, 16–17) × 900 HS (I assume they were paid like the *auxilia*; they are after all described as 'soldiers' in legal texts) = 13.5 million sesterces (taking no account of officers).
- **Praemia** – perhaps about 4000 legionaries discharged each year × 12,000 sesterces = 48 million sesterces; about 280 praetorians discharged each year × 20,000 sesterces HS = 5.6 million sesterces; also about 90 from urban cohorts × 15,000 sesterces = 1.35 million HS; total about 55 million sesterces. Survival rate – see Hopkins (1980, 124); Shaw (1983, 139).

65 The auxiliaries came to receive Roman citizenship as a reward for service; but how long can they have been excluded from monetary *praemia*, since they made up probably half of the armed forces?

66

- **Legions** – 5240 × 30 = 157,200 × 1200 HS = 188.64 million sesterces; add about 720,000 sesterces for 3600 legionary cavalry at 1400 sesterces; centurions – about 36 million sesterces; total – *c.* 226 million sesterces.
- **Praetorians** – 10,000 × 4000 sesterces = 40 million (taking no account of officers' salaries).
- **Urban cohorts** – 4000 × 2000 sesterces = 8 million sesterces (taking no account of officers' salaries).
- **Vigiles** – 7000 × 1200 sesterces = 8.4 sesterces (taking no account of officers); total of about 56.4 million sesterces for the urban troops.
- **Auxilia** – 180,000 × 1200 sesterces = 216 million sesterces; in this there were perhaps *c.* 50,000 cavalrymen at premium rates of 1400 sesterces = 10 million sesterces in addition; total – 226 million sesterces (taking no account of officers' salaries).
- **Fleet** – 20,000 × 1200 sesterces = 24 million sesterces.
- **Praemia** – perhaps *c.* 5000 legionaries discharged each year × 12,000 sesterces = 60 million sesterces; perhaps *c.* 300 praetorians discharged × 20,000 sesterces – 6 million sesterces.

Again this is a conservative estimate and takes no account of transport and ordnance.

67 See Chapter 5, pp. 115ff.
68 Here I follow Alston (1994), who argued that Severus raised pay by 50 per cent from 1200 to 1800 sesterces. M.A.Speidel (1992) argued for 2400 HS. On the lower estimate we have 33 legions × 5240 = 172,920 × 1800 sesterces = 311.256 million sesterces, to which we should add about 60 million sesterces for legionary centurions' pay.
69 See Chapter 2, p. 31.
70 See in general Campbell (1984, 165–71, 186–98).
71 Suetonius, *Claudius*, 10.4; see Campbell (1984, 167–8).
72 *Augustan History, Life of Marcus Aurelius*, 7.9; Campbell (1984, 170).
73 Hopkins (1978, 41 and 39 with n. 52).
74 Hopkins (1980).
75 *Res Gestae*, 17.2; Dio, 55.24.9.
76 77.9.3–5.
77 Dio, 71.3.3.
78 Dio (see Loeb edition, ix, p. 71).
79 Campbell (1994, 143–5).
80 C. Boesch, *JDAI*, 46 (1931), Arch Anz., 422; see also Burnett *et al.* (1992, 7–8).
81 Isaac (1992, 293–5); Chevallier (1989, 42–5).
82 See below, pp. 91–2.
83 For the provision of supplies to the army, see in general Rostovtzeff (1957, 357–9, 694–5, notes 4 and 6). The collection of supplies will often have involved compulsion; under Severus Alexander, Furius Timesitheus was appointed procurator of Syria Palestina and 'requisitioner of the remaining supplies for the revered expedition' (*ILS*, 1330). See MacMullen, *Latomus* (1984, 576–7), for the increased cost of supplying the army on campaign.
84 *ILS*, 5016.

85   *IGR*, 3.173.
86   *Select Papyri* (Loeb), vol. 2, no. 211. We may compare Philo's account of what the emperor Gaius' intended visit to Egypt would mean for the inhabitants (*Embassy to Gaius*, 33).
87   *Augustan History, Life of Antoninus Pius*, 7.11.
88   Lepper and Frere (1988, pls. LIX–LXIII).
89   *IGR*, 3.1054 (AD 130).
90   M.N. Tod, *Annual of the British School at Athens*, 23 (1918–19), no. 7, pp. 72–81.
91   *AE*, 1959.13, and *REG*, 72 (1959), 241; *Forsch. Eph.* iii, p. 161, no. 80. See also *Forsch. Eph.* iii, p. 155, no. 72. For the later empire a papyrus (Skeat (1964, no. 1)) dated to AD 298 deals with the intended visit of the emperor Diocletian to Egypt and the detailed provisions for this including foodstuffs required: lentils, meat, chaff, bread, barley, wheat, wine; an entire bakery was to be at the disposal of the army authorities.
92   *IGR*, 3.62 (from Prusias ad Hypium).
93   *Sylloge* (3rd edn) 869 (AD 165/9). His exotic tastes – *Augustan History, Life of Verus*, 6.9 – orchestras and singing at Corinth, hunting in Apulia.
94   *Sylloge* (3rd edn) 872 (AD 177–80).
95   Dio, 68.24–5.
96   *IGBR*, nos 1689–90.
97   *Annona militaris* – van Berchem (1937, 1977). For the cumulative impact of taxes on local communities in the east and the role of the military, especially in the third century and after, see Isaac (1992, 282–304), who exploits Talmudic sources. It is not always clear, however, that the taxes and impositions he discusses are specifically and directly for the support of the army.
98   For maps of military dispositions, see pp.19–20; the provinces were: Britain (3), Spain (1), Lower Germany (2), Upper Germany (2), Raetia (1), Noricum (1), Upper Pannonia (3), Lower Pannonia (1), Upper Moesia (2), Lower Moesia (2), Dacia (2), Cappadocia (2), Mesopotamia (2), Syria Coele (2), Syria Phoenice (1), Syria Palaestina (2), Arabia (1), Egypt (1), Numidia (1). There was also a legion stationed in Italy at Albanum, north of Rome.
99   Breeze, in Breeze and Dobson (1993, 530).
100 Isaac (1992, 33–53, 139).
101 A. Birley (1987, 169, 176–7). Book Two of Marcus' *Meditations* was written at Carnuntum. For the activity that surrounded an emperor on campaign, see Millar (1977, 3–12).
102 Nijmegen – Bogaers and Rüger (1974, 76–9); consolidation in the eastern provinces – Isaac (1992, 56–67); see also Chapter 3, pp. 72–5. I have discussed some of the following material in 'Power without limit: the Romans always win' (forthcoming).
103 The theme of the Roman army as an army of occupation is discussed in detail by Isaac (op. cit., 101–60).
104 Alston (1995, 33–8); the army and internal security – 74–9.
105 Emphasized by Isaac (op. cit., 160). But the interests of the ruled were sometimes closely linked to those of the Romans, especially in the case of the rich upper classes who ran city government for the benefit of the Romans, and profited from their social and political support.
106 Evidence in MacMullen (1963, 50–6); Isaac (op. cit., 112–13); Alston (1995, 79–86).
107 Tacitus, *Annals*, 4.15.
108 Pliny, *Letters*, 10.19–20.
109 Campbell (1984, 431–5); Davies (1989, 175–85); see now the detailed discussion in Alston (1995, 86–96).

110 Ulpian, in *Digest*, 1.18.6.5–7.
111 Pliny, *Letters*, 10.77–8.
112 For a survey of the evidence see Mitchell (1976); Campbell (1984, 246–54; 1994, 174–80); Isaac (1992, 269–310); for the problems caused by armies on the march, see also above, pp. 87–8.
113 *Discourses*, 4.1.79.
114 *On Agriculture*, 1.5.6–7.
115 *CIL*, III 12336; translation in Campbell (1994, 180).
116 *Select Papyri* (Loeb), vol. 2, no. 221; translation in Campbell (1994, 176–7).
117 Garnsey and Saller (1987, 89).
118 See Breeze, in Breeze and Dobson (1993, 530–4). See also Elton (1996, 67).
119 Whittaker (1994, 102).
120 Jones, in Vetters and Kandler (1990, 100–1); see also Garnsey and Saller (1987, 90–2).
121 *ILS*, 986.
122 Jones (op. cit.) defines three model relationships between the natives of north Britain and the Roman army: import of supplies, managing supply, and economic integration.
123 For example, the Romans imposed a tax of ox hides on the Frisii, who dwelt beyond the Rhine; a revolt occurred when a centurion interpreted this to be the hide of the auroch, or wild ox, which was bigger (Tacitus, *Annals*, 4.72).
124 Jones (op. cit., 107–8) thinks that with the exception of lowland Yorkshire northern Britain failed to achieve thorough integration into the Roman economic system, but that it was at least 'involved in the process of becoming integrated'. Breeze, in Vetters and Kandler (1990, esp. 90–5), has examined the kind of evidence we might expect to find for an expansion of cereal production – increased levels of cereal pollen, the laying out of fields for arable farming, different agricultural tools, the development of a roads network, an increasing presence of Roman goods in local farmsteads. He points out that it is very difficult to establish a clear context for this kind of evidence and to date developments precisely enough. The assessment of change would require a comparison of settlement in the Roman period with pre-Roman and post-Roman settlement.
125 Whittaker (1994, 114).
126 Cunliffe (1988, 132–44, esp. 132–3); Drinkwater (1983, ch. 6, esp. 124–35).
127 *Epitome of Military Science*, 2.11.
128 *Digest*, 50.6.7.
129 MacMullen (1963, 23–32); Breeze, in Breeze and Dobson (1993, 537–9); Whittaker (1994, 103); Coulston, in Austin *et al.* (1998, 170–5), notes the importance of regionality in the supply of weapons to the army, and cultural traditions and levels of urbanization, and argues that in the west and north legionary workshops supplied most of the army's needs up to the third century.
130 MacMullen, op. cit., 28–9.
131 Campbell (1994, no. 238). For supply of the army in Egypt, see Alston (1995, 110–12); Adams, in Goldsworthy and Haynes (1999).
132 Campbell (1994, no. 239); requisitioning in general – Garnsey and Saller (1987, 92–4); Breeze, in Breeze and Dobson (1993, 539–40).
133 Campbell (1994, no. 36).
134 See Le Roux (1977, 368–9).
135 *Digest*, 39.4.4.1, 4.9.7.
136 *FIRA*, 3, no. 137.
137 *CIL*, 3.3653 (fourth century AD). And see above, p. 89
138 There is a useful examination of the evidence by Whittaker in Barrett *et al.* (1989), 69–75; Whittaker (1994, 98–131).

139 See MacMullen (1959; 1963, 32–48); *Diz. epig.*, vol. 4, s.v. *legio*, 618–20.

140 *ILS*, 5795; translation in Campbell (1994, 125–6).

141 Fentress (1979, chs 8 and 9); see also the critical evaluation by Shaw (1983, 149–50).

142 See Breeze, in Breeze and Dobson (1993, 541–2).

143 For examples of peacetime duty rosters, see Campbell (1994, 110–17).

144 Alston (1995, 112–15) argues strongly that in Egypt the army had little impact on the economic structure of the province.

145 Livy, 43.3.

146 See Chapter 2, pp. 26–7.

147 Saller and Shaw (1984, 139–45). By contrast, at the base of the imperial fleet at Misenum, where most of the recruits came from distant areas, inscriptions tend to celebrate conjugal relationships or fellow soldiers – see Parma (1994).

148 Dobson, in Breeze and Dobson (1993, 121–2); and see Chapter 2, p. 35.

149 See Chapter 2, p. 26. Most of these women will not have been Roman citizens, and so any children will also have been non-Roman.

150 *FIRA*, III, no. 19 = Campbell (1994, no. 257(iv)) – the case concerns the children's eligibility for Alexandrian citizenship; see in general Campbell (1978; 1984, 207–29; 1994, 151–60).

151 M. Hassall, in Goldsworthy and Haynes (1999, 35–40), has suggested that some military forts contained a larger civilian element than previously supposed; but the evidence for married quarters seems very slight. See also L. Allason-Jones (in ibid., 41–51) arguing for the greater presence of women in the military zones of Britain than is usually believed; but again there is little evidence.

152 Tacitus (*Annals*, 13.35) notes that the legions in Syria had become slack and that some soldiers had never been on guard and found ramparts and ditches a novelty. However, we must allow for the conventional view that the Syrian legions tended towards indiscipline.

153 See below, p. 102.

154 For Carnuntum, see Swoboda (1958, 75–160); Mócsy (1974, 126–9, 162–5, 218). For army units in towns in the east and the development of settlements around legionary bases, see Isaac (above, n. 100); also 269–82; for the camp at Bostra, ibid., 124, fig. 1. For an attempt to construct a model for development of *canabae* and *vici*, see Jones, in Mattingly (1997, 192–3).

155 Mason (1987). There is no definite evidence that Chester was elevated to municipal or colonial rank.

156 See Laporte (1989); *ILS*, 6885; translation in Campbell (1994, 147–8); other auxiliary forts – Dura Europus – Isaac (1992, 147–52); Vindolanda – Bowman (1994, esp. 51–64). For the role of *vici* in Britain, see Sommer (1984); in Germany, idem, in Goldsworthy and Haynes (1999); the houses in these *vici* were not built by the army but some show signs of an Italian or Mediterranean origin.

157 See Alston (1995, 96–101; see also 117–42).

158 See e.g. soldiers' inscriptions from Pannonia with defective Latin (*CIL*, 6.2662, 32783).

159 Noricum – Alföldy (1974, 195); Pannonia and Upper Moesia – Mócsy (1974, 181–2, 254–9).

160 See Chapter 2, p. 45; Beard *et al.* (1998, 324–8).

161 Note the laws attempting to restrict serving soldiers from acting on behalf of the interests of a third party (Campbell (1984, 260–1)); petition – the people of Scaptopara presented their complaint to the emperor Gordian 'through Aurelius Purrus, soldier of the tenth praetorian cohort . . . fellow villager and fellow possessor' (see above, n. 115).

162 See Campbell (1984, 298–9).

163 Lewis (1989, no. 11) (AD 124).

164 Siculus Flaccus, probably writing in the second century AD (translation in Campbell (2000, 121–2)).

165 For a general account of Roman land survey, see Dilke (1971); Campbell (2000). For the distinctly Roman landscape of Africa, see now Mattingly (1997, 118–24).

166 Keppie (1983, 49–86).

167 Beard and Crawford (1985, 83–4).

168 See Patterson, in Rich and Shipley (1993, 108).

169 Keppie (1983, 205–7).

170 Mann (1983, 59). Several colonies founded in the early empire were on the site of a vacated legionary fortress (see Keppie, 2000); Todisco (2000) has collected evidence relating to Italian legionary veterans who settled in the provinces.

171 Levick (1999, 137). Isaac (1992, 311–33) has argued that most Roman military colonies were not expected to exercise military control in the local area on their own; they could provide support for the regular army but were incapable of withstanding an assault in full-scale war.

172 Mann (1983, 14).

173 See Mann (op. cit., 59–63); Keppie (1983); *PBSR* (1984); Campbell (1994, 210–21).

174 For the limited number of examples from Britain, see E. Birley (1988, 275–81). See also below n. 176.

175 See above, p. 84, and also Chapter 2, p. 34.

176 *ILS*, 2462, 9085 (Campbell, 1994, nos 356–7); *AE*, 1934.226. Alston (1995, 108, and n. 19) is therefore wrong to claim that discharge *praemia* were discontinued in the second century. His argument that no source says that soldiers had *praemia* in the second century has no weight given the fragmentary nature of the ancient source material. He also notes that one wealthy military family in Egypt can be shown to have owned only 7¾ *arourai* of land, much less than could have been purchased with a discharge *praemium*. But this family might have spent the money elsewhere, or invested it in land in a different location, about which we know nothing.

177 *CIL*, 6.37271 (Rome).

178 See Alston (op. cit., 108).

179 *AE*, 1979.412.

180 M.A.Speidel (1992, 101–2).

181 *ILS*, 2637; Tacitus, *Annals*, 3.21; for military decorations, see Chapter 2, p. 40.

182 Keppie (1983, 114–22).

183 Mouterde and Lauffray (1952); Isaac (1992, 318–21).

184 Tacitus, *Histories*, 4.64.

185 Tacitus, *Agricola*, 13, 19, 21.

186 Bowman and Thomas (1986, 122; 1994, 106, no. 3).

187 See in general Brunt (1990, 267–81); Mattingly (1997).

188 For example, in Misenum the veterans from the fleet had only a limited role in civic life – Parma (1994, 52–9); see also Brennan (1990, 499–502) on the limited impact of veteran colonies and individual veterans, and Todisco (2000, 665–6) for the social relations of Italian veterans settled in the provinces.

189 Alston (1995, 117–42) has made a study of the village of Karanis in the Fayum, and concludes that 'the veterans were not in control of the political and economic life of the village. The veterans were not a caste' (140), and seem to have been substantially integrated into the local Egyptian community and

not to have made a major impact on the culture of the village. They included Egyptians in their social circle and their children sometimes married Egyptians. Whitehorne (1990) emphasizes the importance of the Roman status of veterans in Egypt and the skills and contacts acquired during their service, and a possible 'old-boy' network with serving soldiers. He assembles evidence for the activities of veteran soldiers in Oxyrhynchus – investing in grain land, lending money, running river boats, being involved in the weaving industry and renting houses. His overall assessment is that veterans, although having an important niche in the 'micro-economy of first-century Oxyrhynchus', were not the 'movers and shakers of the Roman economic world'.

5 WAR AND POLITICS

1   *Agricola*, 39.2.
2   For discussion of these themes, see Andreski (1968), and further below, pp. 115–21.
3   For a concise analysis of the political decline of the Republic, see Crawford (1992).
4   Discussion in Botermann (1968).
5   53.11.5.
6   Suetonius, *Augustus*, 25.1.
7   *Digest*, 1.4.1; cf. Gaius, *Instit.*, 1.5. See further below, n. 53.
8   Tacitus, *Histories*, 1.90.
9   *Annals*, 12.69.
10 Brunt (1977); see also in general Campbell (1984, 374–82).
11 78.16.2.
12 As argued by Rostovtzeff (1957, ch. IX).
13 Soldiers might hope that under a militarily active emperor they would profit from donatives and booty. On the other hand, they were more likely to be killed under an emperor who fought many wars; see Campbell (1984, 386–7).
14 Tacitus, *Histories*, 1.5.
15 5.2.4.
16 5.3.6, 5.5. There may be something in the idea that the troops eventually turned against Elagabalus because of his behaviour; but Herodian stresses the importance of bribery of the troops by Severus Alexander.
17 Dio, 68.3.3.
18 Tacitus, *Histories*, 1.55, 57.
19 See below, p. 115.
20 Tacitus, *Annals*, 11.20.
21 *Antiquities of the Jews*, 19.365–6.
22 Dio, 72.9.2; Brunt (1973).
23 See Chapter 4, n.161; individual access to the emperor – Campbell (1984, 267–73).
24 Dio, 46.46.7; *Augustan History, Life of Septimius Severus*, 7.6.
25 See below, pp. 113–15.
26 *Digest*, 29.1.1. Although Augustus made a great show of refraining from using 'comrades' to address the soldiers in public after the civil war was over, in private it seems that he attempted to preserve the personal relationship with his men. Thus we hear how he turned up in court to help an old soldier of his, and how he called on a veteran of his praetorian guard for an afternoon visit. At his funeral members of his bodyguard paraded around the funeral pyre and those who had received military decorations from him threw them into the flames (Suetonius, *Aug.*, 56.4; 74; Dio, 56.42).
27 For discussion of all these themes, see Campbell (1984, 17–156).

28　Some emperors spent a considerable part of their reign outside Rome on campaign, notably Domitian, Trajan (who died at Selinus in Cilicia), Marcus Aurelius (who died at Vindobona), Lucius Verus (who died at Altinum in 169 on the way back to Rome from winter quarters), and Septimius Severus (who died at York). Others like Caracalla (Parthia) and Severus Alexander (the Persians; Germany) faced difficult wars at crucial parts of their reign, and both were murdered on campaign.

29　See Chapter 6.

30　Ferguson, in Raaflaub and Rosenstein (1999, 402).

31　See Chapter 1, p. 9.

32　See also below, p. 114; for celebrations, see Chapter 6, pp. 138, 145, 147.

33　See also Chapter 1, p. 15.

34　Andreski (1968, 33–5, 116–23); Andreski's analysis is perhaps too schematic; Keegan (1993, 223–8) argues that the relationship between army and society is more complex than Andreski allows; note also Marwick (1974, esp. 223–4), who criticized the term 'military participation ratio', preferring simply 'participation' to take account of those who contributed to the war effort on the home front; this applies particularly to modern societies.

35　Ibid., 104–7.

36　Suetonius, *Augustus*, 28.2.

37　For Sejanus' career see Levick (1976, 158–79); he was executed in AD 31.

38　*RIC* I², p. 122, nos 7 and 11 (*aurei*, AD 41–2); see Levick (1990, 39; plate 7).

39　In foreign policy, the invasion of Britain may be a reaction to the emperor's political difficulties (see above, p. 112).

40　See Campbell (1984, 365–71).

41　*Histories*, 1.4.

42　Dio, 74.11–12; Herodian, 2.6.12.

43　*CIL*, 3.4037.

44　Dio, 75.1–2, 53.11.5 (27 BC).

45　Ibid., 76.15.2.

46　Ibid., 75.2.3.

47　Ibid. In the view of Herodian, Severus' rule was based on fear and he corrupted the discipline of the army (3.8.5, 8.8).

48　See Campbell (1984, 401–4). For a general account of the reign see A. Birley (1988); for Severus' relationship with the army see E. Birley (1969); Le Roux (1992).

49　For Severus' early helpers see A. Birley (1988, ch. 11).

50　Cappadocia (two legions), Syria Coele (two legions), Syria Phoenice (one legion), Syria Palaestina (two legions), Arabia (one legion).

51　Discussion in Campbell (1984, 404–8).

52　Campbell (op. cit., 408–9); some inscriptions are too damaged for definite conclusions.

53　*Digest*, 1.4.1.

54　76.17.

55　Suetonius, *Tiberius*, 25.1.

56　Andreski (1968, 104).

57　This fragment of text is printed in Loeb, vol. 9, p. 470. Note also the comments of Herodian: 2.6.10–14, 5.4.1–2, 8.1–3, 6.9.4–7, 8.8.1–3. On the murder of Pertinax, he says: 'Since no one took any action against soldiers who had cold-bloodedly murdered an emperor, or prevented the outrageous auction of the imperial power, this was a major reason for the disgraceful state of disobedience that was to persist in the years to come' (2.6.14).

58   Dio, 77.3.
59   Herodian, 6.9.5.
60   See Chapter 1, n. 45; also Chapter 6, n.160.
61   For the role of Odenathus see Millar (1993, 159–73).
62   Op. cit., 107.

6 WAR AND PUBLIC OPINION

1   Suetonius, *Augustus*, 31.5. *Augustan History, Life of Alexander Severus*, 28.6.
2   Aulus Gellius, *Attic Nights*, 9.11.7–10.
3   Dio, 55.10.3.
4   This is also depicted on coins (e.g. *BMC*, I, p. 103 no. 633 – *denarius*, 29 to
      27 BC).
5   Zanker (1988, 192–215); Nicolet (1988, 59–63); Luce, in Raaflaub and Toher
      (1990); Richardson (1992, 160–2); Favro (1996, 96–7, 175, 231); Claridge (1998,
      158–61); Rich (1998, 91–7).
6   *Res Gestae*, 21; Suetonius, *Augustus*, 56. It was claimed that the plan for the
      forum had to be altered since some landowners refused to sell. However, some
      now argue that the curious shape of the rear wall of the forum was caused
      by the direction of an existing road and sewer; see Patterson (1992, 209).
7   Suetonius, *Augustus*, 31; *Res Gestae*, 35.
8   See Simpson (1977). Rich (1998, 79–97) shows that Dio's reference to a temple
      of Mars Ultor on the Capitol was the result of a confused assumption that all
      honours granted to Augustus by the senate in 20 BC were initiated.
9   Dio, 54.8, 55.10.3. The standards may have been temporarily placed in the
      temple of Jupiter on the Capitol (see Simpson, op. cit.).
10   Dio, 55.10.2–4; Suetonius, *Augustus*, 29.2.
11   Suetonius, *Augustus*, 21.2.
12   Tacitus, *Annals*, 2.64; *CIL*, 6.911–12.
13   See Campbell (1994, 129).
14   Dio, 49.15.1, 51.19.1, 54.8.3; Schol. Veron. *Ad Verg. Aen.*, 7.606. I here follow
      Rich (1998, 97–115), who argues that of the three arches voted to Augustus
      he accepted only the one in celebration of Actium but agreed to a compro-
      mise by which it was modified in 19 BC. In this way he would avoid excessive
      honours where there had been no actual military engagement. See also Claridge
      (1998, 99); Patterson (1992, 194).
15   See Roullet (1972, 43–5); Zanker (1988, 144–5); *ILS*, 91; Pliny, *Natural History*,
      36.72–3. Both obelisks have identical inscriptions and were dedicated to the
      Sun. Further discussion in Patterson (1992, 199).
16   See Claridge (1998, 70). For the temple of Victory on the Palatine, see
      Richardson (1992, 420).
17   Zanker (1988, 187–92).
18   Ibid., 187. For his own signet ring Augustus adopted the seal of Alexander the
      Great, renowned as a great conqueror (Suetonius, *Augustus*, 50).
19   Ovid, *Fasti*, 1.709–22.
20   See Toynbee (1961); Simon (1967); Zanker (1988, 120–3, 158–9); Elsner (1991);
      Richardson (1992, 287–9); Claridge (1998, 185–9). Note that the identifica-
      tion of the figures is disputed. Gruen, in Winkes (1985), noting that *Pax* appears
      infrequently on the coinage of Augustus, emphasizes that in the Augustan
      message peace derived from force of arms; for *Pax* in Roman ideology see
      also Woolf, in Rich and Shipley (1993).
21   Suetonius, *Augustus*, 28.3.
22   MacMullen (1959); Mierse, in Raaflaub and Toher (1990); Zanker (1988,
      297–333, esp. 323–33).

23   Strabo, 7.7.5–6 (324–5); Pliny, *Natural History*, 4.1.5; Pausanias, 10.38.4; Dio, 51.1.2–3 (Actium); Strabo, 17.1.10 (795); Dio, 51.18.1 (Alexandria).

24   Mierse, in Raaflaub and Toher (1990, 321).

25   Pliny, *Natural History*, 3.4; text of inscription – Formigé (1949, 61).

26   For a general survey, see Crawford, 'Numismatics' (1983).

27   On the intelligibility of Roman imperial coin types see Crawford, *Studies* (1983); Howgego (1995, 62, 67–87). Levick (1982) argued that lesser men in the mint were offering, through their choice of coin types, symbols of respect to the emperor.

28   See Crawford, *Studies* (1983).

29   Wallace-Hadrill (1986, 76); see also below, p. 141.

30   Wallace-Hadrill, op. cit.

31   For coinage in the Republic, see Crawford, *RRC*; also Howgego (1995, 67–9).

32   *RRC*, 359/2 (*denarius*, 84 to 83 BC), 367/3 (*denarius*, 82 BC).

33   Dio, 47.25.3; cf. *RRC*, 508/3 (*denarius*, 43 to 42 BC).

34   Crawford, *Studies* (1983, 54–5), argued that it could be more important than the pictures on the reverse.

35   See Burnett *et al.* (1992, 38–51).

36   *RIC*, I² 275a (*denarius*, 28 BC).

37   *BMC*, I, p. 109, no. 672 (*denarius*, 20 or 19 to 18 BC); *Res Gestae*, 27.2.

38   *RIC*, I² 288 (*denarius*, *c.* 19 BC); see also p. 9.

39   See above, p. 124.

40   On emperors and public shows, see in general Yavetz (1969); Wiedemann (1992, 165–83).

41   *Res Gestae*, 4. For the triumphal way, see Claridge (1998, 250).

42   Suetonius, *Augustus*, 101.4; Dio, 56.34.

43   Ibid., 56.42.

44   Suetonius, *Augustus*, 101.4.

45   There is a useful discussion in Nicolet (1988, 28–40).

46   1.1.16 (9).

47   6.4.2 (288), 17.3.24 (839).

48   2.5.8 (115–16); see also Chapter 1.

49   2.101, 111.3–4, 124.3–4.

50   2.89.3.

51   2.90–1, 101.

52   2.96.2, 110, 113, 114.4.

53   2.97, 106.

54   2.120.

55   2.109.

56   The best discussion of the nature of Augustus' foreign policy and its relationship to the literature of the day, especially the poets Horace, Ovid, Propertius and Virgil, is still that of Brunt (1963); see also Wells (1972, 3–13; 1992, 69–78); Gruen, in Raaflaub and Toher (1990); Campbell, in Rich and Shipley (1993, 226–7); Cloud, in Rich and Shipley (1993), argues that there was no anti-militarist culture among the poets in Augustan Rome.

57   Tacitus, *Annals*, 1.2.

58   See Chapter 2, p. 26.

59   For a vigorous argument (in my view too schematic) that interest in military affairs was declining in this period, see Cornell, in Rich and Shipley (1993, 164–8; see Chapter 1, n.70).

60   Respect for military culture among the élite – Campbell (1984, 317–25, 348–62). For a very useful discussion of upper-class attitudes to imperialist expansion, see Brunt, 'Roman imperial illusions' (1990).

61 *Praef.*, 7.
62 1.9.5.
63 See Chapter 1, p. 13.
64 *Res Gestae*, 26. Cf. Suetonius, *Augustus*, 21.2 – 'He made no war on any people without just and necessary reasons.'
65 For what follows see also the discussion in Chapter 1, pp. 9–16.
66 49.36.
67 *Agricola*, 11–12, 24.3.
68 *Germania*, 37.3. The Elder Pliny's history of the German wars extended to twenty books.
69 *Agricola*, 41.
70 4.32, 6.31.
71 6.32.
72 54.9 – Augustus' eastern settlement in 20 BC.
73 60.19–21, 68.7.5, 68.17.
74 75.3.2.
75 *Oration*, 4.43ff. *On Kingship*. On philosophers and war, see Sidebottom, in Rich and Shipley (1993). He argues that the 'relegation of warfare to the geographic periphery may have facilitated a flirtation with pacifism' (262).
76 *Oration*, 12.20.
77 Eutropius, 8.5.3.
78 68.29.1, 29.4–33.1.
79 69.5.1, 9.4–5.
80 Haines (Loeb), vol. 2, 206.
81 Quoted in the *Epitome*, 14.10. See in general Campbell (1984, 398–400).
82 Claridge (1998, 164–7); also Richardson (1992, 176–7).
83 68.16.3, 69.2.3; *ILS*, 294.
84 Aulus Gellius, 13.25.1; Claridge (1998, 162). Other emperors also placed statues of famous people in Trajan's forum – *Augustan History, Life of Marcus Aurelius*, 22.7; *Life of Severus Alexander*, 26.4; an example is the statue of Claudius Fronto, depicted in armour (*ILS*, 1098).
85 For analysis of the scenes see Rossi (1971); Settis *et al.* (1988); Lepper and Frere (1988); for carved columns in general, see Becatti (1960).
86 *Epitome* (13.4) sums up Trajan: 'he displayed integrity in domestic matters, and courage in military matters.'
87 Zanker (1988) argued that the world of images was one side of a relationship or dialogue in which artists and people could respond.
88 This is the height of the column; the height of the entire monument was greater (Claridge, 1998, 193–8).
89 See Caprino *et al.* (1955); Richardson (1992, 95–6); Claridge (1998); Pirson (1996) emphasizes the themes of battle, violence and Roman superiority expressed in the resolution and efficiency of the Roman soldiers in contrast to their desperate and humiliated opponents; resistance is futile and brings violent retribution. The menacing circumstances in Marcus' reign demanded different images from those on Trajan's column to restore lost confidence in Roman power (174).
90 *ILS*, 5920.
91 See *RE*, VII.A.1 (1939) cols 373–493, s.v. *Triumphbogen*; MacDonald, in Winkes (1985); De Maria (1988); Kleiner (1989); Richardson (1992, 21–31); Favro (1996, 157–60); Claridge (1998, 75–6) (Septimius Severus), 116–18 (Titus), 272–6 (Constantine); Brilliant (1967) (Septimius Severus). Trajan's arch at Beneventum includes (with his civil achievements) a memorial to the Dacian

Wars and shows the emperor being crowned by Victory – Hannestad (1986); for arches as a manifestation of the language of power in the early empire, see Wallace-Hadrill (1990); for Augustus see above, p. 124.

92 See esp. Wallace-Hadrill, op. cit.
93 Dio, 60.22.1 (two arches, one in Rome, one in Gaul); *ILS*, 216.
94 *ILS*, 265; see Claridge (1998, 116–18).
95 *ILS*, 264.
96 *ILS*, 425.
97 Brilliant (1967).
98 This is shown on a coin; see Claridge (1998, 76).
99 *ILS*, 694; see Richardson (1992, 24–5); Claridge (1998, 272–6).
100 Alföldy (1996, no. 40454a); Claridge (1998, 278).
101 Reckoned at 50,000kg of gold and silver from the temple.
102 See above, p. 124.
103 Cassiodorus, *Var.*, 3.51; Humphrey (1986, 56–294); above, n. 95.
104 Nepos, 25.20.3; Livy, 4.20.7; Augustus, *Res Gestae*, 19.
105 Dio, 71.33.3; cf. Ovid, *Fasti*, 6.205–8.
106 See above, pp. 124–5.
107 Bergemann (1990, 107).
108 For example, Tiridates laid his crown before a statue of Nero – Tacitus, *Annals*, 15.29.
109 Campbell (1984, 98–9).
110 For the desire to identify with imperial family and for stylistic developments in portraiture in Rome, see Zanker (1988, 292–5).
111 Howgego (1995, 75); for Augustus see above, pp. 126–7.
112 *BMC*, III, p. 189, no. 892 (*sestertius*, AD 104 to 111).
113 See above, pp. 124–5; *BMC*, III, p. 161, no. 765 (*as*, AD 103).
114 For the importance of the emperor's portrait on coins, see above, p. 127.
115 For the importance of gesture in imperial imagery, see Brilliant (1963).
116 Discussion in Campbell (1984, 142–8).
117 *BMC*, II, p. 362, no. 294 (*sestertius*, AD 85).
118 *BMC*, II, p. 117, no. 543 (*sestertius*, AD 71).
119 *BMC*, III, p. 65, no. 242 (*aureus*, AD 103 to 111), no. 245 (*aureus*, AD 103 to 111), cf. p. 221, no. 1033 (*sestertius*, AD 116–117 – 'Armenia and Mesopotamia brought into the power of the Roman People').
120 *RIC*, II, p. 241 no. 667 (*sestertius*, AD 114 to 117); cf. *BMC*, III, p. 115, no. 588 ('The Bestowal of Kingdoms', AD 112 to 117).
121 *BMC*, III, p. 65, no. 244 (*aureus*, AD 103 to 111); p. 38 (five-*denarius* piece, AD 98 to 99).
122 *BMC*, IV, p. 629, no. 1449 (*sestertius*, AD 172 to 173).
123 *BMC*, III, p. 500, no. 1679 (*sestertius*, AD 119 to 138).
124 See above, p. 135.
125 See Howgego (1995, 83).
126 Burnett *et al.* (1992, 1–26); Howgego (1995, 84–7).
127 See Versnel (1970); Campbell (1984, 133–42). An *ovatio* (minor triumph) or triumphal decorations (the attributes of a *triumphator* without the procession) were given to those outside the imperial family. Augustus held three triumphs; see above, pp. 127–8.
128 Suetonius, *Claudius*, 17.1; Tacitus, *Annals*, 12.20.
129 Vespasian and Titus chose their triumphal route so that more people could see them (Josephus, *Jewish War*, 7.131).
130 Tertullian, *Apologeticus*, 33.4; Philostratus, *Lives of the Sophists*, 488. We may note the bizarre posthumous triumph of Trajan when a statue of the dead emperor was placed in the triumphal chariot (*Augustan History*, *Life of Hadrian*, 6.3).

131 *Jewish War*, 7.157.
132 Dio, 68.15.1.
133 Dio, 76.1.1–5.
134 See Brilliant (1963); e.g. *BMC*, III, p. 215, no. 1014 (Trajan; sestertius, AD 114–115 (?); *profectio Aug.*).
135 Tacitus, *Annals*, 12.21, 36–7.
136 Suetonius, *Nero*, 13; Dio, 63.1–7.
137 Syme, *Historia* (1958).
138 *Res Gestae*, 4.
139 Tacitus, *Annals*, 3.74. As Augustus directly controlled most of the legions he was effectively commander-in-chief; therefore other commanders were not acting under their own auspices and not in a position to receive military honours. See the discussion in Campbell (1984, 349–51).
140 Vespasian 20; Titus 17; Domitian 22 (one more than Augustus). For acclamations in general, see Campbell (op. cit., 122–8).
141 12.1.
142 Dio, 60.21.4–5. His acclamations had been increased from three to at least five, and perhaps eight or nine (Levick (1990, 144)).
143 Lepper and Frere (1988, scene CXXV).
144 Kneissl (1969); Campbell (1984, 128–33).
145 68.28.2.
146 Smallwood (1966, no. 23 (*Fasti Ostienses*)).
147 The last example of a senator receiving an honorary *cognomen* was Publius Gabinius Cauchius under Claudius (Suetonius, *Claudius*, 24.3).
148 See above, p. 42.
149 Dio, 69.14.3, referring to Hadrian.
150 See Campbell (1984, 148–9).
151 Suetonius, *Caligula*, 44.2.
152 Smallwood (1967, no. 369); translation in Braund (1985, no. 570).
153 *IGBR*, 659.
154 Reynolds (1982, document 17).
155 Smallwood (1966, no. 39); see also Speidel (1970).
156 *ILS*, 371.
157 Augustus – above, pp. 128–9. Augustus also wrote an autobiography in thirteen volumes covering his life up to 25 BC (Suetonius, *Augustus*, 85.1); Vespasian and Titus – Josephus, *Life*, 342, 358–9; cf. *Against Apion*, 1.56; Trajan – Priscianus, *GL*, 2.205.7–8; Severus – Dio, 75.7.3.
158 Rosenberger (1992, 128–33). The use of the word *expeditio* to describe a campaign indicates increasing emphasis on the emperor's personal military role; combined with an adjective (e.g. *expeditio Parthica*), it showed that the emperor had been present for a time (133–40; see also 78, 100, 111, 166).
159 *ILS*, 1006; Rosenberger (op. cit., 89).
160 See Chapter 1, p. 8; Chapter 4, p. 78. The emotional and psychological impact of Varus' defeat can be seen in Tacitus' re-creation of the discovery of the battle site by Germanicus in AD 16 (*Annals*, 1.61).
161 Suetonius, *Augustus*, 23. We find the same message in the *clades Lolliana*, where Lollius, Augustus' commander in Gaul, was defeated and lost a military standard. See Rosenberger (op. cit., 68–70, 145–9). Note that P. Caelius, who set up a memorial to his brother, a centurion killed in Varus' defeat, ignored official terminology and referred to the *bellum Varianum*, using the traditional word for 'war' or 'battle' (see Chapter 3, n. 165).
162 Severianus was probably from Gaul or the Rhineland; see A. Birley (1988, 121–2).

163   Dio, 51.23–4; discussion in Rosenberger (op. cit., 172–3).

164   See above, n. 56.

165   Statius, *Silvae*, 1.1.25–7, 78–81, 1.2.180–1, 4.1.13–14, 39–43, 4.2.66–7; *Thebaid*, 1.17–24; Martial, 2.2, 5.1.7, 7.5, 7.80.1–2, 8.11.

166   *Letters*, 8.4.

167   Haines (Loeb), vol. 2, 196–218.

168   Ibid., 194–6.

169   *Apocolocyntosis*, 12–13.

170   See Chapter 1, p. 10; Fuscus – 4.111–12; for satire 16 see Campbell (1984, 255–63).

171   *How to Write History*, 7, 14, 20.

172   *Agricola*, 39.2; *Germania*, 37.6; Dio, 67.4.1.

173   *Panegyric*, 16.

174   Gilliver, in Lloyd (1996) discusses the theme of morality in war in the Roman world, noting that while commentators did debate the relative value of severity and mercy in military tactics, this was mainly from the point of view of achieving the desired outcome. In fact there seems to be no clear moral imperative in the thinking of Roman commanders: 'brutality and mercy were both tools of conquest' (235).

175   In Virgil's words (*Aeneid*, 1.279).

BIBLIOGRAPHY

Adams, C.E.P. 'Supplying the Roman army: bureaucracy in Roman Egypt', in Goldsworthy and Haynes (1999), 119–26.

Adams, J.N. 'Latin and Punic in contact? The case of the Bu Njem ostraca', *JRS* 84 (1994), 87–112.

—— 'The poets of Bu Njem: language, culture and the centurionate', *JRS* 89 (1999), 109–34.

Alföldy, G. *Noricum* (1974).

—— (ed.) *Corpus Inscriptionum Latinarum* VI. *Inscriptiones Urbis Romae Latinae* VIII. Fasc. 2 (Berlin, 1996).

Alston, R. 'Roman military pay from Caesar to Diocletian', *JRS* 84 (1994), 113–23.

—— *Soldier and Society in Roman Egypt* (London and New York, 1995).

Andreski, S. *Military Organization and Society* (2nd edn, London, 1968).

Ardevan, R. 'Veteranen und städtische Decurionen im römischen Dakien', *Eos* 77 (1989), 81–90.

Ash, R. *Ordering Anarchy. Armies and Leaders in Tacitus' Histories* (London, 1999).

Austin, M., Harries, J. and Smith, C. (eds) *Modus Operandi. Essays in Honour of Geoffrey Rickman* (London, 1998).

Austin, N.J.E. and Rankov, N.B. *Exploratio. Military and Political Intelligence in the Roman World from the Second Punic War to the Battle of Adrianople* (London and New York, 1995).

Bagnall, R.S. 'Army and police in Roman upper Egypt', *JARCE* 14 (1977), 67–86.

Balty, J.-C. 'Apamea in Syria in the second and third centuries AD', *JRS* 78 (1988), 91–104.

Balty, J.-C. and Van Rengen, W. *Apamea in Syria: Winter Quarters of Legio II Parthica: Roman Gravestones from the Military Cemetery* (Brussels, 1993).

Barrett, J.C., Fitzpatrick, A.P, and Macinnes, L. (eds) *Barbarians and Romans in Northwest Europe*. BAR S471 (Oxford, 1989).

Beard, M. and Crawford, M.H. *Rome in the Late Republic* (London, 1985).

Beard, M., North, J. and Price, S. *Religions of Rome* Vol. 1: *A History* (Cambridge, 1998).

Becatti, G. *La colonna coclide istoriata* (Rome, 1960).

Bérard, F. 'Vie, mort et culture des vétérans d'après les inscriptions de Lyon', *REL* 70 (1992), 166–92.

—— 'Territorium legionis: camps militaires et agglomérations civiles aux premiers siècles d'empire', *CCG* 3 (1993), 73–105.

Berchem, D. van. 'L'annone militaire dans l'empire romain au IIIe siècle', *Mémoires de la Société nationale des Antiquaires de France* 10 (1937), 117–202.

—— 'L'annone militaire est-elle un mythe?', in *Armées et fiscalité dans le monde antique. Colloques nationaux du Centre national de la Recherche scientifique*, no. 936 (Paris, 1977), 331–9.

Bergemann, J. *Römische Reiterstatuen: Ehrendenkmäler im öffentlichen Bereich* (Mainz am Rhein, 1990).

Berger, F. *Kalkriese 1: Die römischen Fundmünzen* (Mainz am Rhein, 1996).

Birley, A. *Marcus Aurelius* (London, revised edn, 1987)

—— *The African Emperor, Septimius Severus* (London, revised edn, 1988).

—— 'Roman frontier policy under Marcus Aurelius', in Applebaum, S. (ed.), *Roman Frontier Studies 1967* (Tel Aviv, 1971), 7–13.

—— 'The economic effects of Roman frontier policy', in King, A. and Henig. M. (eds), *The Roman West in the Third Century*, BAR S109 (Oxford, 1981), 39–53.

—— *Hadrian. The Restless Emperor* (London and New York, 1997).

Birley, E. 'Promotions and transfers in the Roman army II: the Centurionate', *Carnuntum Jahrbuch* (1963–64), 21–33.

—— 'Septimius Severus and the Roman army', *Epigraphische Studien* 8 (1969), 63–82.

—— 'The religion of the Roman army: 1895–1977', *ANRW* II.16.2 (1978), 1506–41.

—— *The Roman Army. Papers 1929–86: Mavors IV* (Amsterdam, 1988).

Bishop, M.C. 'The military *fabrica* and the production of arms in the early principate', in Bishop, M.C. (ed.), *The Production and Distribution of Roman Military Equipment*, BAR S275 (Oxford, 1985), 1–42.

Bishop, M.C. and Coulston, J.C.N. *Roman Military Equipment from the Punic Wars to the Fall of Rome* (London, 1993).

Blagg, T.F.C. and King, A.C. (eds) *Military and Civilian in Roman Britain*, BAR 136 (Oxford, 1984).

Bogaers, J.E. and Rüger, C.B. *Der niedergermanische Limes: Materialen zu seiner Geschichte* (Cologne, 1974).

Botermann, H. *Die Soldaten und die römische Politik in der Zeit von Caesars Tod bis zur Begründung des Zweiten Triumvirats* (Munich, 1968).

Bowersock, G. *Roman Arabia* (Cambridge, Mass., and London, 1983).

Bowman, A.K. *Life and Letters on the Roman Frontier. Vindolanda and its People* (London, 1994).

Bowman, A.K. and Thomas, J.D. 'Vindolanda 1985: the new writing-tablets', *JRS* 76 (1986), 120–3.

—— 'A military strength report from Vindolanda', *JRS* 81 (1991), 62–73.

Bowman, A.K., Thomas, J.D. and Adams, J.N. 'Two letters from Vindolanda', *Britannia* 21 (1990), 33–52.

Braund, D.C. *Rome and the Friendly King. The Character of Client Kingship* (London, Canberra and New York, 1984).

—— *Augustus to Nero. A Sourcebook on Roman History 31 BC–AD 68* (London and Sydney, 1985).

—— 'The Caucasian frontier: myth, explanation and the dynamics of imperialism', in Freeman and Kennedy (1986), 31–49.

—— 'Coping with the Caucasus: Roman responses to local conditions in Colchis', in French and Lightfoot (1989), 31–43.

—— 'Piracy under the principate and the ideology of imperial eradication', in Rich and Shipley (1993), 195–212.

Breeze, D.J. 'The impact of the Roman army on north Britain', in Barrett, J.C. *et al.* (1989), 227–34.

—— 'The impact of the Roman army on the native peoples of north Britain', in Vetters and Kandler (1990), 85–97.

Breeze, D.J. and Dobson, B. *Roman Officers and Frontiers* (*Mavors Roman Army Researches* X) (Stuttgart, 1993).

Brennan, P. 'A Rome away from Rome: veteran colonists and post-Augustan Roman imperialism', in Descoeudres, J.-P. (ed.), *Greek Colonists and Native Populations* (Canberra and Oxford, 1990), 491–502.

Brilliant, R. *Gesture and Rank in Roman Art* (New Haven, Conn, 1963).

—— *The Arch of Septimius Severus in the Roman Forum*, *MAAR* 29 (Rome, 1967).

Brunt, P.A. 'Pay and superannuation in the Roman army', *PBSR* 18 (1950), 50–71.

—— 'Augustan imperialism', *JRS* 53 (1963), 170–6 = *Roman Imperial Themes* (1990), 96–109.

—— *Italian Manpower 225 BC–AD 14* (Oxford, 1971).

—— 'The fall of Perennis: Dio-Xiphilinus 72.9.2', *Classical Quarterly* 23.1 (1973), 172–7.

—— 'C. Fabricius Tuscus and an Augustan *dilectus*', *ZPE* 13 (1974), 161–85.

—— 'Conscription and volunteering in the Roman imperial army', *SCI* 1 (1974), 90–115 = *Roman Imperial Themes* (1990), 188–214.

—— 'Did imperial Rome disarm her subjects?', *Phoenix* 29 (1975), 260–70 = *Roman Imperial Themes* (1990), 255–66.

—— '*Lex de imperio Vespasiani*', *JRS* 67 (1977), 95–116.

—— 'Roman imperial illusions', in *Roman Imperial Themes* (1990), 433–80.

—— *Roman Imperial Themes* (Oxford, 1990).

Burnett, A., Amandry, M. and Ripollès, P.P. *Roman Provincial Coinage* I: *From the Death of Caesar to the Death of Vitellius* (*44 BC–AD 69*) (London and Paris, 1992).

Burnham, B.C. and Johnson, H.B. (eds) *Invasion and Response: The Case of Roman Britain*, BAR S73 (Oxford, 1979).

Cameron, A. *The Later Roman Empire AD 284–430* (London, 1993).

Campbell, J.B. 'The marriage of soldiers under the empire', *JRS* 68 (1978), 153–66.

—— *The Emperor and the Roman Army 31 BC–AD 235* (Oxford, 1984; reprinted with corrections 1996).

—— 'Teach yourself how to be a general', *JRS* 77 (1987), 13–29.

—— 'War and diplomacy: Rome and Parthia, 31 BC–AD 235', in Rich and Shipley (1993), 213–40.

—— *The Roman Army 31 BC–AD 337: A Sourcebook* (London and New York, 1994).

—— *The Writings of the Roman Land Surveyors. Introduction, Text, Translation and Commentary* (London, 2000).

—— 'Diplomacy in the Roman world (*c.* 500 BC–AD 235)', *Diplomacy and Statecraft* 12.1 (2001), 1–22.

Caprino, C. *et al. La colonna di Marco Aurelio* (Rome, 1955).

Carrié, J.M. 'Il soldato', in *L'uomo romano* (ed. Giardina, A.), 99–142 (Rome, 1989).

Castagnol, A., Nicolet, C. and van Effenterre, H. (eds) *Armées et fiscalité dans le monde antique* (Paris, 1977).

Chaumont, M.L. 'Un document méconnu concernant l'envoi d'un ambassadeur Parthe vers Septime Sévère (P. Dura 60B)', *Historia* 36 (1987), 422–47.

Cheesman, G.L. *The Auxilia of the Roman Imperial Army* (Oxford, 1914; reprinted 1971).

Cherry, D. 'Soldiers' marriages and recruitment in Upper Germany and Numidia', *AHB* 3.6 (1989), 128–30.

—— *Frontier and Society in Roman North Africa* (Oxford, 1998).

Chevallier, R. *Roman Roads* (London, revised edn, 1989).

Claridge, A. *Rome. An Oxford Archaeological Guide* (Oxford, 1998).

Cloud, D. 'Roman poetry and anti-militarism', in Rich and Shipley (1993), 113–38.

Coleman, K.M. 'Fatal charades: Roman executions staged as mythological enactments', *JRS* 80 (1990), 44–73.

Connolly, P. *Greece and Rome at War* (London, 1981).

Cornell, T. 'The end of Roman imperial expansion', in Rich and Shipley (1993), 139–70.

Coulston, J.C.N. 'Roman, Parthian and Sassanid tactical developments', in Freeman and Kennedy (1986), 59–75.

—— 'How to arm a Roman soldier', in Austin *et al.* (1998), 167–90.

Crawford, M.H. *Roman Republican Coinage* (Cambridge, 1974).

—— 'Roman imperial coin types and the formation of public opinion', in Brooke, C.N.L. *et al.* (eds), *Studies in Numismatic Method presented to P. Grierson* (Cambridge 1983), 47–64.

—— 'Numismatics', in *Sources for Ancient History* (ed. Crawford, M.H., Cambridge, 1983), 185–233.

—— *The Roman Republic* (2nd edn, London, 1992).

Cunliffe, B. *Greeks, Romans and Barbarians: Spheres of Interaction* (London, 1988).

Curchin, L.A. *Roman Spain. Conquest and Assimilation* (London, 1991).

Dabrowa, E. 'Les rapports entre Rome et les Parthes sous Vespasien', *Syria* 58 (1981), 187–204.

—— *Legio X Fretensis. A Prosopographical Study of its Officers I–III c. AD* (Stuttgart, 1993).

Daris, S. *Documenti per la storia dell'esercito romano in Egitto* (Milan, 1964).

Dauge, Y.A. *Le Barbare: recherches sur la conception romaine de la barbarie et de la civilisation*, Collection Latomus 176 (Brussels, 1981).

Davies, R. 'Joining the Roman army', *BJ* 169 (1969), 208–32 = *Service in the Roman Army* (1989), 3–30.

—— 'The Roman military medical service', *Saalburg Jahrbuch* 27 (1970), 84–104.

—— 'Some more military *medici*', *Epigraphische Studien* 9 (1972), 1–11.

—— 'The daily life of the Roman soldiers under the principate', in *ANRW* II.1 (1974), 299–338 = *Service in the Roman Army* (1989), 33–70.

—— *Service in the Roman Army* (ed. Breeze, D. and Maxwell, V.) (Edinburgh, 1989).

De Maria, S. *Gli archi onorari di Roma e dell'Italia romana* (Rome, 1988).

Dennis, G.T. *Maurice's Strategikon. Handbook of Byzantine Military Strategy* (Philadelphia, Pa, 1984).

De Souza, P. *Piracy in the Graeco-Roman World* (Cambridge, 1999).

De Ste Croix, G.E.M. *The Class Struggle in the Ancient Greek World* (London, 1981).

Devijver, H. *Prosopographia militiarum equestrium quae fuerunt ab Augusto ad Gallienum*, IV, Suppl. 1 (Leuven, 1987).

Dilke, O.A.W. *The Roman Land Surveyors* (Newton Abbot, 1971).

Dixon, K.R. and Southern, P. *The Roman Cavalry* (London, 1992).

Dodgeon, M.H. and Lieu, S.N.C. *The Roman Eastern Frontier and the Persian Wars, AD 226–363. A Documentary History* (London, 1991).

Drinkwater, J.F. *Roman Gaul. The Three Provinces, 58 BC–AD 260* (London, 1983).

Dupuis, X. 'La participation des vétérans à la vie municipale en Numidie Méridionale aux le IIe et IIIe siècles', in *Histoire et archéologie de l'Afrique du Nord. Actes du IV Colloque International*, Vol. II, *L'armée et les affaires militaires* (Paris, 1991), 343–54.

Durry, M. *Les cohortes prétoriennes* (Paris, 1938).

Dyson, S.L. 'Native revolts in the Roman empire', *Historia* 20 (1971), 239–74.

—— 'Native revolt patterns in the Roman empire', *ANRW* II.3 (1975), 138–75.

—— *The Creation of the Roman Frontier* (Princeton, 1985).

Eadie, J.W. 'The development of Roman mailed cavalry', *JRS* 57 (1967), 161–73.

Edmonds, M. *Armed Services and Society* (Leicester, 1988).

Elsner, J. 'Cult and sculpture: sacrifice in the Ara Pacis Augustae', *JRS* 81 (1991), 50–61.

Elton, H. *Frontiers of the Roman Empire* (London, 1996).

Favro, D. *The Urban Image of Augustan Rome* (Cambridge, 1996).

Fentress, E. *Numidia and the Roman Army. Social, Military and Economic Aspects of the Frontier Zone*, BAR S53 (Oxford, 1979).

Ferguson, B. 'A paradigm for the study of war and society', in Raaflaub and Rosenstein (1999), 389–437.

Ferguson, B. and Whitehead, N. (eds) *War in the Tribal Zone. Expanding States and Indigenous Warfare* (Santa Fe, N. Mex., 1992).

Ferrill, A. *Roman Imperial Grand Strategy* (New York, 1991).

Fink, R. *Roman Military Records on Papyrus* (Cleveland, Ohio, 1971).

Finley, M.I. *Studies in Roman Property* (Cambridge, 1976).

Fishwick, D. 'Soldier and emperor', *AHB* 6 (1992), 63–72.

Florescu, F.B. *Das Siegesdenkmal von Adamklissi: Tropaeum Traiani* (Bucharest and Bonn, 1965).

—— *Die Trajanssaüle: Grundfragen und Tafeln* (Bucharest and Bonn, 1969).

Formigé, J. *Le trophée des Alpes (La Turbie)*, Gallia Suppl. 2 (Paris, 1949).

Forni, G. *Il reclutamento delle legioni da Augusto a Diocleziano* (Milan and Rome, 1953).

—— 'Estrazione etnica e sociale dei soldati delle legioni nei primi tre secoli dell'impero', in *ANRW* II.1 (1974), 339–91 = *Esercito* (1992), 339–91.

—— *Esercito e marina di Roma antica* (Stuttgart, 1992).

Freeman, D. and Kennedy, D.L. (eds) *The Defence of the Roman and Byzantine East*, BAR S297 (Oxford, 1986).

French, D.H. and Lightfoot, C.S. (eds) *The Eastern Frontier of the Roman Empire*, BAR S553 (Oxford, 1989).

Frere, S. *Britannia. A History of Roman Britain* (3rd edn, London, 1987).

Gabba, E. *Republican Rome, the Army and the Allies* (transl. P.J. Cuff) (Oxford, 1976).

—— 'Le strategie militari, le frontiere imperiali', in Schiavone, A. (ed.), *Storia di Roma*, Vol. 4 (Turin, 1989), 487–513.

Gabler, D. 'The structure of the Pannonian frontier on the Danube and its development in the Antonine period', in Hanson and Keppie (1980), 637–54.

Garlan, Y. *War in the Ancient World* (London, 1975).

Garnsey, P. *Famine and Food Supply in the Graeco-Roman World. Responses to Risk and Crisis* (Cambridge, 1988).

Garnsey, P. and Saller, R. *The Roman Empire. Economy, Society and Culture*, (Berkeley and Los Angeles, Calif., 1987).

Garnsey, P. and Whittaker, C.R. (eds) *Imperialism in the Ancient World* (Cambridge, 1978).

—— *Trade and Famine in Classical Antiquity* (Cambridge, 1983).

Gichon, M. 'Cestius Gallus' campaign in Judaea', *Palestine Exploration Quarterly* 113 (1981), 39–62.

Gilliam, J. F. *Roman Army Papers. Mavors Roman Army Researches* II (Amsterdam, 1986).

Gilliver, C.M. 'The Roman army and morality in war', in Lloyd (1996), 219–38.

Goldsworthy, A.K. *The Roman Army at War 100 BC–AD 200* (Oxford, 1996).

Goldsworthy, A.K. and Haynes, I. (eds) *The Roman Army as a Community* (Portsmouth, RI, 1999).

Goodman, M. *The Ruling Class of Judaea. The Origins of the Jewish Revolt against Rome AD 66–70* (Cambridge, 1987).

—— *The Roman World 44 BC–AD 180* (London and New York, 1997).

Gracey, M. 'The armies of the Judaean client kings', in Freeman and Kennedy (1986), 311–23.

Grelle, F. and Silvestrini, M. 'P. Babullius C.f. H[or] Sallu[vius—] e la deduzione delle colonie nel principato', in *Preatti dell'XI Congresso internazionale di Epigrafia Greca e Latina (settembre 1997)*, 349–56.

Groenman-van Waateringe, W. 'Food for soldiers, food for thought', in Barrett *et al.* (1989), 96–107.

Gruen, E.S. 'Augustus and the ideology of war and peace', in Winkes (1985), 51–72.

—— 'The imperial policy of Augustus', in Raaflaub and Toher (1990), 395–416.

Halfmann, H. *Itinera Principum. Geschichte und Typologie der Kaiserreisen im römischen Reich* (Stuttgart, 1986).

Hannestad, N. *Roman Art and Imperial Policy* (Aarhaus, 1986).

Hansen, M.H. 'The battle exhortation in ancient historiography. Fact or fiction?', *Historia* 42 (1993), 161–80.

Hanson, W.S. 'The organisation of Roman military timber supply', *Britannia* 9 (1978), 293–305.

—— 'The nature and function of Roman frontiers', in Barrett *et al.* (1989), 55–63.

Hanson, W.S. and Keppie, L. (eds) *Roman Frontier Studies XII, 1979*, BAR S71 (Oxford, 1980).

Hanson, W.S. and Maxwell, G.S. *Rome's North-West Frontier. The Antonine Wall* (Edinburgh, 1983).

Harmand, J. *L'Armée et le soldat à Rome de 107 à 50 avant notre ère* (Paris, 1967).

Harris, W.V. *War and Imperialism in Republican Rome 327–70 BC* (Oxford, 1979).

—— (ed.) *The Imperialism of Mid-Republican Rome* (Rome, 1984).

Haynes, I.P. 'The Romanisation of religion in the auxilia of the Roman imperial army from Augustus to Septimius Severus', *Britannia* 24 (1993), 140–57.

Helgeland, J. 'Roman army religion', *ANRW* II.16.2 (1978), 1470–1505.

Hodgson, N. 'The east as part of the wider Roman imperial frontier policy', in French and Lightfoot (1989), 177–89.

Holder, P.A. *Studies in the Auxilia of the Roman Army from Augustus to Trajan*, BAR S70 (Oxford, 1980).

Holmes, R. *Firing Line* (London, 1985).

Hopkins, K. *Conquerors and Slaves. Sociological Studies in Roman History* 1 (Cambridge, 1978).

—— 'Taxes and trade in the Roman empire (200 BC–AD 400)', *JRS* 70 (1980), 101–25.

Hopwood, K. 'Bandits, élites and rural order', in A. Wallace-Hadrill (1989), 171–87.

Howard, M. *War in European History* (Oxford, 1976).

Howgego, C. *Ancient History from Coins* (London and New York, 1995).

Humphrey, J.H. *Roman Circuses: Arenas for Chariot Racing* (London, 1984).

Hyland, A. *Training the Roman Cavalry. From Arrian's Ars Tactica* (Stroud, 1993).

Isaac, B. 'Bandits in Judaea and Arabia', *HSCP* 88 (1984), 171–203.

—— *The Limits of Empire. The Roman Army in the East* (revised edn, Oxford, 1992).

Jarret, M.J. 'Non-legionary troops in Roman Britain', *Britannia* 25 (1994), 35–77.

Johnston, S. *Hadrian's Wall* (London, 1989).

Jones, A.H.M. *The Later Roman Empire 284–602* (Oxford, 1964).

Jones, B.W. *The Emperor Domitian* (London and New York, 1992).

Jones, G.D.B. '"Becoming different without knowing it": The role and development of *vici*', in Blagg and King (1984), 75–91.

—— 'From *Brittunculi* to Wounded Knee: a study in the development of ideas', in Mattingly (1997), 185–200.

Jones, R.F.J. 'Natives and the Roman army: three model relationships', in Vetters and Kandler (1990), 99–110.

Junkelmann, M. *Die Legionen des Augustus. Den römische Soldat im archäologischen Experiment* (Mainz am Rhein, 1986).

Keegan, J. *The Face of Battle* (London, 1976).

—— *The Mask of Command* (London, 1987).

—— *A History of Warfare* (London, 1993).

Kennedy, D.L. 'The frontier policy of Septimius Severus: new evidence from Arabia', in Hanson and Keppie (1980), 879–88.

—— *Archaeological Explorations on the Roman Frontier in North-east Jordan: The Roman and Byzantine Military Installations and Road Networks on the Ground and from the Air*, BAR S134 (Oxford, 1982).

—— 'The garrisoning of Mesopotamia in the late Antonine and early Severan period', *Antichthon* 21 (1987), 57–66.

—— (ed.) *The Roman Army in the East*, *JRA* Supplementary Series 18 (Ann Arbor, Mich., 1996).

Kennedy, D.L and Riley, D. *Rome's Desert Frontier from the Air* (London, 1990).

Keppie, L. 'The legionary garrison of Judaea under Hadrian', *Latomus* 32 (1973), 859–64.

—— 'Vexilla veteranorum', *PBSR* 41 (1973), 8–17.

—— *Colonisation and Veteran Settlement in Italy 47–14 BC* (London, 1983).

—— *The Making of the Roman Army* (London, 1984; updated edn, 1998).

—— 'Colonisation and veteran settlement in Italy in the first century AD', *PBSR* 52 (1984), 77–114.

—— 'The army and the navy', in Bowman, A.K., Champlin, E. and Lintott A.W. (eds), *Cambridge Ancient History*, Vol. X (2nd edn, Cambridge, 1996), 371–96.

—— 'The changing face of the Roman legions (49 BC–AD 69)', *PBSR* 65 (1997), 89–102.

—— 'From legionary fortress to military colony', in *Legions and Veterans. Roman Army Papers 1971–2000* (Stuttgart, 2000).

Kleiner, F.S. 'The study of Roman imperial and honorary arches 50 years after Kähler', *JRA* 2 (1989), 195–206.

Kneissl, P. *Die Siegestitulatur der römischen Kaiser* (Göttingen, 1969).

Knight, D.J. 'The movements of the auxilia from Augustus to Hadrian', *ZPE* 85 (1991), 189–208.

Kraft, K. *Zur Rekrutierung von Alen und Kohorten an Rhein und Donau* (Bern, 1951).

Laporte, J.-P. *Rapidum. Le camp de la cohorte des Sardes en Maurétanie Césarienne* (Sassari, 1989).

Le Bohec, Y. *L'Armée romaine* (Paris, 1989).

—— *La IIIe Légion Auguste* (Paris, 1989)

—— *Les unités auxiliaires de l'armée romaine en Afrique Proconsulaire et Numidie sous le haut empire* (Paris, 1989).

Lee, A.D. 'Morale and the Roman experience of battle', in Lloyd (1996), 199–217.

Lepper, F.A. *Trajan's Parthian War* (Oxford, 1948).

Lepper, F.A. and Frere, S. *Trajan's Column* (Gloucester, 1988).

Le Roux, P. 'L'Armée de la péninsule ibérique et la vie économique sous le haut-empire romain', in *Armées et fiscalité dans le monde antique* (Paris, 1977), 341–71.

—— *L'Armée romaine et l'organisation des provinces ibériques d'Auguste à l'invasion de 409* (Paris, 1982).

—— 'L'Armée romaine sous les Sévères', *ZPE* 94 (1992), 261–8.

Levi, M.A. 'Le iscrizioni di Lambaesis e l'esercito di Adriano', *RAL* 9.5 (1994), 711–23.

Levick, B.M. *Tiberius the Politician* (London, 1976)

—— 'Propaganda and the imperial coinage', *Antichthon* 16 (1982), 104–16.

—— *Claudius* (London, 1990).

—— *Vespasian* (London and New York, 1999).

Lewis, N. 'Soldiers permitted to own provincial land', *BASP* 19 (1982), 143–8.

—— *The Documents from the Bar Kokhba Period in the Cave of Letters. Greek Papyri* (Jerusalem, 1989).

Lightfoot, C.S. 'Trajan's Parthian war and the fourth-century perspective', *JRS* 80 (1990), 115–26.

Lightfoot, C.S. and Healey, J.F. 'A Roman veteran on the Tigris', *Epigraphica Anatolica* 17 (1991), 1–7.

Link, S. *Konzepte der Privilegierung römischer Veteranen* (Stuttgart, 1989).

Lintott, A. 'What was the "Imperium Romanum"?', *Greece and Rome* 28 (1981), 53–67.

Lloyd, A.B. (ed.), *Battle in Antiquity* (London and Swansea, 1996).

Luce, T.J. 'Livy, Augustus, and the Forum Augustum', in Raaflaub and Toher (1990), 123–38.

Luttwak, E.N. *The Grand Strategy of the Roman Empire from the First Century AD to the Third* (Baltimore, Md, and London, 1976).

MacDonald, W.L. 'Empire imagery in Augustan architecture', in Winkes (1985), 137–48.

Macinnes, L. 'Settlement and economy: East Lothian and the Tyne–Forth province', in Micket and Burgess (1984), 176–98.

MacMullen, R. 'Roman imperial building in the provinces', *HSCPh* 64 (1959), 207–35.

—— *Soldier and Civilian in the Later Roman Empire* (Cambridge, Mass., 1963).

—— *Enemies of the Roman Order* (Cambridge, Mass., 1966).

—— 'How big was the Roman army?', *Klio* 62 (1980), 451–60.

—— 'The legion as society', *Historia* 33 (1984), 440–56.

—— 'The Roman emperors' army costs', *Latomus* 43 (1984), 571–80.

—— 'How to revolt in the Roman empire', *RSA* 15 (1985), 67–76.

Mann, J.C. 'The raising of new legions during the principate', *Hermes* 91 (1963), 483–9.

—— 'The frontiers of the principate', *ANRW* II.1 (1974), 508–31.

—— 'Power, force and the frontiers of the empire', *JRS* 69 (1979), 175–83.

—— *Legionary Recruitment and Veteran Settlement during the Principate* (London, 1983).

—— 'Epigraphic consciousness', *JRS* 75 (1985), 204–6.

Marsden, E.W. *Greek and Roman Artillery: Historical Development* (Oxford, 1969).

—— *Greek and Roman Artillery: Technical Treatises* (Oxford, 1971).

Marwick, A. *War and Social Change in the Twentieth Century* (London, 1974).

Mason, D.J.P. 'Chester: the *canabae legionis*', *Britannia* 18 (1987), 143–68.

Mattern, S.P. *Rome and the Enemy. Imperial Strategy in the Principate* (Berkeley, Los Angeles, Calif., and London, 1999).

Mattingly, D.J. 'War and peace in Roman Africa: observations and models of state–tribe interaction', in Ferguson and Whitehead (1992), 31–60.

—— *Tripolitania* (London, 1995).

—— (ed.) *Dialogues in Roman Imperialism. Power, Discourse and Discrepant Experience in the Roman Empire* (Portsmouth, RI, 1997).

Maxfield, V.A. *The Military Decorations of the Roman Army* (London, 1981).

Messer, W.S. 'Mutiny in the Roman army. The Republic', *Classical Philology* 15 (1920), 158–75.

Micket, R. and Burgess, C. (eds) *Between and Beyond the Walls: Essays on the Prehistory and History of Northern Britain in Honour of G. Jobey* (Edinburgh, 1984).

Middleton, P. 'Army supply in Roman Gaul', in Burnham and Johnson (1979), 81–97.

Mierse, W. 'Augustan building programs in the Western provinces', in Raaflaub and Toher (1990), 308–33.

Millar, F. *The Roman Empire and its Neighbours* (London, 1967).

—— *The Emperor in the Roman World (31 BC–AD 337)* (London, 1977).

—— 'Emperors, frontiers and foreign relations, 31 BC to AD 378', *Britannia* 13 (1982), 1–23.

—— 'The political character of the classical Roman Republic 200–151 BC', *JRS* 74 (1984), 1–19.

—— 'Politics, persuasion and the people before the Social War (150–90 BC)', *JRS* 76 (1986), 1–11.

—— 'Government and diplomacy in the Roman empire during the first three centuries', *International History Review* 10.3 (1988), 345–77.

—— *The Roman Near East 31 BC–AD 337* (Cambridge, Mass., 1993).

—— *The Crowd in Rome in the Late Republic* (Ann Arbor, Mich., 1998).

Milner, N.P. *Vegetius: Epitome of Military Science* (Liverpool, 1993).

Mitchell, S. 'Requisitioned transport in the Roman empire: a new inscription from Pisidia', *JRS* 66 (1976), 106–31.

—— (ed.) *Armies and Frontiers in Roman and Byzantine Anatolia*, BAR S156 (Oxford, 1983).

Mócsy, A. 'Die origo castris und die Canabae', *AArchHung* 13 (1965), 425–31 = *Pannonien und das römische Heer* (1992), 174–80.

—— *Pannonia and Upper Moesia* (London, 1974).

—— *Pannonien und das römische Heer, Ausgewählte Aufsätze*, Mavors VII (Stuttgart, 1992).

Momigliano, A.D. *Studies in Historiography* (London, 1966).

Morgan, M.G. '*Imperium sine finibus*: Romans and world conquest in the first century BC', in Burstein, S.M. and Okin, L.A. (eds), *Panhellenica: Essays in Ancient History and Historiography in Honor of Truesdell S. Brown* (Lawrence, Kan. 1980), 143–54.

Mor, M. 'The Roman army in Eretz-Israel in the years AD 70–132', in Freeman and Kennedy (1986), 575–602.

Mouterde, R. and Lauffray, J. *Beyrouth ville romaine* (Beirut, 1952).

Mrozewicz, L. 'Die veteranen in den Munizipalräten an Rhein und Donau zur hohen Kaiserzeit (I–III Jh.)', *Eos* 77 (1989), 65–80.

Nicolet, C. *L'Inventaire du monde: Géographie et politique aux origines de l'Empire romain* (Paris, 1988).

North, J.A. 'The development of Roman imperialism', *JRS* 71 (1981), 1–9.

Ober, J. 'Tiberius and the political testament of Augustus', *Historia* 31 (1982), 306–28.

Ogilvie, R.M. and Richmond, I.A. *Cornelii Taciti, De Vita Agricolae* (Oxford, 1967).

Ott, J. *Die Beneficiarier. Untersuchungen zu ihrer Stellung innerhalb der Rangordnung des römischen Heeres und zu ihrer Funktion* (Stuttgart, 1995).

Owens, E.J. *The City in the Greek and Roman World* (London, 1991).

Paret, P. *Understanding War* (Princeton, NJ, 1992).

Parker, H.M.D. *The Roman Legions* (reprinted Cambridge, 1958).

—— *A History of the Roman World AD 138 to 337* (2nd edn, London, 1958).

Parker, S.T. 'Peasants, pastoralists, and the *Pax Romana*: a different view', *BASO* 265 (1987), 35–51.

Parma, A. 'Classiari, veterani e società cittadina a Misenum', *Ostraka* 3 (1994), 43–59.

Passerini, A. *Le coorti pretorie* (Rome, 1939).

Patterson, J. 'The city of Rome: from Republic to empire', *JRS* 82 (1992), 186–215.

—— 'Military organization and social change in the later Roman Republic', in Rich and Shipley (1993), 92–112.

Pavan, M. *Dall'Adriatico al Danubio* (Padua, 1991).

Picard, G.C. *Les trophées romains* (Paris, 1957).

Pirson, F. 'Style and message on the column of Marcus Aurelius', *PBSR* 64 (1996), 139–79.

Pitts, L.F. 'Relations between Rome and German "kings" on the middle Danube in the first to fourth centuries AD', *JRS* 79 (1989), 45–58.

Pontiroli, G. 'Stele di *T. Aponius signifer legionis IX Hispaniensis* nel territorio cremonese', *Rend. Ist. Lomb.* 105 (1971), 149–56.

Purcell, N. 'Maps, lists, money, order and power', *JRS* 80 (1990), 178–82.

Raaflaub, K. 'The political significance of Augustus' military reforms', in Hanson and Keppie (1980), 1005–25.

Raaflaub, K. and Rosenstein, N. *War and Society in the Ancient and Medieval Worlds. Asia, the Mediterranean, Europe, and Mesoamerica* (Cambridge, Mass., and London, 1999).

Raaflaub, K. and Toher, M. (eds) *Between Republic and Empire. Interpretations of Augustus and his Principate* (Berkeley, Los Angeles, Calif., and London, 1990).

Rajak, T. *Josephus. The Historian and his Society* (London, 1983).

Reddé, M. *Mare nostrum. Les infrastructures, le dispositif et l'histoire de la marine militaire sous l'empire romain* (Rome, 1986).

Reynolds, J. *Aphrodisias and Rome* (London, 1982).

Ricci, C. *Soldati delle milizie urbane fuori di Roma. La documentazione epigrafica* (Rome, 1994).

Rich, J. 'Fear, greed and glory: the causes of Roman war-making in the middle Republic', in Rich and Shipley (1993), 38–68.

—— 'Augustus's Parthian honours, the temple of Mars Ultor and the arch in the Forum Romanum', *PBSR* 66 (1998), 71–128.

Rich, J. and Shipley, G. (eds) *War and Society in the Roman World* (London and New York, 1993).

Richardson, J.S. *Hispaniae. Spain and the Development of Roman Imperialism 218–82 BC* (Cambridge, 1986).

—— '*Imperium Romanum*: empire and the language of power', *JRS* 81 (1991), 1–9.

—— *The Romans in Spain* (Oxford, 1996).

Richardson, L. jr. *A New Topographical Dictionary of Ancient Rome* (Baltimore, Md, and London, 1992).

Richmond, I.A. 'Trajan's army on Trajan's column', *PBSR* 13 (1935), 1–40 (reprinted in *Trajan's Army on Trajan's Column*, ed. Hassall, M.) (London, 1982).

—— 'The Roman siege works at Masàda, Israel', *JRS* 52 (1962), 142–55.

—— 'Adamklissi', *PBSR* 35 (1967), 29–39 = Hassall (1982), 43–54.

—— (ed.) *Roman and Native in North Britain* (Edinburgh, 1958).

Rivet, A.L.F. *Gallia Narbonensis. Southern France in Roman Times* (London, 1988).

Romer, F.E. 'Gaius Caesar's military diplomacy in the east', *TAPHA* 109 (1979), 199–214.

Rosenberger, V. *Bella et expeditiones. Die antike Terminologie der Kriege Roms* (Stuttgart, 1992).

Rosenstein, N. *Imperatores Victi. Military Defeat and Aristocratic Competition in the Middle and Late Republic* (Berkeley and Los Angeles, Calif., 1990).

Rossi, L. *Trajan's Column and the Dacian Wars* (London, 1971).

Rostovtzeff, M. *The Social and Economic History of the Roman Empire* (2nd edn, Oxford, 1957).

Roth, J. 'The size and organization of the Roman imperial legion', *Historia* 43 (1994), 346–62.

—— *The Logistics of the Roman Army at War (264 BC–AD 235)* (Brill, 1999).

Roullet, A. *The Egyptian and Egyptianizing Monuments of Imperial Rome* (Leiden, 1972).

Roxan, M.M. *Roman Military Diplomas 1954–1977* (London, 1978).

—— *Roman Military Diplomas 1978–84* (London, 1985).

—— *Roman Military Diplomas 1985–1993* (London, 1994).

Roymans, N. *From the Sword to the Plough: Three Studies on the Earliest Romanisation of Northern Gaul* (Amsterdam, 1996).

Rubin, Z. *Civil War Propaganda and Historiography*, Collection Latomus 173 (Brussels, 1980).

Sabin, P. 'The face of Roman battle', *JRS* 90 (2000), 1–17.

Saddington, D.B. 'The development of the Roman auxiliary forces from Augustus to Trajan', *ANRW* II.3 (1975), 176–201.

Saller, R.P and Shaw, B.D. 'Tombstones and Roman family relations in the principate: civilians, soldiers and slaves', *JRS* 74 (1984), 124–56.

Saxer, R. *Untersuchungen zu den Vexillationen des römischen Kaiserheeres von Augustus bis Diokletian* (= *Epigraphische Studien* 1) (Cologne and Graz, 1967).

Scarborough, J. *Roman Medicine* (London, 1969).

Schlüter, W. (ed.) *Kalkriese, Römer im Osnabrücker Land: archäologische Forschungen zur Varusschlacht* (Bramsche, 1993).

Schlüter, W. and Wiegels, R. (eds) *Rom, Germanien und die Ausgrabungen von Kalkriese* (Osnabrück, 1999).

Schönberger, H. 'The Roman frontier in Germany: an archaeological survey', *JRS* 59 (1969), 144–97.

Schürer, E. *The History of the Jewish People in the Age of Jesus Christ* (revised by G. Vermes, F. Millar, M. Black and M. Goodman), 3 vols (Edinburgh, 1973–87).

Settis, S. *et al. La colonna traiana* (Turin, 1988).

Shaw, B. 'Soldier and society: the army in Numidia', *Opus* 2 (1983), 133–52.

—— 'Bandits in the Roman empire', *Past and Present* 105 (1984), 3–52.

Sherk, R.K. 'Roman geographical exploration and military maps', *ANRW* II.1 (1974), 534–62.

Sherwin-White, A.N. 'Rome the aggressor?', *JRS* 70 (1980), 177–81.

—— *Roman Foreign Policy in the East 168 BC to AD 1* (London, 1984).

Sidebottom, H. 'Philosophers' attitudes to warfare under the principate', in Rich and Shipley (1993), 241–64.

Simon, E. *Ara Pacis Augustae* (Tübingen, 1967).

Simpson, C.J. 'The date of the dedication of the temple of Mars Ultor', *JRS* 67 (1977), 91–4.

Skeat, T.C. *Two Papyri from Panopolis* (Dublin, 1964).

Smallwood, E.M. *Documents Illustrating the Principates of Nerva Trajan and Hadrian* (Cambridge, 1966).

—— *Documents illustrating the Principates of Gaius Claudius and Nero* (Cambridge, 1967).

—— *The Jews under Roman Rule* (Leiden, 1976).

Smith, C.J. 'Onasander on how to be a general', in Austin *et al.* (1998), 151–66.

Snape, M.E. 'Roman and native: *vici* on the north British frontier', in *Limeskongress XV. Roman Frontier Studies 1989* (Exeter, 1991), 468–71.

Sommer, C.S. *The military vici in Roman Britain*, BAR 129 (Oxford, 1984).

—— 'The Roman army in SW Germany as an instrument of colonisation: the relationship of forts to military and civilian *vici*', in Goldsworthy and Haynes (1999), 81–93.

Southern, P. *Augustus* (London, 1998).

Southern, P. and Dixon, K.R. *The Late Roman Army* (New Haven, Conn., and London, 1996).

Speidel, M.A. 'Roman army pay scales', *JRS* 82 (1992), 87–106.

Speidel, M. P. 'The captor of Decebalus', *JRS* 60 (1970), 142–53 = *Roman Army Studies*, 173–87.

—— 'The pay of the *auxilia*', 63 (1973), 141–7.

—— 'The Roman army in Arabia', *ANRW* II.8 (1977), 687–730.

—— *Guards of the Roman Armies* (Bonn, 1978).

—— *Roman Army Studies* I (Amsterdam, 1984).

—— 'Catafractarii Clibanarii and the rise of the later Roman mailed cavalry', *Epigraphica Anatolica* 4 (1984), 151–6.

—— 'The later Roman field army and the guard of the high empire', *Latomus* 46 (1987), 375–9.

—— *The Framework of an Imperial Legion* (Caerleon, 1992).

—— *Riding for Caesar. The Roman Emperors' Horse Guards* (London, 1994).

—— (ed.) *Roman Army Studies* II = *Mavors. Roman Army Researches* VIII (Stuttgart, 1992).

Sperber, D. 'The centurion as a tax collector', *Latomus* 28 (1969), 186–8.

Starr, C.G. *The Roman Imperial Navy 31 BC–AD 324* (Cambridge, 1960).

—— *The Influence of Sea Power on Ancient History* (Oxford, 1989).

Swoboda, E. *Carnuntum. Seine Geschichte und seine Denkmäler* (3rd edn, Graz and Cologne, 1958).

Syme, R. *Tacitus* (Oxford, 1958).

—— 'Imperator Caesar. A study in nomenclature', *Historia* 7 (1958), 172–88 = *Roman Papers* I (1979), 361–77.

—— *History in Ovid* (Oxford, 1978; reprinted 1997).

—— 'Military geography at Rome', *Classical Antiquity* 7 (1988), 227–51.

Talbert, R.J.A. 'Rome's empire and beyond: the spatial aspect', in *Gouvernants et gouvernées dans l'Imperium Romanum, Cahiers des Études Anciennes* 26 (1990), 215–23.

Todisco, E. 'Rassegna di studi militari 1989–1994', in *Epigrafia e territorio. Politica e società. Temi di antichità romana*, ed. Pani, M., IV (Bari, 1996), 373–422.

—— 'Veterani a Lucera', in *Epigrafia e territorio* (1996), 163–87.

—— *I Veterani in Italia in età imperiale* (Bari, 1999).

—— 'I veterani italici nelle province: l'integrazione sociale', in Le Bohec, Y. and Wolff, C. (eds), *Les légions de Rome sous le haut-empire. Actes du congrès de Lyon (17–19 septembre 1998). Collection du Centre d'Études romaines et gallo-romaines*, NS 20 (Lyon, 2000), 663–73.

Toynbee, J.M.C. 'The "ara pacis Augustae"', *JRS* 51 (1961), 153–6.

Versnel, H.S. *Triumphus. An Enquiry into the Origin, Development, and Meaning of the Roman Triumph* (Leiden, 1970).

Vetters, H. and Kandler, M. (eds) *Der römische Limes in Österreich. Akten des 14. Internationalen Limeskongresses 1986 in Carnuntum* (Vienna, 1990).

Wallace-Hadrill, A. 'Civilis princeps: between citizen and king', *JRS* 72 (1982), 32–48.

—— 'Image and authority in the coinage of Augustus', *JRS* 76 (1986), 66–87.

—— 'Roman arches and Greek honours: the language of power in Rome', *PCPhS* n.s. 36 (1990), 143–81.

—— (ed.) *Patronage in Ancient Society* (London and New York, 1989).

Ward-Perkins, J.B. 'The Roman west and the Parthian east', *PBA* 51 (1965), 175–99.

Watson, G.R. *The Roman Soldier* (London, 1969).

Webster, G. *The Roman Imperial Army* (London, 1969; 2nd edn, London, 1979; 3rd edn, Oklahoma, 1998).

Wells, C.M. *The German Policy of Augustus* (Oxford, 1972).

—— *The Roman Empire* (2nd edn, London, 1992).

Wheeler, R.E.M. *Maiden Castle, Dorset* (Oxford, 1943).

Whitehorne, J.E.G. 'Soldiers and veterans in the local economy of first-century Oxyrhynchus', in Capasso, M. *et al.* (eds), *Miscellanea Papyrologica (Papyrologica Florentina* 19) (Florence, 1990), 543–57.

Whittaker, C.R. '*Agri Deserti*', in Finley (1976), 137–65.

—— 'Trade and frontiers of the Roman empire', in Garnsey and Whittaker (1983), 110–25.

—— 'Supplying the system: frontiers and beyond', in Barrett *et al.* (1989), 64–80.

—— *Frontiers of the Roman Empire. A Social and Economic Study* (Baltimore, Md, and London, 1994).

—— 'Where are the frontiers now?', in Kennedy (1996), 25–41.

Wiedemann, T. *Emperors and Gladiators* (London and New York, 1992).

Wightman, E.M. *Gallia Belgica* (London, 1985).

Wilkes, J.J. *Dalmatia* (London, 1969).

Williams, S. *Diocletian and the Roman Recovery* (London, 1985).

Winkes, R. (ed.) *The Age of Augustus. Proceedings of an Interdisciplinary Conference held at Brown University April 30–May 2, 1982 = Archaeologia Transatlantica* V (Providence, RI, and Louvain-la-Neuve, 1985).

Woodman, A. 'Self-imitation and the substance of history', in West, D. and Woodman, A. (eds), *Creative Imitation and Latin Literature* (Cambridge, 1979), 143–55.

Woolf, G. 'Roman Peace', in Rich and Shipley (1993), 171–94.

Yavetz, Z. *Plebs and Princeps* (Oxford, 1969).

Zanker, P. *The Power of Images in the Age of Augustus* (trans. A. Shapiro), Ann Arbor, Mich., 1988).

INDEX